Beyond
THE BULL

*A 100 year celebration of kickin' it up
with good food and great parties
at the Pendleton Round-Up*

Published by
The Pendleton Round-Up Association
1910-2010
Pendleton, Oregon

The purpose of publishing a cookbook in celebration of the Round-Up's 100 year anniversary is to present a little different side of what goes on in Pendleton during the second full week in September. That is, beyond the rodeoing, there's a lot of cooking, a lot of partying, a lot of entertaining, and a lot of stories that haven't been written down anywhere else.

Each purchase of BEYOND THE BULL will help build and restore the front entrance of the Round-Up Grounds. In celebration of the Centennial, the façade will have a whole new look, something like the drawing below. All of us who have worked on the Cookbook Committee hope to put our name on the big gate right up there in front, to recognize and pay tribute to the many, many hosts and hostesses who have extended the warm hand of hospitality to visitors from all around the world, making them feel truly special when they visit the Round-Up City.

FIRST EDITION
First Printing: 5,000 copies

To order additional copies of BEYOND THE BULL,
use the order blanks provided in the back of the book or write to:

BEYOND THE BULL
Post Office Box 609
Pendleton, Oregon 97801
Telephone: (800) 457-6336
www.pendletonroundup.com

ISBN number 978-0-692-00219-3
Library of Congress Control Number: 2008925255

WIMMER
COOKBOOKS

A CONSOLIDATED GRAPHICS COMPANY

800.548.2537   wimmerco.com

We welcome you to

Beyond THE BULL

This has been a labor of love and, true to our mission, a whole bunch of parties!

The Pendleton Round-Up started in 1910 and has grown to a four-day extravaganza that brings more than 50,000 visitors to this cozy Eastern Oregon town of 16,000. Food has played an important role in Round-Up celebrations over the decades and each organization and family has added their own spin. The participation of the Umatilla, Cayuse and Walla Walla tribes, dating back to the very first rodeo, makes the Pendleton gathering a unique event and adds to the diversity of food that's associated with Round-Up. Whether it's fry bread, the cowboy breakfast, a barbeque, or a special baked beans dish that is served to guests in the backyard, food has become an important tradition. We wanted to document these traditions in a cookbook commemorating the Round-Up's 100th Anniversary.

We began the project by asking for recipes: we wanted to include recipes that spoke to us of Round-Up, those that may have been a mainstay or staple back in the olden days, like the quintessential Cheese Ball, which we've dressed up with the addition of Pendleton Whisky. We asked old-timers for their favorite recipes. How could we have anticipated ending up with Roy Rogers' favorite banana cake? We asked the pickup crew (those brave souls who ride around plucking riders from bucking broncs and who usher the wild animals out of the arena) for their favorites, and got recipes like Jody Rempel's Spicy Lasagna. But mostly the recipes have come from those men and women who have opened their homes and their hearts and fed the visitors, many times not knowing when they left for the Round-Up Grounds in the morning that the party was going to be at their house that night.

After the recipes were catalogued, a group of just under 100 volunteered to be testers. Recipes were distributed to these willing cooks and bakers, served to their families and friends. Neighborhood parties were put together with everyone bringing a recipe to try. And every recipe that has been included in the book has been tested at least twice (some, like Adam West's Holy Batman Sawtooth Pot Roast, got more than two testings — we just liked it a lot).

The committee needed guinea pigs, so we held parties, charged a nominal fee, and invited folks to come taste! We did an appetizer and dessert party, we did barbecues with all the trimmings, we did parties featuring soups and breads and desserts, but the one that people are still talking about is the Pitchfork Barbecue. We served over 75 people and each steak was briefly simmered in hot lard (yes!) on a pitchfork. Barby-Master Bob Mumm was the overseer of the operation, and the recipe (or instruction) is indeed included in this book. We also used these parties to introduce some wild and wacky new drinks, featuring our own Pendleton Whisky.

Some recipes are originals, some are not. We've tried to include recipes that showcase local flavors and include ingredients that are easily obtainable. Not many are difficult; most are pretty easy, and we believe that they ALL are tasty and will speak well to your family and guests.

We think this book will be a terrific keepsake that will help memorialize those who have contributed to the richness of Round-Up and allow future generations to carry on some of these traditions.

The making of BEYOND THE BULL has truly been a creative journey and the committee has loved every minute of it. We hope that you will enjoy using it as much as we've enjoyed putting it together.

COMMITTEE

Chairman	Mary Alice Ridgway
Vice Chairman	Suzie Barhyte
Testing Chairman	Raphael Hoffman
Graphic Design	Pam Forrester
	Caryn Appler
Historians	Betty Branstetter
	Pat Terjeson
Treasurer	Carolyn Gerberding

EDITORS AND TYPISTS

Carolyn Gerberding	Norma Rickman
Judy Dickey	Judy Malcolm
Rachel Florip	Mike Forrester
Cindy Criswell	Shannon Criswell
Julie Denny	Mary Alice Ridgway

COMMITTEE MEMBERS

Julie Reese	Susan Corey
Corrin Graybeal	June Mohrland
Linda Neuman	Betty Lou Holeman

PHOTOGRAPHERS

Ron Cooper (cover)	Ric & Pat Walters
Lee Farren	Marilyn Lieuallen
Laura Davis	Pam Forrester
E.J. Harris	Matt Johnson

COVER PHOTOGRAPH

Rodeo Clown JJ Harrison	Crystal Pond
John Green	Mary Alice Ridgway,
	Suzie Barhyte

*A special thanks to Marilyn Lieuallen for
letting us use many of her personal photos, taken over many years.*

Susan Olsen Corey presenting the 1984 Steer Roping Award to Pake McEntire.

Historically speaking, round-ups, spring brandings, weighing time, and gatherings have been part of our western heritage since the early 1800's. It's a time when family, neighbors, hired hands and volunteers come together to experience the "harvest" time of the fall. They labor hard together. Then at a break in the day…whether it is dinner or supper, they stop and "celebrate" a meal together. Not only were favorite family recipes shared but also many different techniques/styles of cooking.

The McEntire family's involvement at the Pendleton Round-Up began in 1933 when John McEntire first came to the Northwest. His son Clark remembers that now by when President Roosevelt brought into law that banks guarantee federal deposits. Clark first competed at the Pendleton Round-Up in 1946 (first year he used nylon ropes) and won the all around in 1947 at the age of 19. He continued to return to Pendleton until 1972. John's grandson and Clark's son, Pake won the steer roping in 1984 and was awarded the steer head tooled by Bill Severe. It just so happened that the snapshot in the background was of Clark on Heel Fly in 1961 when he won 2nd in the steer roping competition. That was also the year the Pendleton Round-Up honored Clark by inducting him into the Hall of Fame.

Reba, Pake, and Susie played the dance at the Happy Canyon in 1978, Reba performed at the night show in 1984 and Susie sang for Cowboy Church services in 1985.

Most everybody in the rodeo business has a desire to go to the Pendleton Round-Up. They love the beauty of that part of the country but you'd better believe if they do go, they've visited the Let'er Buck room before they go home!

Souvenirs are a very special thing to take home and now you'll be able to take home this special recipe book that you can use for years to come.

Enjoy,

Jacqueline, Alice, Reba, and Susie McEntire

REBA

May 19th, 2009

Dear Mr. Hawkins,

Please find the forward to the Pendleton Round-Up Cookbook along with this letter. I hope it's what you were wanting. Mama, Alice, Susie and I were on a week road trip when we put it together. That's why everyone's name is on it

Thanks for asking us to do it. The Pendleton Round-Up is very special to all the McEntires.

Always,

Reba McEntire

40 Music Square West • Nashville, Tennessee 37203 • (615) 259-0001

C H U T E

Appetizers & Beverages

CHEDDAR CHEESE SPREAD WITH
OREGON RASPBERRY MUSTARD SAUCE

The Cheese Ball for the 21st Century — a colorful, tasty canapé to serve with drinks — which can be made in advance and refrigerated.

10–12 servings

CHEESE SPREAD

1	8-ounce package cream cheese, softened
1½	cups grated sharp Cheddar cheese, (white or yellow)
2	tablespoons sherry

¾	teaspoon curry powder
½	cup finely chopped green onion
½	cup toasted and chopped walnuts

RASPBERRY MUSTARD SAUCE

1	14-ounce can red raspberries, drained (reserve ½ cup syrup)
1	tablespoon cornstarch

1	tablespoon plus 1 teaspoon old style whole grain Dijon mustard
	Chopped green onion for garnish

★ Blend the cream cheese, Cheddar cheese, sherry, curry powder, and chopped green onion and shape into a round flat disk, 1½-inches thick and 6-inches in diameter. Lightly press in the walnuts all over the spread. Place on serving dish.

★ In a saucepan, heat the reserved raspberry syrup, cornstarch, and mustard until thickened, stirring every 5 minutes. Gently stir in the drained raspberries and cool.

★ Spread the topping on the cheese disk and garnish with chopped green onions.

★ Serve with your favorite crackers and a cheese spreader.

This was a recipe sent to me by a neighbor when I lived in Arlington, Virginia. She knew I came from Oregon and thought I would like it...*Harriet Isom*

1929 Round-Up Princess Kathryn Furnish Ramey and Harriet Isom

PENDLETON WHISKY CHEESE BALL

Popular in the 50's, we've jazzed it up with a little Pendleton Whisky.

4 cheese balls

1	5-ounce jar Roka cheese spread	1	teaspoon dry mustard
1	5-ounce jar Pimento cheese spread	¼	teaspoon garlic powder
2	5-ounce jar Old English cheese spread	1	tablespoon Pendleton Whisky
1	8-ounce package cream cheese		Dash of hot sauce
			Chopped pecans

✱ In large bowl cream cheeses together. Stir in mustard, garlic powder, whisky, hot sauce, and mix until well blended.

✱ Place in freezer for 20 minutes for easier handling.

✱ Form into 4 balls and roll each ball in chopped pecans. Wrap and store in refrigerator. Serve with crackers.

Having the cheeses all at room temperature makes for much easier mixing.

SMOKED UMATILLA SALMON SPREAD

This got rave reviews from our guests at one of our tasting parties.

One Salmon Ball

2	8-ounce packages cream cheese, softened	½	tablespoon lemon juice
8	ounces smoked salmon, flaked (reserve about 2 tablespoons of flaked salmon for garnish)	1	tablespoon horseradish
		1	tablespoon grated sweet onion
		5	drops hot sauce
			Parsley or other greens

✱ Stir cream cheese until smooth. Add salmon, lemon juice, horseradish, onion, hot sauce, and blend thoroughly. Form into a ball, wrap in plastic wrap and refrigerate for at least 1 hour.

✱ Place unwrapped salmon ball onto a serving dish, top with reserved flaked salmon and garnish with parsley or other greens.

✱ Serve with crackers.

SMOKED SALMON HORS D'OEUVRE

This recipe was submitted by Sara Mautz Danzelaud to the East Oregonian when she was a Round-Up Princess in 1987, and again as her submission to the Round-Up Centennial Cookbook. You can see it has staying power!

One Salmon Ball

1	15-ounce can salmon	2	tablespoons lemon juice
12	ounces cream cheese, softened	1	tablespoon horseradish (grated type, not creamy)
2	tablespoons liquid smoke		Parsley for garnish
2	tablespoons grated onion		Crackers

✱ Drain salmon in colander. Pick out skin and bones. Mix salmon with cream cheese, liquid smoke, onion, lemon juice, and horseradish until thoroughly blended.

✱ Roll into ball shape. Place in bowl, cover with plastic wrap and leave in refrigerator for at least 1 hour.

✱ When ready to serve, place salmon ball on platter, garnish with parsley, and serve with crackers.

Can be made ahead, wrapped in plastic and placed in the freezer. Allow 1 hour to thaw before serving. Freezing enhances the flavor.

ISLAND CRAB SPREAD

This one is great. You'll get fantastic reviews from your guests.

2½ cups

1	8-ounce package crabmeat	2	tablespoons green onions, minced
1	8-ounce can sliced water chestnuts, drained and julienned	½	cup mayonnaise
		1	tablespoon soy sauce

✱ Place crabmeat, water chestnuts, and green onion in bowl.

✱ In separate bowl mix mayonnaise and soy sauce until smooth. Pour mayonnaise mixture over crab mixture and mix well.

✱ Chill until ready to serve. Serve with crackers.

Sara Mautz

Many people may not realize that concert entertainers often provide the directors with lists of items they want in their dressing rooms. Some were a gallon of "real" spring water, Royal Crown Cola, an unopened bottle of Jack Daniels, M&M's with peanuts, cashews (not peanuts), celery and carrot sticks...some performers were very demanding, and their food choices were even included in their contracts. We no longer provide liquor of any kind for them. One group wanted pizza for the bus on their way out of town. What goes on behind the scenes can be quite entertaining...*Evelyn Huston and Dennis Hunt*

I grew up in Pendleton in the 1950's and have fond memories of attending the rodeo, Happy Canyon, and many other Round-Up events with friends and family who visited our home during the Round-Up. As teenagers we would go behind the bucking chutes to get glances of the "handsome" cowboys. Both of my daughters were born in Pendleton. Here is a photograph of them dressed in their "Round-Up Western Clothes" right before attending the rodeo in 1966...*Sharon Bishop*

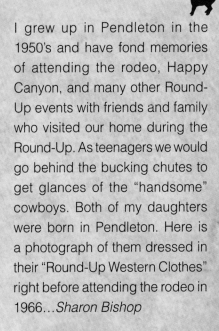

FIRESIDE CRAB DIP

This is very rich and very good.

8 servings

1 8-ounce package cream cheese	½ cup mayonnaise
1 5-ounce jar Old English sharp cheese spread	⅛ teaspoon hot sauce
8-10 ounces Dungeness crabmeat	¼ teaspoon white pepper
1 tablespoon grated onion	½ teaspoon lemon juice
	Corn chips

✶ Put cream cheese, cheese spread, crab, onion, mayonnaise, hot sauce, pepper, and lemon juice in the top of a double boiler until melted. Do not stir until ready to serve.

✶ Serve in a chafing dish with corn chips.

May substitute two 6-ounce cans chopped clams, drained, for the crabmeat.

CHEDDAR CHEESE & CRAB FONDUE

Dig out that old fondue pot and give this a whirl — it's great!!!

2¾ cups

¼ cup butter	1 6.5-ounce can crab or one 6-ounce package frozen crabmeat, drained and flaked
2 tablespoons all-purpose flour	
1 cup Sauterne	¼ teaspoon caraway seed
2½ cups shredded Cheddar cheese (10-ounces)	Chunks of French bread for dipping

✶ Melt butter in heavy 1-quart saucepan. Stir in flour and remove from heat. Gradually stir in the Sauterne. Cook over medium heat, stirring constantly until thickened.

✶ Stir in cheese and heat until cheese is melted. Add crab and caraway seed.

✶ Serve warm from fondue pot.

Fondue may be made ahead and frozen. Reheat over hot water.

RODEO SHRIMP SPREAD

This is as good as it looks.

20 servings

1	8-ounce package cream cheese, softened	8	ounces shredded mozzarella cheese
½	cup sour cream	1	red pepper, chopped
¼	cup mayonnaise	1	2½-ounce can sliced black olives
1	pound salad shrimp, thawed (if frozen) and patted dry	3	green onions with tops, sliced
1	12-ounce bottle zesty seafood cocktail sauce		Assorted crackers

✶ Stir cream cheese until smooth. Add sour cream and mayonnaise and mix until blended. Spread on a 12-inch serving platter.

✶ Sprinkle with shrimp. Pour cocktail sauce over the shrimp. Sprinkle mozzarella cheese over the cocktail sauce, then top with red pepper, olives, and green onion. Cover and refrigerate until serving.

✶ Serve with crackers.

LONGHORN TACO DIP

You don't have to tell anyone how easy this is.

3½ cups

1	1-ounce package dry onion soup mix	¾	cup shredded Cheddar or Monterey Jack cheese
2	cups sour cream	1	cup shredded lettuce
1	8-ounce package cream cheese, softened	2	tomatoes, seeded and chopped
¼	pound ground beef, cooked, drained, and crumbled	½	cup sliced green onions
			Tortilla chips

✶ In shallow 1-quart casserole, combine onion soup mix, sour cream, cream cheese, ground beef, and ½ cup shredded cheese. Sprinkle remaining ¼ cup cheese over top. Bake uncovered at 350° for 30 minutes or until heated through.

✶ Top with lettuce, tomato, and onions. Serve with tortilla chips.

The Happy Canyon wives have provided the appetizers and snacks served in the Happy Canyon hospitality room, and they were all delicious. I well remember the carrots, radishes, turnips, etc. that Betty Critchlow (Mrs. Bob) created and made into beautiful flowers and decorations. They were admired and enjoyed by many of our guests. Our potluck lunches when we attended the regional parades and rodeos were truly gourmet delights...*Evelyn Huston*

Hall of Fame Board Members Matt Duchek and Tim O'Hanlon

If you only have rock-hard avocados and you need some for a recipe rightaway, pierce them several times with a sharp knife and place them in a microwave oven at 50% power for 20 seconds. Turn them over and microwave them for another 20 seconds. Let them rest at room temperature for an hour or so.

SONORA MEXICAN DIP

A beautiful dish with great flavor!

8–10 servings

2	avocados
4	teaspoons lemon juice
½	teaspoon salt
¼	teaspoon black pepper
¾	cup sour cream
6	tablespoons mayonnaise
1	1-ounce package taco seasoning mix
1½	15-ounce cans refried beans

Hot taco sauce, to taste
¾ cup chopped green onions
2 tomatoes, seeded and chopped
½ cup sliced black olives
1½ cups Monterey Jack cheese, shredded
Tortilla chips

✶ Cut avocados in half, remove seed, and scoop out the pulp into a medium bowl. Mash with fork, stir in lemon juice, salt, and pepper. Set aside.

✶ Combine sour cream, mayonnaise, and taco seasoning mix in a bowl. Set aside.

✶ Mix refried beans with hot taco sauce to taste.

✶ To assemble: Spread refried bean mixture in a 9x13-inch serving dish; top with seasoned avocados, layer with sour cream-taco mixture. Mix together onions, tomatoes and olives and sprinkle over sour cream. Cover with shredded cheese.

✶ Serve chilled with tortilla chips.

Dish can be placed under broiler to melt cheese before serving if desired (but only if you used an ovenproof serving dish!).

BAKED JALAPEÑO CHEESE DIP

Great do-ahead recipe and terrific to take to a party because there are no worries about forgetting to take home your serving dish.

8-12 servings

1   10-inch round sourdough bread, hollowed out, save "lid"

1   6-ounce jar marinated artichoke hearts, drained and chopped

1   cup shredded extra sharp Cheddar cheese

1   cup shredded Monterey Jack cheese

1   cup shredded Parmesan cheese

1   clove garlic, minced

1   small sweet onion, chopped fine

1   cup mayonnaise

2   heaping tablespoons jalapeño mustard

1   baguette loaf, cubed

✱ Mix artichoke hearts, cheeses, garlic, onion, mayonnaise, and mustard together. Place mixture in bread bowl. Replace the "lid" and bake for 1¼ hours at 350°.

✱ Serve with cubed baguette and forks for dipping.

BUSHWHACKER BREAD BOWL

Good to the last drop because you can eat the bowl!

8-12 servings

3   8-ounce packages cream cheese, softened

1   4-ounce can diced green chiles

1   8-ounce package ham, finely cubed

6   green onions, thinly sliced

1   10-inch round loaf sourdough bread, hollowed out, save "lid"

1   loaf French bread, cubed for dipping

✱ Mix together the cream cheese, chiles, ham, and green onions. Put mixture into bread bowl, replace lid, and wrap in foil.

✱ Bake 1 hour at 350°. Serve with bread cubes.

Can be made day ahead and refrigerated. Adjust baking time if refrigerated.

If you need to take an appetizer to a party and you're crunched for time, think antipasto. Just swing by the supermarket and grab some really good olives from the deli, a package of pepperoni, a couple of Italian cheeses (one softer, one firmer) cut into bite size pieces, and some hard Italian salami. Get some fresh basil as you go through the produce section for garnish. Arrange everything on a large platter and toss the basil leaves around. This is great with a good Italian bread, but it's good all by itself too.

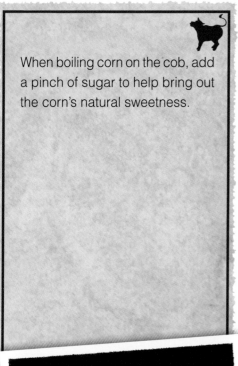

When boiling corn on the cob, add a pinch of sugar to help bring out the corn's natural sweetness.

FRESH CORN SALSA

This salsa variation combines sweet and spicy and it's ideal for Round-Up parties, since you make it well ahead of time.

3 cups

LIME DRESSING

¼	cup freshly squeezed lime juice	2	teaspoons ground cumin
3	tablespoons honey	1	teaspoon chili powder
3	tablespoons vegetable oil	1	teaspoon salt
2	cloves garlic, minced		

SALSA

2	cups fresh corn (from 4 ears)	5	stalks celery, finely chopped
1	small red onion, diced	1	cup chopped fresh cilantro leaves
1	red or orange bell pepper, diced		Tortilla chips

✶ Combine lime juice, honey, oil, garlic, cumin, chili powder, and salt for lime dressing; shake or blend well.

✶ Briefly cook ears of corn in a small amount of water. Plunge into ice water to stop cooking, drain. Cut corn from cobs.

✶ Combine corn, onion, pepper, celery, and cilantro, toss with lime dressing. Chill several hours or overnight. Serve with tortilla chips.

*Happy Canyon Princess
Claudette Enos*

Cowboy Caviar

This is such a Pendleton favorite that we received several variations ... you can add or subtract ingredients according to your tastes and what you have on hand.

12–16 servings

DRESSING

2	tablespoons red wine vinegar	1	teaspoon garlic salt
2	tablespoons hot sauce	½	teaspoon freshly ground black pepper
1	tablespoon vegetable oil		
1	clove garlic, minced		

CAVIAR

2	avocados, firm and ripe	3	Roma tomatoes, seeded and finely chopped
1	15-ounce can black beans		Salt to taste
1	11-ounce can white corn		Corn or tortilla chips
⅔	cup thinly sliced green onion		
⅔	cup chopped fresh cilantro		

✶ In small mixing bowl combine vinegar, hot sauce, oil, garlic, garlic salt, and pepper, mix well and set aside.

✶ Peel, pit, and cut avocados into ½-inch cubes. Place in a large bowl, add dressing and mix gently to coat.

✶ Drain and rinse beans and corn. Add beans, corn, onion, cilantro, and tomatoes to avocado mixture and gently mix to coat. Add salt.

✶ Serve with corn chips. (The large "scooper" kind work best.)

When I started dating my husband over 30 years ago, he introduced me to the Round-Up. We started bringing his co-workers, and as they moved on, we kept adding people to our annual trek from Portland. Now it is a combination of friends from over the years, usually about 15 of us and there are so many parts of Round-Up we enjoy, but for sure we are seated for the Opening Ceremonies and the Grand Entry. We love to eat at Hamley's and Raphael's and make the Buckle Club an annual event. Cowboy Caviar has been one of our favorite appetizers...
Sandy Patchin

1998 Round-Up Queen Megan Corey

COWGIRL CAVIAR

The black beans look like caviar, and it has a southwestern, cowboy look with all the colors. Also can be used as a salad ... just serve it with forks.

enough for a crowd

Angela Boston was introduced to this recipe by the daughters of long-time Pendleton musician, Rob Roy. She is frequently requested to make it. It has become a favorite of the parents and coaches of the Pendleton Swim Association for the hospitality tent at large swim events in Pendleton, and she's happy to share it with the cookbook. Angela says an unshared recipe is a lost recipe!!

To ripen avocados (and bananas), enclose them in a brown paper bag with an apple for 2-3 days.

DRESSING

3   tablespoons red wine vinegar

3   tablespoons vegetable oil

1   teaspoon black pepper and/or cumin, to taste

CAVIAR

1   15-ounce can whole kernel yellow corn

1   15-ounce can white corn

1   15-ounce can black beans

1   15-ounce can black-eyed peas

1   15-ounce can garbanzo beans (chickpeas)

1   15-ounce can dark red kidney beans

1   15-ounce can light red kidney beans

1   15-ounce can white kidney beans (cannellini)

3   teaspoons hot sauce

3   cloves garlic, minced, or 2 heaping tablespoons minced garlic

6   avocados, peeled and chopped

1   bunch green onions, chopped, or one Walla Walla Sweet onion, chopped

⅔   cup chopped fresh cilantro

1   pound Roma tomatoes, chopped

   Tortilla chips

✳   Mix vinegar, vegetable oil, black pepper and/or cumin and set aside.

✳   Drain and rinse the yellow corn, white corn, black beans, black-eyed peas, garbanzo beans, dark red kidney beans, light red kidney beans, and white kidney beans; place in a large bowl. Add the hot sauce, minced garlic, avocados, onions, cilantro, and Roma tomatoes. Toss with the dressing. Serve cold with tortilla chips.

I like to squeeze fresh limes over the vegetables — it helps keep the avocados from browning.
This bean-based side dish goes well with pasta salads.

Happy Canyon SEPT. 15 – 18, 2004

SANTA ANA GARLIC DIP

Good with crackers or cauliflower. Make it in the morning and enjoy it in the afternoon.

2½ cups

1	8-ounce package cream cheese, softened
½	cup sour cream
1	cup mayonnaise
¼	teaspoon Worcestershire sauce
¼	teaspoon hot sauce
5	(or more) garlic cloves, chopped
	Salt and black pepper

✸ In a medium bowl mix cream cheese with sour cream and mayonnaise. Stir in Worcestershire sauce, hot sauce, and garlic. Mix well. Salt and pepper to taste.

Cut the root end off garlic and soak in tap water for 15 minutes. Skins come off easily.

CHEF ROB'S SAUTÉED WILD MUSHROOMS

These are requested for just about every party catered at Round-Up and year round.

4 servings

3	tablespoons butter
12-16	mixed mushrooms (button, shiitake, portabella)
5	ounces heavy cream
1	tablespoon sour cream
1½	ounces dry sherry
1	teaspoon garlic seasoning
1	teaspoon seasoned salt (or Chef Rob's All Purpose Seasoning, if you're lucky enough to have some)

✸ Sauté mushrooms in butter until tender. Add cream and sour cream, and mix. Add sherry (carefully — remember, it's flammable), garlic seasoning and seasoned salt, and simmer gently until sauce starts to thicken.

✸ Serve with slices of French bread.

My friend, Bob Fetsch, brought me to the Pendleton Round-Up from Yuma, Arizona. We went to rodeos from Bel Fouche, South Dakota to the Pendleton Round-Up, explored the Oregon coast and visited friends everywhere in between. I managed to take my garlic dip with fresh cauliflower to all the parties. It was a hit and since everyone's breath was about the same, nobody had to leave. I made a lot of new friends and left my recipe for others to enjoy. Oregon is truly a beautiful state and I loved meeting everyone in Pendleton. Good food, good times, great people. Let 'er Buck...
Ruby Levandowski

To get the most juice out of fresh lemons, bring them to room temperature and roll them under your palm against the kitchen counter before squeezing.

ASPARAGUS WITH AÏOLI CHIVE SAUCE

This is excellent with asparagus, but try it with other vegetables too.

6–8 servings

¼	cup Aïoli Mustard	2	tablespoons minced fresh chives
1	cup sour cream		
1	cup mayonnaise	2	tablespoons minced fresh parsley
	Grated peel from ½ lemon		
	Juice from ½ lemon	2	pounds fresh asparagus, washed and trimmed

✷ To make sauce, mix mustard, sour cream, mayonnaise, lemon peel, lemon juice, chives, and parsley. Chill thoroughly.

✷ Place asparagus in a pan of boiling water, boil about 2 minutes or until crisp tender. Remove asparagus and immediately plunge into a bowl of ice water. Remove from ice water and place on towel to dry. Chill until ready to serve.

✷ Serve chilled asparagus with mustard sauce.

Use a 6-quart pasta pot so that it is easy to lift the asparagus out of the boiling water and into the ice water.

PROSCIUTTO ASPARAGUS

Hot off the grill, these are reminiscent of a summer day in Tuscany.

6–8 servings

1	pound fresh asparagus	½	pound prosciutto, thinly sliced

✷ Snap off and discard lower ends of asparagus. Blanch asparagus in boiling water for 30 seconds or until bright green. Remove from boiling water immediately and chill in cold water. Pat asparagus dry.

✷ Slice prosciutto in half lengthwise. Wrap each piece of prosciutto around a piece of asparagus in a spiral. Grill on medium heat until prosciutto starts to crisp, turning frequently. Serve immediately.

PANCETTA-WRAPPED DATES

You don't even have to like dates to become a fan of these.

6–8 servings

½	pound small pitted dates	½	pound pancetta, thinly sliced
¼	pound Marcona almonds		Toothpicks

✸ Insert an almond into each date. Cut pancetta into strips, just long enough to go around the date. Wrap each date with a strip of pancetta and secure with a toothpick.

✸ Grill for just a few minutes, long enough for the pancetta to start to crisp and dates to warm. Serve immediately.

CRAB STUFFED ARTICHOKES

Very elegant, very rich!

6 servings

6	artichokes	1	cup mayonnaise
2	tablespoons lemon juice	2	tablespoons grated onion
2	8-ounce cans crabmeat (flaked) or the equivalent of fresh crab	1	teaspoon salt
		1	tablespoon lemon juice
		2	tablespoons olive oil
1	cup grated Provolone or Gruyère cheese		

✸ Break stems off artichokes, cut off top third and wash. Snip off points of each leaf. Place in large kettle and add several inches of water. Cook until just slightly done. Scoop out the thistle.

✸ Combine crabmeat, cheese, mayonnaise, onion, salt, and 1 tablespoon lemon juice. Spoon crab mixture into center of each artichoke.

✸ Arrange artichokes in a shallow baking dish just large enough to hold them standing upright. Pour boiling water into baking dish to a depth of 1-inch; add 2 tablespoons of lemon juice. Brush artichokes with olive oil. Bake at 350° for 30 minutes.

✸ Serve hot or cold.

To scoop out the thistle: after slightly cooking the artichoke, remove the small inner leaves so that the thistle in the bottom of the artichoke can be removed to make an opening to fill with crab mixture.

Native only to Spain, crunchy Marcona almonds are smooth and juicy with an incomparably sweet delicate taste. Usually lightly sautéed in oil and sprinkled with sea salt, these large flat almonds have a richer and more intense flavor than ordinary almonds.

Jacqueline Brown, Rosemary Thorpe Lockhart, and Penny Belts Tallman

I've always thought it was intuitive of the founders of the Round-Up to invite Native people to participate, because back in the early days, the relationships between Native people and the Pendleton Community were not always congenial. Don't miss the part of the rodeo when little children to adults parade into the grounds wearing their gorgeous and colorful handmade regalia. Watch how graceful the women are, and how proudly the chiefs step to the beat of the drums. You'll see spots of young men looking like birds, twirling and jolting. It's mesmerizing. The younger girls are swirling with their newly made jingle dresses. The smaller children are fun, some so serious, others so shy, and then there are those who are hitting each other, the mothers putting them in their place with a sharp look from their eyes...*Raphael Hoffman*

RANCH PARTY PINWHEELS

These will hit the spot, and if you like them a little spicier, add a touch of hot sauce.

36 pinwheels

2	8-ounce packages cream cheese, softened	4	12-inch flour tortillas
1	1-ounce package dry ranch salad dressing mix	½	cup finely diced red pepper
2	green onions, finely minced	½	cup finely diced celery
		1	2½-ounce can sliced black olives, drained

✱ Stir together the cream cheese, salad dressing mix, and green onion. Spread on tortillas. Sprinkle with red pepper, celery, and olives. Roll and wrap tightly in plastic wrap. Chill at least 2 hours.

✱ Cut off roll ends. Cut roll into 1-inch slices.

POW-WOW ROLL-UPS

These roll ups can be frozen and made ahead, just perfect for the Round-Up crowd!

48 roll-ups

4	ounces cream cheese, softened	½	cup sliced green onions
1	cup shredded Cheddar cheese	½	cup pitted ripe olives, chopped
1	4-ounce can diced green chiles	4	6-inch flour tortillas
			Salsa, optional

✱ In bowl, blend cheeses, chiles, green onions, and olives. Spread ½ cup cheese mixture on each tortilla. Roll up each tortilla jelly-roll fashion. Wrap each roll in plastic wrap and chill at least 1 hour.

✱ To serve, cut each roll into 12 slices. Serve with salsa if desired.

BACON STUFFED MUSHROOMS

An explosion of flavors.

8-10 servings

4 slices bacon, cut up
¼ cup finely minced onion
2 tablespoons finely chopped green pepper
1 3-ounce package cream cheese, softened
½ teaspoon salt

1 teaspoon Worcestershire sauce
1 pound medium mushrooms, wiped clean
2 tablespoons lemon juice
½ cup soft bread crumbs
1 tablespoon butter or margarine
Parsley to garnish

* In a sauté pan, cook bacon, onion, and green pepper until bacon begins to crisp. Drain grease from mixture and set aside. Mix cream cheese, salt, and Worcestershire sauce together and stir until smooth. Fold in bacon mixture.

* Remove stems from mushrooms. Chop stems and add to bacon mixture. Dip mushroom caps in lemon juice to prevent turning brown.

* Place bread crumbs and butter in small bowl. Place in microwave for 1 minute to melt butter. Add to bacon mixture. Press bacon mixture into mushroom caps. Arrange in a glass pan and bake at 350° 20-25 minutes or until mushrooms are tender.

* Serve with parsley garnish.

Frank and Virginia Tubbs

Traditionally, Denver is where rodeo board directors meet in January with stock suppliers, clowns, and specialty acts such as trick-riders and ropers, and representatives of the cowboy union to plan the shows for the coming year. Negotiations are always rigorous, bidding intense, calendar dates hammered out. Finally when agreements are reached, the contracts are signed. It is a nervous time and everyone is more than ready for the relaxation, partying and dinners that follow.

Frank and his fellow Round-Up board members ended up most nights at the popular top floor restaurant in the Brown Palace, their headquarters hotel. Weather in the dead of winter in the mile-high city can be brutal and everyone is warned to dress warmly. Frank was, but as the evening went on, he became increasingly warm and fidgety, so he excused himself and left. A short while later he reappeared and seemed to be much more comfortable and at ease.

When the evening finally ended, everyone went to claim their hats from among the dozens and dozens of Stetsons at the hat check stand. The counter girl had no trouble identifying Frank's. His was the only Stetson that had been checked with a neatly folded pair of long johns in it!...*Virginia Tubbs*

If you make guacamole ahead of time be sure to press plastic wrap directly on the surface of the guacamole to keep it fresh looking. And put the pit in the dip...somehow the pit keeps it from turning brown.

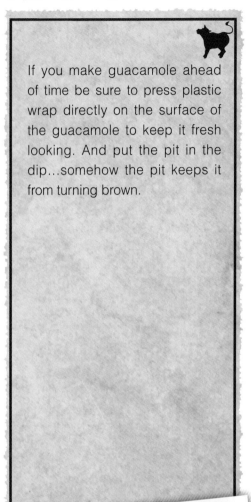

GUACAMOLE FRESCA

A pretty basic guacamole recipe, but the jalapeños give it an added dimension.

6–8 servings

4	ripe avocados	1	4-ounce can diced jalapeños
¾	cup chopped red onion	1	tablespoon seasoned salt
3	tomatoes, seeded and chopped	½	lime
			Tortilla chips

★ Cut avocados in half, remove seed and scoop out pulp into a bowl. Mash with a spoon. Mix in the chopped onion, chopped tomatoes, diced jalapeños, and seasoned salt. Squeeze lime juice over the mixture and stir.

★ Serve with tortilla chips.

RODEO CHICKEN WINGS

Delicious, sticky chicken wings.

6–8 servings

CHICKEN WINGS

3	pounds chicken wings	1	cup all-purpose flour for coating
1	egg, lightly beaten	1	cup butter

SAUCE

3	tablespoons soy sauce	½	teaspoon garlic powder, or to taste
3	tablespoons water	1	teaspoon salt
1	cup white granulated sugar		
½	cup white vinegar		

★ Discard wing tip, cut wings in half and dip in egg and coat with flour. Heat butter in a large, deep skillet over medium-high heat. Fry wings until deep brown. Place in a shallow roasting pan.

★ In a small pan combine soy sauce, water, sugar, vinegar, garlic powder, and salt. Heat and stir until sugar is dissolved. Pour over wings. Bake at 350° for 30-45 minutes, basting wings with sauce often.

SHRIMP PUFFS

Once you get the hang of these puffs, you can stuff them with just about anything. For now, try the wonderful shrimp filling!

24 puffs

SHRIMP FILLING

1	8-ounce package cream cheese, softened	1½	teaspoons Worcestershire sauce
¼	cup mayonnaise	1	teaspoon minced onion
2	teaspoons lemon juice	6	ounces salad shrimp, chopped

PUFFS

½	cup margarine or butter	1	cup all-purpose flour
1	cup boiling water	4	eggs
¼	teaspoon salt		

✱ Mix cream cheese, mayonnaise, lemon juice, Worcestershire sauce, onion, and shrimp until well blended. Set aside.

✱ Melt butter in boiling water in medium saucepan. Bring to boil again. Add salt and flour all at once. Cook over medium heat, stirring constantly, until mixture leaves sides of pan and forms a stiff ball. Remove from heat. Blend in eggs, one at a time, beating vigorously after each addition until mixture is smooth and glossy.

✱ Drop 24 mounds of dough by teaspoonfuls on ungreased baking sheets. Bake at 425° for 20-25 minutes, or until golden brown. Remove from oven, cut slits in sides of puffs. Return to oven for 3-5 minutes to dry out center. Cool.

✱ Cut tops from puff shells. Fill with shrimp filling, and replace tops.

It was the 1934 Round-Up that cowboy and trick roper Montie Montana first appeared in the Round-Up. He was 23.

Jarred Livingston taking a big chance, roping his mom, Annie Livingston, in the 2008 Westward Ho! Parade

Betty Belle Tubbs, 1934 Round-Up princess, was supposed to be a boy. Her parents, Lois and Clarence Tubbs, wanted a boy and so they called her "Bill." Maybe that's why she excelled in everything — just to show 'em! She taught her horse to rear up, and right before the Round-Up, she thought he was going over backwards, so she bailed. And broke her arm. And that's the way she rode in the Round-Up. It was the 1934 Round-Up when the Queen and Court staged the first galloping entry.

Betty Belle Tubbs

AVOCADO QUICHE

This was a specialty at the Dallas, Texas Hyatt Regency Hotel and a favorite of Betty Belle Tubbs Walzek

12 servings

SHELL

2	cups all-purpose flour	3	tablespoons shortening
½	teaspoon salt	¼	cup ice water
½	cup cold butter, cut into pieces		

FILLING

½	pound bacon, chopped	3	avocados, peeled and diced
1	small onion, chopped	¼	pound cooked ham, minced
1	small green pepper, chopped	¾	cup Parmesan cheese
12	large eggs	½	teaspoon nutmeg
1½	cups milk	¼	teaspoon salt
¾	pound shelled shrimp, chopped	¼	teaspoon black pepper

✶ For shell, blend flour, salt, butter, and shortening until mixture resembles meal. In a bowl, gently toss mixture with ice water, just enough to form into a ball. Dust with flour, wrap in waxed paper, and chill for 1 hour. Roll into 14-inch round and fit into a 10-inch springform pan. Crimp edges.

✶ For filling, cook bacon for 1-2 minutes. Add onion and green pepper. Cook until bacon is crisp, stirring occasionally. Drain on paper towels.

✶ In large bowl, beat eggs with milk. Stir in bacon mixture, shrimp, avocados, ham, Parmesan, nutmeg, salt, and pepper. Pour filling into shell and bake in lower third of a 350° oven, 1 hour and 15 minutes or until filling is golden and puffed slightly. Cool on rack 15 minutes and serve warm.

OLD-TIMER'S DEVILED EGGS

These eggs have been a favorite at the Northwest Old Timer's Rodeos. They travel well and can be made ahead of time...Shirley Warner Dickerson

16–60 deviled eggs

FOR A SMALL PARTY

8	eggs, hard-boiled, cooled, and peeled	1½	tablespoons canned, minced jalapeño peppers
3	tablespoons mayonnaise		Paprika
1	tablespoon Dijon mustard		

FOR A LARGE PARTY

30	eggs, hard-boiled, cooled, and peeled	½	cup canned, minced jalapeño peppers
1	cup mayonnaise		Paprika
⅓	cup Dijon mustard		

✳ Cut eggs in half and remove yolks.

✳ Crumble yolks in a bowl, add mayonnaise, Dijon mustard, and peppers. Mix well.

✳ Fill egg white halves with yolk mixture. Garnish with paprika and chill until serving time.

To prevent egg shells from cracking, add a pinch of salt to the water before hard-boiling.

Queen Kathryn Lazinka's Court 1950. Francine Hisler, Shirley Warner, Bette Belle Lieuallen, Nancy Collins

Ike C. Whitely on Golden King

For the 1950 Pendleton Round-Up, they tried some different things. There was a Sunday performance. The court rode on a float in the Rose Festival Parade. It was a colorful war bonnet covered with flowers and it was beautiful!

In the late 40's, they burned the wagon on the hill north of the grounds. Along with the Indian pageantry was a serpentine ride in the arena with cowboys, riding clubs, royalty, and visitors such as the King County Sheriff's Posse in silver on palominos...*Shirley Warner*

Without fanfare, a string of covered wagons appeared on the hill on the north side of the Umatilla River across from the Round-Up grounds. Drawn by oxen, the wagons were followed by mounted Indians in "war dress." An attack ensued, and a wagon was left burning. This act, the Over the Hill Pageant, became a great favorite and was part of the Round-Up pageantry until housing developments took over the north side.

PRAIRIE BACON SMOKIES

We can't get enough of these! Keep them warm in a crockpot.

8-10 servings

1   pound miniature smoked sausage links

½   pound regular sliced bacon

½   cup brown sugar

Hot mustard

✱   Cut bacon slices into quarters. Wrap each sausage link in a piece of bacon, secure with a toothpick, and arrange in a single layer in a 9x9-inch baking dish.

✱   Sprinkle brown sugar over the top to cover. Bake at 350° for 45-60 minutes or until bacon is crisp and brown sugar is dissolved.

✱   Serve with mustard on the side. Or just eat 'em one right after the other.

JALAPEÑO JELLY

This versatile dish can be used as jelly on toast, poured over a softened cream cheese brick, or mix 3-4 tablespoons jelly to 8 ounces cream cheese and use as a dip with crackers.

5-6 half pints

6   cups granulated sugar

1½   cups cider vinegar

2   medium green peppers, chopped or puréed

1   3½-ounce can jalapeño peppers (if using fresh, approximately 4 jalapeño peppers; use gloves while removing seeds)

¼   teaspoon green food coloring

1   6-ounce bottle liquid pectin

✱   In a medium sized saucepan, combine sugar and cider vinegar and warm to dissolve sugar.

✱   Add green peppers and jalapeño peppers. Bring to a boil and boil for 1 minute. Remove from heat and cool slightly.

✱   Stir in green food coloring and liquid pectin. Pour into ½ pint canning jars, straining through a double layer of cheesecloth, adjust lids, and process in water bath canner for 10 minutes.

If you like little bits of the peppers left in the jelly, omit the straining step.

ARTICHOKE GRATIN WITH PITA CHIPS

A favorite offering of Chef Brian von Eggers of The Plateau Restaurant at Wildhorse Resort and Casino.

8–12 servings

GRATIN

1	14-ounce can artichoke hearts	1	cup grated Asiago cheese
¼	cup roasted garlic	2-3	tablespoons chopped fresh thyme
1	cup sour cream		
1	cup mayonnaise		

PITA CHIPS

1	12-ounce bag pita bread	1	tablespoon Chef's salt (see note below)
¼	cup olive oil		

✳ Drain artichoke hearts and dice in food processor with garlic. Add sour cream, mayonnaise, ⅔ cup of the Asiago cheese and thyme. Blend well.

✳ Transfer from food processor to a shallow 1-quart baking dish and sprinkle with remaining cheese. Slide dish under broiler or in hot oven for about 10 minutes, until cheese starts to brown.

✳ Cut pita rounds into 6 equal pie-shaped parts. Place in large bowl and toss with oil and Chef's salt.

✳ Lay on sheet pan and bake about 15 minutes at 325° or until golden brown. Serve immediately with the gratin.

Chef Brian's Chef Salt is a mixture of salt, pepper, powdered garlic, and paprika. It is important to make the chips the same day they will be used, to hold their crispness.

ROASTED GARLIC: preheat the oven to 400°. Peel away the outer layers of the garlic bulb skin, leaving the skins of the individual cloves intact. Using a knife, cut off ¼ to a ½-inch of the top of cloves, exposing the individual cloves of garlic. Place the garlic heads in a baking pan; muffin pans work well for this purpose. Drizzle a couple teaspoons of olive oil over each head, using your fingers to make sure the garlic head is well coated. Cover with aluminum foil. Bake at 400° for 30-35 minutes, or until the cloves feel soft when pressed. Allow the garlic to cool enough so you can touch it without burning yourself. Use a small knife, cut the skin slightly around each clove. Use a cocktail fork or your fingers to pull or squeeze the roasted garlic cloves out of their skins. Eat as is or mash with a fork and use for cooking. Can be spread over warm French bread, mixed with sour cream for a topping for baked potatoes, or mixed in with Parmesan cheese and pasta.

My Dad, the ultimate rodeo fan, was so excited when my family and I moved to Pendleton. He would have a place to stay for THE PENDLETON ROUND-UP, which to him was about the best rodeo on earth. Dad was a cowboy at heart. We teased him that he had been born about 50 years too late for the life he would have loved. Within two weeks of setting up housekeeping, here came my Dad and Mom, Uncle Arnold, and Aunt Mae and several other relatives for the Round-Up. Of course, we bought tickets after arriving. Although they were not the best seats, no one complained as this was pretty much the ultimate for rodeoing in the Northwest as far as they were concerned. So in 1977 when the addition was built on the north grandstand, I stayed in Roy Raley Park overnight to obtain front row seats. I lined up with lots of others at 4 p.m. the day before the tickets went on sale and my husband Jim brought me dinner. That was quite a party, no sleeping, and even a few scuffles between some line holders as some folks thought others were trying to cut-in. I was about eighth in line and,

(continued on next page)

FRED SPREAD

This is a standard and a tradition at our house during Round-Up as it's a "ready-in-a-minute" appetizer when coming home after the rodeo...Marlene Krout

8 servings

½   cup chopped onion
2   cloves garlic, minced
½   cup ketchup
½   teaspoon salt
1   tablespoon dry mustard
2   tablespoons cider vinegar
½   teaspoon black pepper
2   tablespoons steak sauce
¼   cup freshly squeezed lemon juice
1   cup honey

✶ Combine onion, garlic, ketchup, salt, mustard, vinegar, pepper, steak sauce, lemon juice, and honey in a small pan. Simmer 15 minutes over low heat. Cool. Store in a pint jar in the refrigerator.

✶ To Serve: Place an 8-ounce brick of cream cheese on a small, flat dish. Pour ½ to 1 cup Fred Spread over top. Place dish in center of a larger platter and arrange crackers around the dish.

It's easy to double or triple this recipe and will keep up to two months in the refrigerator.

SWEET AND SOUR MEATBALLS

Kids especially have loved the sauce that this makes.

4–5 servings

MEATBALLS

1	pound ground beef	¼	teaspoon pepper
1	egg, beaten	2	tablespoons chopped onion
1	tablespoon cornstarch	2	tablespoons vegetable oil
1	teaspoon salt		

SAUCE

1	tablespoon vegetable oil	½	cup granulated sugar
1	cup pineapple juice (use juice from canned chunks)	1	tablespoon soy sauce
		6	tablespoons water
2	tablespoons cornstarch	1	14-ounce can pineapple chunks, drained
3	tablespoons vinegar		

✶ Mix ground beef, egg, 1 tablespoon cornstarch, salt, and pepper together and shape into 18 small meatballs. Brown in hot oil. Drain.

✶ In a small saucepan, combine oil and pineapple juice. Heat over low heat. Mix 2 tablespoons cornstarch, vinegar, sugar, soy sauce, and water. Add to saucepan, and stir over medium heat until thickened. Add meatballs and pineapple chunks. Heat through.

WRANGLER WATER CHESTNUTS

This is a trophy winner every time.

10–12 servings

2	8-ounce cans water chestnuts, drained	⅛	cup honey
¼	cup soy sauce	8	slices bacon, cut into quarters

✶ Marinate water chestnuts in a mixture of soy sauce and honey for at least 1 hour. Wrap each marinated chestnut in a quarter slice of bacon and secure with a toothpick.

✶ Place in a baking dish and bake at 450° for 15 minutes or until bacon is done. Remove from oven and drain on paper towel before serving.

(continued)

per my father, very successful, as I was able to purchase first and second row seats over Chute 3. He thought he had died and gone to heaven and I am not exaggerating. He loved those seats and he and my Mom attended all four days of Round-Up, plus slack time, every year until the year before he passed away when he was too sick to walk the distance to the north side; 33 years, never missing one performance from 1968 through 2001. He definitely believed in bragging rights as he was overheard many times describing the view from his front row "bucking chute" seats at the Pendleton Round-Up...*Marlene Krout*

✶ ✶ ✶

To easily remove honey from a measuring spoon, first coat the spoon with nonstick cooking spray.

To quickly use that frozen juice concentrate, simply mash it with a potato masher — no need to wait for it to thaw.

Rob Hoffman and Bob Ridgway

Until the building burned in 1999, this office was a perfect place for a parade party — right on Court Street, across from the Courthouse with a big parking lot, and the only official invitation was a sign above the blender station that read, "Come back again next year." We used to run milkshakes out to friends who were in the Westward Ho! Parade, and it was a really big deal when our daughter and her friends all turned 21 and could come for milkshakes...*Bob Ridgway*

VODKA SLUSH

A great summertime drink!

approximately 35 servings

1	46-ounce can peach nectar	1	6-ounce can frozen pink lemonade
1	46-ounce can unsweetened pineapple juice	½	fifth vodka
1	6-ounce can frozen orange juice	½	fifth peach schnapps
			Ginger ale or lemon lime soda

✻ Mix all ingredients together (do not dilute) in large plastic container and place in freezer until slushy.

✻ To serve, place several tablespoonfuls of slush into glass and pour ginger ale or lemon lime soda over the slush.

Leftover Vodka Slush should be stored in the freezer. (What? There could be leftovers?)

MILKSHAKES WESTWARD HO! STYLE

This milkshake was served for many years at Bob Ridgway's parade party.

4-6 cups per "blenderful"

1	12-ounce can frozen lemonade	¾	cup soda water
1	12-ounce can frozen limeade	1	tablespoon granulated sugar
24	ounces water	3-4	scoops vanilla ice cream
½	cup gin		Ice

✻ Mix thawed lemonade and limeade in gallon jug. Add water.

✻ In a blender, blend 2 cups of the lemon-lime-water mixture with gin, soda, sugar, ice cream, and about a cup of ice. Serve when frothy and make another batch.

APPLE PIE SCHNAPPS

Tastes great on ice cream or mixed with cranberry juice.

2 gallons

2	quarts apple cider	1	7-ounce bag hot red cinnamon candies
1	gallon apple juice		
3	cups granulated sugar	1	750 ml bottle (1 fifth) 190 proof grain alcohol
8	cinnamon sticks		

✳ Combine cider, apple juice, sugar and cinnamon sticks in large pan. Bring to a boil and boil for 30 minutes.

✳ Remove the cinnamon sticks after 30 minutes and add the red cinnamon candies. Let cool completely and then add alcohol.

Great for filling small corked containers for your Round-Up guests or for special occasions.

Jack & Dani Urick (AZ), Danise & Ken Parrish (WA), Dianne Conway & Rick Schaub (CA)

BLACKBERRY CORDIAL

We like to give these to our guests as well, and the screw-top wine cooler bottles work well for bottling.

1 gallon

4½	cups granulated sugar	¾	gallon blackberries
4	cups 100-proof vodka		

✳ Combine sugar and vodka in large pan and heat to dissolve sugar.

✳ Place berries in a gallon jar and pour vodka mixture over berries and seal with a lid. Let sit for 8 hours, turn jar over. Repeat for 10 days, turning the jar every 8 hours or so. After 10 days strain the liquid through cheesecloth. Bottle liquor in small bottles.

The Ransier family section in the grandstand seats dates back to the efforts of our Uncle Merwyn Ransier who was born in Pendleton in 1910. Uncle Merwyn owned a wheat ranch in an area known as Stage Gulch. Family members have come from Washington, California, and Arizona since 1970 for the Pendleton Round-Up. The three Ransier sisters, daughters of former Pendleton area native Dan Ransier, have promoted "Horse Pucky Bingo" at the Westward Ho! Parade each year. The annual event has had as many as 112 circles drawn on the parade route to predict where the "deposits" will fall.

All three sisters and their husbands have always dressed alike in red, white, and blue on Saturday in memory and recognition of September 11, 2001. For the other days of the Round-Up, you'll see us and can't miss us in our other coordinated or matching outfits. We've been long fans of Apple Pie Schnapps...*Dianne Ransier Conway*

Crazy Aunt Sue (above) with nieces Laura and Julie

★ ★ ★

HANGOVER REMEDY #1

Drink lots and lots of water and take an aspirin before you go to bed, and you'll be just fine (well, a little better) in the morning. The more water you drink, the better (although we did hear of some guy who drowned himself by drinking waaaaaay too much water). Don't drink that much. Orange juice works really well too.

CRAZY AUNT SUE'S SANGRÍA

Go easy with these, especially if you've come back from the Let 'er Buck Room!

8–10 servings

1	750 ml bottle hearty, dry, red wine	1	ounce lemon juice or juice of fresh lemon
2	ounces orange liqueur	¼	cup powdered sugar
1	ounce brandy		Orange wedges for garnish
2	ounces orange juice		

★ In a large pitcher combine wine, orange liqueur, brandy, orange juice, lemon juice, and sugar. Stir until sugar is dissolved. Chill completely.

★ When ready to serve, pour over ice in a glass and garnish with orange wedge.

CRAZY AUNT SUE'S BEER MARGARITAS

Delicious on a hot day after the performance!

8–12 servings

1	12-ounce can frozen limeade concentrate, thawed	1	12-ounce can beer, chilled
12	ounces tequila		Margarita salt
1	12-ounce can lemon-lime flavored soda, chilled		Limes

★ Pour thawed limeade concentrate into large pitcher. Fill empty limeade can with tequila and pour into pitcher. Slowly add soda and then beer. Mix gently.

★ Salt rim of glass, add ice. Pour mixture over ice and garnish with lime wedges.

In a pinch, lemonade can be substituted for limeade.

Our testers wrote: "We tried this on some friends. They all loved it and were very surprised that beer was an ingredient. We decided we'd like to go to Aunt Sue's for a party."

BLOODY MARY BAR

Great for a brunch!!

6-8 servings

1	46-ounce can tomato juice
2	tablespoons Worcestershire sauce
⅓	cup lime juice
1	teaspoon hot sauce
1	tablespoon sweet paprika
2	teaspoon salt
1	teaspoon freshly ground black pepper
½	teaspoon celery salt

Serrano lime salt (a blend of Serrano pepper and lime flavored salt)

Gin

Garnishes: Jalapeño, garlic and pimento stuffed olives, cocktail onions, pepperoncinis, pickled green beans, pickled asparagus, cherry tomatoes, lemon and lime wedges, celery, and carrot sticks.

✱ Combine tomato juice, Worcestershire sauce, lime juice, hot sauce, paprika, salt, black pepper, and celery salt in large pitcher. Chill until serving time.

✱ To serve, rim an 8-ounce glass with lime salt. (Run a lime wedge around the rim and then dip the glass in a saucer of the salt.)

✱ Pour 1½ ounces gin into each glass. Drop in a few ice cubes and fill glass with tomato juice mixture.

✱ Place gin, pitcher of tomato mixture and garnishes on "Bloody Mary Bar" and let guests garnish their drinks as desired.

It is far easier to use long wooden skewers for those folks who like a whole salad in their Bloody Mary.
The original Bloody Mary was made with gin. Some think it makes a superior drink.

HANGOVER REMEDY #2

We've heard that a bacon sandwich really does cure a hangover. Scientists say bacon boosts the level of amines in your body which clears your head. The carbohydrates in the bread speeds up your metabolism, helping your body get rid of all of that alcohol. Besides the bacon just smells so darn good. And tomatoes have lots of Vitamin C, which helps cure a hangover. Heck, just make yourself a good old BLT for breakfast.

✱ ✱ ✱

HANGOVER REMEDY #3

There are those who claim there is nothing better than a big old greasy breakfast which should contain bacon.

Judge Henry Kaye, Everett Stroble,
Don Hawkins, Dr. Donald (Bud) Smith

Over 20 years ago, we started having a Gin Fizz party Saturday morning 10 to noon, for James' relatives that come for Round-Up. There are no written invitations or RSVP's. Just come if you can. Relatives and their guests come from all over Oregon, Washington, California, Texas, Ireland, and any place a guest is from.

The first year we made 30 batches of the Fizz and about 60 people came. We've never fixed any food, as you notice from the recipe ... with orange juice, eggs and cream, it seems like a full breakfast. It tastes like a milkshake, but has the kick of a mule. And we warn the guests. Some are what we call generic as they have no gin.

We've blown up four or five blenders, which is a small price to pay for having so much fun and seeing all the relatives every year. We've had between 40-70 people here each year and we feel it keeps the family together.

We love Round-Up...*Marilyn & James Terjeson*

LIQUID BREAKFAST (GIN FIZZ)

Use 2 mixers: one for the gin fizz and one for the non-alcoholic mix.

6–8 servings

2   eggs
1   6-ounce can frozen orange juice concentrate, thawed
1   6-ounce can gin (use empty orange juice can for measure)

½   cup carbonated soda water
½   cup half-and-half
    Mint leaves

✶   Blend eggs, orange juice, gin, soda water, and half-and-half with a small amount of ice.

Can be garnished with mint leaves.

Terjeson relatives at Gin Fizz Party: Robin Terjeson, James Terjeson, Jan Terjeson Hoffman, Charlotte Brown Dickerson, Carla Krinklaw, and Liz Brown Stoddart

CHOCOLATE LIQUEUR

Easy to make and very good!!

1 quart

3   eggs
1   12-ounce can sweetened condensed milk
2   teaspoons coconut syrup

2   tablespoons chocolate syrup
3   teaspoons vanilla
5   ounces Pendleton Whisky

✶   Mix eggs, condensed milk, coconut syrup, chocolate syrup, vanilla, and whisky in blender. Store in refrigerator.

"THE BIG CHILL" KAHLÚA HUMMER

2 drinks

2   scoops chocolate ice cream
1   ounce Kahlúa
1   ounce light rum

✷   Put 2 scoops chocolate ice cream into blender. Mix briefly. Add Kahlúa and rum. Mix briefly.

✷   Pour into apéritif glasses and serve.

Gladys, Jennifer, and Ruff Raymond

COMPANY KAHLÚA

Make ahead and serve to your guests after a long day, right before bed.

2 quarts

4   cups granulated sugar
4   cups water
4   tablespoons instant coffee granules
3   tablespoons vanilla or ½ split vanilla bean
4   tablespoons chocolate syrup
1   fifth Pendleton Whisky

✷   In large kettle combine sugar, water, coffee granules, vanilla, and chocolate syrup. Bring to a boil, stirring until sugar and coffee granules are dissolved. Remove from heat and cool. Remove vanilla bean, if using.

✷   Stir in 1 fifth Pendleton Whisky and pour into gift bottles and store in refrigerator.

This drink was a favorite of Raphael (Ruff) Raymond, Happy Canyon Director in the late 40's, Grand Marshall of the Westward Ho! Parade in 1983, and Grandfather of 1977 Queen Jennifer Raymond

✷   ✷   ✷

HANGOVER REMEDY #4

You've heard of the "hair of the dog that bit you." If you subscribe to that school of thought, try a Bloody Mary. It has the benefit of vitamins in the tomato juice and the hot sauce to get you kick-started. In addition to being a prevention remedy, tomato juice contains fructose, a type of sugar that helps your body metabolize alcohol more quickly. This is probably why the morning-after Bloody Mary seems to work. We figure you're just giving your body some new alcohol to deal with so it can ignore the alcohol from the night before.

✷   ✷   ✷

HANGOVER REMEDY #5

We have heard that drinking pickle or sauerkraut juice works, but haven't tried that, so we can't say. We do have doubts about taking in all the salt found in those juices. It kind of turned our stomach just thinking about it, but hey, to each his own.

This drink was a favorite of Royal Raymond, Round-Up Director 1971-1978, President of Round-Up Board of Directors 1979-1980, and father of 1973 Queen Becky Raymond.

Royal, Becky, and Wilma Raymond

✳ ✳ ✳

Some rancher friends of my husband's came for a visit and asked if they could use my blender for some tumbleweeds. I was stunned and said, "Oh, it's too small." After they finished laughing, they told me what they needed to make it, and I was amazed at how good it tasted...*Grace Lund*

✳ ✳ ✳

HANGOVER REMEDY #6

Jack Shaw swears by beer and brownies.

CADILLAC AFTER DINNER DRINK

1 serving

1   ounce Kahlúa
1   ounce rum

1   cup vanilla ice cream

✳   Put the ice cream into a blender and blend a little. Add the Kahlúa and rum, mixing lightly.

CHUTE THE BULL

Undoubtedly, this will help your ride on the mechanical bull!!

2 drinks

2   ounces Pendleton Whisky
1   ounce apple jack brandy
1   ounce orange liqueur

Crushed ice
Lime wedges

✳   Combine whisky, brandy, and orange liqueur in cocktail shaker. Mix well. Pour into martini glasses.

✳   Garnish with a generous squeeze of lime.

TUMBLEWEED

It's easy to drink too many of these, so go easy. Oh my.

Serves 8

3   ounces Kahlúa
1½ ounces brandy
1½ ounces white crème de cocoa

4   ice cubes
1½ pints vanilla ice cream

✳   In a blender, combine Kahlúa, brandy, crème de cocoa, ice cubes, ice cream, and press blend for 5 minutes or until mixed. Serve immediately.

PENDLETON CHERRY BOUNCE

Infusions of Grandeur at its finest. The resulting Cherry Cordial is absolutely exquisite Sadly, this recipe is still doing its "thing" at Round-Up time, and isn't really ready until mid-November, but you can ask your guests to help you in the bouncing.

2 fifths

3 pounds pie cherries, washed, stemmed and pitted	1½ pounds granulated sugar 2 fifths Pendleton Whisky

★ Put all ingredients in a glass gallon jug and seal tightly with a lid.

★ Set the jug near your most used door and bounce daily from cherry season until Thanksgiving. If you need to leave home for a time, pass the jug off to neighbors to "babysit".

★ Strain through many layers of cheesecloth back into the whisky bottles and stopper tightly. Serve in small liqueur glasses.

The cherries will have turned brown, but are delightfully preserved. They may be used in fruit cakes, plum puddings, or chocolate covered cherries.

Cherry Bounce is traditionally an after dinner liqueur with the first being served after Thanksgiving dinner. It's primo over ice cream too. Might also be interesting to dab some behind your ears and see who follows you home...*Ginnie Hardie*

ROSE MARY ALICE MARTINI

Only one, only one!

1 drink

1 ounce good gin	2 Blue cheese stuffed olives
1 ounce citrus vodka	Lemon peel
1 6-inch rosemary sprig	

★ In martini shaker, mix gin and vodka with ice. Shake or stir until very cold. Pour into martini glass.

★ Thread olives onto sprig of rosemary and place in glass with lemon peel.

Last Hangover Remedy — And then there is the method some Round-up goers use. Just keep drinking until Sunday.

This drink was developed by Raphael Hoffman of Raphael's Restaurant, and it made its debut at the 2006 Annual Rotary Meeting. It is named for Roy Raley, one of the founders of the Pendleton Round-Up.

Teepee Raising Party

RALEY MANHATTAN

1 drink

2   ounces Pendleton Whisky
¼   ounce huckleberry liqueur
    Dash Angostura bitters

Orange slice
Red maraschino cherry

✷ Put whisky, liqueur, and bitters into a glass. Garnish with a slice of orange and a cherry, which just happen to be the colors of the Round-Up.

BANANA SLUSH PUNCH

This was particularly popular in the 70's and still makes a thirst-quenching non-alcoholic cooler.

24–30 servings

4   cups granulated sugar
6   cups water
1   46-ounce can pineapple juice
2   12-ounce cans frozen orange juice concentrate, thawed

1   12-ounce can frozen lemonade concentrate, thawed
5   ripe bananas
2   16-ounce bottles of lemon lime soda

✷ Boil the sugar and water to dissolve the sugar completely. Cool by adding the pineapple juice, orange juice, and lemonade concentrates. Mash ripe bananas well with a fork, or pulverize in a food processor and add to the juice mixture. Freeze in 9x13-inch pans, well covered.

✷ Scoop frozen mixture into punch bowl or pitcher, add soda and enjoy.

The frozen juice mixture keeps well for months, and is great to have made ahead for unexpected guests.

HIKE, FISH, AND GO CAMPING PUNCH

It's so light and refreshing ... you'll want another!!

4 servings

HUCKLEBERRY SYRUP
2 cups water
1 cup granulated sugar

2 cups huckleberries

DRINK
5 ounces Pendleton Whisky
4 ounces frozen lemonade concentrate
4 ounces frozen limeade concentrate

4 ounces Huckleberry Syrup (see above)
2 12-ounce bottles Terminal Gravity IPA Beer
Mint sprigs

✷ Bring water, sugar, and berries to a boil and simmer 20-30 minutes. Cool slightly. Strain through a fine-mesh sieve, discarding skins. Refrigerate leftover syrup.

✷ Mix Pendleton Whisky, lemonade, limeade, and huckleberry syrup in a pitcher. Slowly stir in the beer. Pour into ice-filled glasses. Top with a mint sprig. Serve.

LAVENDER LEMONADE

For an afternoon pick-you-up! And get ready to go again!

6 servings

½ cup lavender
2 cups freshly squeezed lemon juice

2 cups granulated sugar
10 cups water

✷ Boil 2 cups water, steep lavender in the water for 30 minutes. Strain into another bowl.

✷ In another pan, bring to a boil 2 cups water, 2 cups sugar, and 2 cups lemon juice. Boil until the sugar is melted.

✷ Mix lavender water and lemon juice mixture together and add the remaining 6 cups of water. Cool and serve over ice.

This pink drink won the title Unofficial Official Oregon Cocktail in a contest sponsored by Travel Oregon, the state's tourism commission. Cheryl Meloy of Portland beat more than 200 contestants with this frothy blend after using her friends as her guinea pigs. It was hard work, but somebody had to do it. Her friends agreed that one isn't enough.

Make giant ice cubes in muffin tins or plastic margarine bowls. These are perfect for using in picnic coolers or punch bowls. Add pansies or nasturtiums or other edible flowers to make them festive.

Before you let lemons shrivel up in your vegetable crisper, try freezing them if you don't have plans for using the lemons soon. When you're ready to use them, just thaw in a microwave at regular power for about 30 seconds. They are great to use for juice and if you need grated lemon peel it's easier to grate the peel while the lemons are still frozen. In fact we found the peel easier to grate on a frozen lemon than a fresh one.

Cindy Insko with her mother Ruth and Jill Thorne

After breaking my jaw at the Heppner rodeo during a run in collision with another horse, I consumed many a smoothie with my jaws wired shut for six weeks. I still like this recipe and now add 1 tablespoon flaxseed. While "wired-up" for six weeks, the shakes couldn't have anything in them that would get caught in the wires, so definitely no flaxseed! And my doctor told me in no uncertain terms NOT to ride in the run-ins during Round-Up week. Broken in three places, my jaw was still very fragile and a little painful. I told the Court Chaperone that I wanted to try to ride during a run-in practice to see if I could stay on, since I had become kind of weak. Needless to say, I was in a bit of trouble when I showed up for my next doctor's appointment, and he showed me the East Oregonian article about my riding!...*Cindy Insko, 1984 Round-Up Princess*

FRUIT SMOOTHIES

Everyone likes these!

4 smoothies

1½ cups skim milk or fruit juice (apple, white grape, cranberry mix, etc.)

1 cup non-fat vanilla yogurt

2 cups frozen fruit mixtures (blueberries, strawberries, raspberries, bananas, peaches, etc.)

✱ Blend skim milk, yogurt, and fruit in blender.

PENDLETON SUNRISE

A great way to get your citrus in the morning! Actually, this drink is good any time of the day.

Serves 30

1¼ cups blood orange juice (about 5 oranges)

5 cups orange juice

2 cups orange liqueur

1 cup Pendleton Whisky

½ cup granulated sugar

Champagne

Blueberries

Grenadine

✱ Mix orange juices, orange liqueur, whisky, and sugar. Chill.

✱ Place 3 or 4 blueberries in bottom of champagne flute. Add 1 teaspoon grenadine to each flute. Pour ⅓-½ cup mixture in flute (fill glass half full). Top with champagne (add gently to avoid frothing over!).

C H U T E

Breakfast & Brunch

Front: Betty Duff, Joan Rugg, Jackie Purchase, Lavelle Morrison, Donna Johns, Virginia Tubbs, and Marlene Davis; Back: Mary Jane Stangier, Doris Stetcher, Helen Hawkins, Natalie Anderson, Marilyn Lieuallen, Barbara Hawkins, Pat Terjeson, and Pauline Thompson

PENDLETON VFW LET 'ER BUCK POST 922 COWBOY BREAKFAST PANCAKES

Expecting a crowd of hungry cowpokes for the Pendleton Round-Up? The Pendleton VFW Let' er Buck Post 922 feeds over 6,000 hungry cowboys and cowgirls each Pendleton Round-Up with this special pancake recipe. The batter crew has used this crowd pleasing recipe for over 60 years.

6,000 servings

700	pounds all-purpose flour	1,188	eggs (separated)
50	pounds granulated sugar	33	cups vegetable oil
25	pounds salt	33	quarts water
22	pounds baking soda	396	ounces secret VFW batter crew beverage ingredient (beer is the suspected secret ingredient)
22	pounds baking powder		
165	gallons buttermilk		
132	pounds margarine, melted		

✶ Whip egg whites until stiff peaks form.

✶ Place buttermilk in large mixing container.

✶ Sift together flour, sugar, salt, baking soda, and baking powder. Add to the buttermilk and mix until blended. Gradually blend into the buttermilk batter the melted margarine, egg yolks, vegetable oil, water, and secret beverage ingredient. Mix gently, being careful not to over mix.

✶ Gently fold the egg whites into the batter and lightly blend.

✶ After donning your favorite straw hat and green apron, head on outside to the grill. Ladle batter (approximately ¼ cup per pancake) onto lightly oiled heated grill. Test the temperature of grill by letting a few drops of cold water fall on it. If water bounces and sputters, grill is ready to use. If water just sits and boils the grill is not ready. And it's way too hot if the water vanishes!

✶ Cook pancakes until bubbles appear on the upper surface but before they break, about 2-3 minutes. Turn the pancake and cook until second side is golden, approximately 1-2 minutes. Serve with a pat of butter, slab of ham, fried eggs and lots of black coffee.

LET' ER BUCK!

During Round-Up week, one of the events most anticipated by locals and visitors is the Cowboy Breakfast at Stillman Park. Between 6 and 10, members of the VFW Post 922 and Women's Auxiliary serve a mouth-watering breakfast to long lines of people.

This tradition began over 60 years ago and gets bigger and better every year. It's a wonderful way for visitors to start their day, and it helps those who live here feed their hungry guests. On Wednesday and Thursday, almost 1,000 folks eat at one of the tables set up on the grass. Friday and Saturday mornings, 1500-1700 hungry Round-Up revelers are served while a live band entertains them with lively Western songs and jokes.

Buttermilk pancakes, ham, eggs and coffee are prepared on gas grills at the park (in earlier years, the grills were fueled by wood).

Two weeks before the breakfasts, VFW members prepare huge quantities of the dry ingredients for the pancakes. And they really do separate those 1,188 eggs themselves. The batter is delivered to Stillman Park early the morning it is to be used and more than 300 gallons of batter are used during the four days of Round-Up. More than one old cowboy has been heard to say, "That breakfast is the only square meal I get all day."

The next time a few friends drop in, you might want to try the buttermilk pancake recipe given to us by the VFW boys.

One Friday evening of Round-Up about six years ago, my husband Dale and I decided to go to the Rainbow to see the Round-Up crowd. We found a table, but it was crowded, and we offered to share it with three young guys who came in looking for a place to sit. As it turned out, they were wrestlers and they remembered Dale from his coaching career at Pendleton. We had a great conversation and found out that they had arrived in Pendleton the evening before without hotel reservations! They were sleeping in the park on Despain. We invited them to our house for breakfast the next morning, never thinking that they would really show up. Saturday morning they showed up at our house. We had other guests, so it was no problem to include them. We had a great meal and great conversation.

Now we see them every year. They come up for breakfast or stop by on Friday or Saturday evening. One year, two bottles of excellent Willamette Valley wine came from our Rainbow friends with a thank-you note for our hospitality. This past year we saw them again in the Rainbow and we had a chance to catch up. It just goes to show that opportunities are endless to meet interesting and fun people at the Pendleton Round-Up. You never know when new friends are right at your table...*Amy Freeman*

GERMAN PANCAKES

These are good with butter and syrup, huckleberries, gooseberries or applesauce.

12 pancakes

2	eggs, well beaten	1¼	cups all-purpose flour
2	cups milk	1	teaspoon salt

✷ Beat together eggs, milk, flour, and salt.

✷ Pour ½ cup batter into a lightly greased pan and tip pan from side to side to spread batter thinly. Cook until batter is done; then turn and cook on other side just enough to brown slightly. The pancakes can be stacked and cut in quarters or left single and rolled.

WONDERFUL WESTERN WAFFLES

A great and tasty "Stick-to-Your-Ribs" food to start off a "Round-Up-Going Day!" A real guest pleaser!

4–6 servings

1	cup all-purpose flour	2	eggs, lightly beaten
½	cup yellow cornmeal	½	cup melted butter (or bacon drippings)
1	cup rolled oats		
2	tablespoons baking powder	3	cups buttermilk
½	teaspoon salt		

✷ Put flour, cornmeal, oats, baking powder, and salt into a bowl. Add lightly beaten eggs, melted butter (or bacon drippings), and buttermilk. Mix well. Batter should be bubbly, and of pouring consistency. Let batter stand for a short time (15-30 minutes) to allow the baking powder to work. Batter will almost double in volume.

✷ Pour onto waffle iron and cook until golden.

PENDLETON ROUND-UP COURT BREAKFAST

This is the traditional dish served the December morning when the new court is announced. Thanks to Susan Olsen Corey and Heather Hales Corey for sharing this!

8-10 people

1	7-ounce can diced green chiles	3	eggs
2	pounds ground sausage (1 hot & spicy), browned and drained	2	cups 2% or whole milk
4-6	green onions, chopped	¼-½	cup biscuit baking mix
1	pound Cheddar cheese, shredded	3	tomatoes, sliced
1	pound Monterey Jack cheese, shredded		Salsa
			Diced avocado
			Sour cream
			Sliced black olives

✶ In buttered 9x13-inch baking dish layer green chiles, browned and drained sausage, chopped green onions, and both shredded cheeses.

✶ Beat eggs, milk, and biscuit baking mix together. Pour egg mixture over layers. Bake at 325° for 35 minutes, uncovered. Add the sliced tomatoes and bake for 10 minutes more. Let rest 10 minutes before serving. Serve with the above condiments.

1994 Round-Up Princess Mary Wachter

The talk of the town is always "who will be on next year's Round-Up court?" The announcement is made in mid-December at a breakfast hosted by the Corey family. The location is either at the century farm home of Doug and Heather Hales Corey near Adams, or at the home of Steve and Susan Olsen Corey on the outskirts of Pendleton. They have hosted the party since 1993 and even the hosts never know who is coming to breakfast until the court and their parents walk in the door.

Each girl has been told by the Court Director that she is on the court, but doesn't know who the other court members are until the entire court comes together for the announcement breakfast.

Like the court selection process, this casserole has been kept a secret until now...*Susan Olsen Corey and Heather Hales Corey*

When I was a little girl in the 1940's and we lived on Carden Street. From our garage roof, my brother and I could see Teepee Town and watch the cannon go off at the beginning of the show. The 1950's were my teen years, and that's when Round-Up became so special to me. We were cute young girls then, and looking for a cowboy was great fun. I'm in my sixties now, and still enjoy looking for those cowboys in cowboy hats! I have had the opportunity to move around these western states, but my heart and wonderful memories will always be in Pendleton and I'll always call it home. Such sweet memories of the Pendleton Round-Up...*Dicey Strom Graham*

O'Rourke's Buckaroo Bunkhouse, North Hill, Buckaroo Flats

CHEESE SOUFFLÉ

Strata Simplified!

10–12 servings

4	slices sourdough bread	1½	cups milk
1	pound sharp Cheddar cheese, grated	1	teaspoon dry mustard
4	eggs, beaten	1	teaspoon salt

✱ Cut up the bread into chunks and put in greased 9x12-inch casserole dish. Mix cheese, eggs, milk, mustard, and salt and pour over cubed bread. Cover and refrigerate overnight.

✱ Bake uncovered at 350° for 1 hour.

Add ½ cup chopped onion or 1 cup cubed ham. Or both!

NO PAN OMELET

Great for camp-outs, no pan, no plates, no clean up!

Enough for as many campers as you have.

Quart-size zipper lock freezer bags (1 per person)

Eggs (2 per person)

Cooked meat of your choice, bacon, sausage (link or bulk), ham (diced)

Chopped vegetables, onions, mushrooms, peppers (green or hot), tomatoes-etc.

Grated or crumbled cheese

Salt and black pepper or spices of your choice

✱ Bring a large pot of water to a boil.

✱ Crack 2 eggs into the zip lock bag. Carefully scramble with a fork. Add the meat and vegetables, salt and pepper or spices (not the cheese). Squeeze the air out and zip shut. Drop into the boiling water and cook for 12-13 minutes. Remove bag, add cheese, reseal the bag and put back in the boiling water for 1 more minute.

✱ Enjoy your omelet right out of the bag or slide out onto plate and serve.

Be very cautious — the bag will be hot, hot, hot.

COOK AND HOLD SCRAMBLED EGGS

An electric frying pan is needed. These eggs work great for those sleepyheads who stayed at the Let 'er Buck Room too long yesterday.

Enough for 2 cowboys or 6 people.

½	cup margarine or butter	¼	teaspoon white pepper
12	eggs	2	tablespoons instant blending flour
1⅓	cups milk		
1	teaspoon salt		

✱ Melt margarine or butter in electric frying pan on 175°.

✱ Combine eggs, milk, salt, pepper, and flour in large mixing bowl. Beat with rotary beater until well blended. Pour into electric frying pan and turn temperature gauge to 250°. Stir eggs with rubber spatula from outside edge toward center, allowing uncooked eggs to flow to outside edge of frying pan. Continue stirring until all the eggs have cooked and look creamy. BE CAREFUL NOT TO OVERCOOK.

✱ Lower temperature gauge to 170°. Cover the pan. The eggs may be held up to 2 hours. If you need the frying pan for another batch of eggs, transfer the eggs to another pan. Cover it and put it in a 175° oven for up to 2 hours.

When I moved to Pendleton in 1994, I was definitely a "foreign body." I was born and raised in Cincinnati, and I had worked in England for 29 years before coming to Pendleton. I wasn't worried about this however, as I had become well acquainted with folks like Creagh Brennan, George and Joan Corey, Creagh Hawes, Teddie and Verne Pearson, and Margaret and Verner Troedson when they visited me in England. When Round-Up activities were in high gear in September 1994, I was included in all of them, starting with a breakfast party by the river on the Pearson's patio: Cook Ahead Scrambled Eggs, grilled lamb chops, and gin fizzes! Let 'er Buck!...*Sylvia Clawson*

Teepee Raisers

Glenn Thorne was a Round-Up Director from 1968 to 1976. He was President in 1975 and 1976. He was the Director of Queen and Court in 1969 and 1970 and Margaret assisted him as chaperone. She was a marvelous cook and liked to entertain during all of those years. One of the traditions they started was the brunch to announce the new queen and court. This tradition has continued to this day and is now hosted by the Corey Family...
Jill Thorne

2007-2008 Round-Up President Butch Thurman and Round-Up Director Tygh Campbell

HUEVOS RANCHEROS

Sauce can be made ahead of time for fast and easy meal.

6 servings

2	tablespoons vegetable oil
½	cup chopped onion
¼	cup chopped green pepper
1	clove garlic, minced
2	canned green chiles, drained, seeded and chopped
2	tablespoons chopped cilantro
½	teaspoon salt
2	cups chopped tomatoes or one 14.5-ounce can chopped tomatoes
6	6-inch corn tortillas
1	tablespoon vegetable oil
6	eggs
½	cup shredded Monterey Jack cheese

✱ In a 2-quart saucepan over medium-high heat, heat 2 tablespoons oil. Sauté onion, green pepper, garlic, chiles, cilantro, and salt until tender, about 5 minutes. Stir in tomatoes, and reduce heat to low. Simmer, uncovered, 20 minutes or until thickened, stirring often. Keep warm.

✱ Wrap tortillas in foil. Heat at 325° for 10 minutes or until warm.

✱ In a 10-inch skillet over medium heat, add remaining 1 tablespoon oil, and fry eggs to desired doneness.

✱ To serve: Place warm tortilla on plate, and top each with one egg. Spoon sauce over each egg, and top with cheese. Serve immediately.

OVERNIGHT SAUSAGE SOUFFLÉ

This is as good plain as it is served with a salsa or mushroom sauce of your choice.

8-10 servings

1	pound link sausage	4	eggs, beaten
6	slices bread, cubed	2	cups milk
1	cup grated sharp Cheddar cheese	½	teaspoon salt
		½	teaspoon dry mustard

✱ Cook sausage links, drain and cut into thirds. Alternate layers of bread cubes, sausage, and cheese in buttered 2½-quart baking dish.

✱ Beat eggs, add salt, mustard, and milk. Mix together. Pour mixture over bread cubes, and sausage. Cover and refrigerate overnight.

✱ Bake uncovered in a 325° oven for 45 minutes to 1 hour.

Substitute 3 cups cooked diced ham for the sausage.

This dish can be frozen after assembling and before baking.

JACK CHEESE OMELET CASSEROLE

This dish is a specialty of 2005 Round-Up Court Chaperone, Patty DeGrofft.

6 servings

8	eggs	1	small bunch green onions, thinly sliced
1	cup milk		
½	teaspoon seasoned salt	2½	cups shredded Monterey Jack cheese
1	12-ounce package bacon, cooked and coarsely chopped		

✱ Beat eggs with milk and seasoned salt. Stir in crumbled bacon, sliced green onions, and 2 cups of cheese. Pour into a greased 2-quart baking dish.

✱ Bake uncovered at 350° for 45 minutes. When lightly browned, add remaining cheese and bake 10 more minutes. Let rest 10 minutes before serving.

The Teepee Raising party was the kickoff event for the Round-Up that was given by Gwen and Steve Thompson, our parents, the weekend of the Dress-Up Parade. The tradition began when our father acquired an authentic, hand-painted teepee from the Umatilla Indian Reservation. It took many "chiefs" to raise the teepee, thus the reason for a party. The stories told mention that sometimes it took several tries before it was secure, but as the years went by, new tricks were learned, and it became easier to raise.

There were usually 20-45 guests and with this many people it was important to have a menu that could be made ahead of time and frozen. The Overnight Sausage Soufflé was a hit and traditionally served with Salty Dogs or Bloody Marys. This is a family favorite that we still prepare for many occasions. The teepee could accommodate several guests when Gwen and Steve's home was filled with company. These guests were usually last minute invitees that Jan would happen on who needed a place to rest...
Judy Thompson Schneider, Jan Thompson Bliss-Beach

ROUND-UP CHICKEN BRUNCH SOUFFLÉ

20-25 servings

I've used this recipe several times when our family hosted a brunch for the Round-Up and Happy Canyon courts and chaperones. Our family has had a number of young women on the courts over the years. This recipe works well for schedules that are hard to predict, as sometimes happens during Round-Up! This can stay on warm in the oven until everyone arrives. It's just been a big hit and goes nicely with fresh fruit and rolls...*Mary Lou Lazinka*

24	slices stale bread, with or without crusts, diced	12	eggs
5	pounds cooked chicken, diced	3	cups milk
3	cups chopped celery	2-3	10.5-ounce cans cream of chicken soup
2	onions, diced	3	cups Cheddar cheese
1½	cups mayonnaise		

✷ Place half of diced bread on bottom of 2 medium casserole dishes.

✷ Mix chicken with celery, onion, mayonnaise, spread over bread. Sprinkle the rest of the diced bread on top.

✷ Beat the eggs and milk together and pour over both pans and refrigerate overnight.

✷ Remove from refrigerator 30 minutes before baking. Bake in 325° oven 15 minutes. Spoon soup over, then sprinkle with cheese.

✷ Return to 325° oven and bake 1 hour. Let stand for 10-15 minutes before serving.

Judy Lazinka Currin, Kathryn Lazinka Thorne, Jean Lazinka Barbouletos, Patti Healy Adair, Annie Hisler Weygandt before the Westward Ho! Parade, 2005 Round-Up

ROMPIN' STOMPIN' EGGS

After the first baking time, and the cheeses have been added, you can freeze and bake later.

6 servings

1½ 12-ounce tubes ground sausage
¼ pound fresh mushrooms, sliced
1 medium onion, chopped
Salt and black pepper to taste
12 eggs
6 tablespoons sour cream

1 small can green chiles
⅓ cup salsa
1 8-ounce package processed cheese loaf, sliced
1 8-ounce package medium Cheddar cheese, sliced
1 8-ounce package mozzarella cheese, sliced

✳ Cook crumbled sausage with mushrooms, onions, salt, and pepper. Drain well on paper towels.

✳ Combine eggs and sour cream in blender and blend for 1 minute. Add green chiles and blend, slightly. Pour eggs into a greased 9x13-inch baking dish. Bake at 400° for 8-10 minutes until set in the middle.

✳ Spoon salsa over eggs and add sausage mix. Then layer the 3 cheeses beginning with the processed cheese loaf, medium Cheddar, and then mozzarella cheese. Bake uncovered at 300° for 45 minutes. Remove from oven and let sit 5-10 minutes before cutting.

This picture was taken at the original Happy Canyon grounds on S.W. Emigrant Street in 1947, before Happy Canyon moved to its present location next to the Round-Up grounds. Helping remove a tooth with a state of the art tooth removing tool are: Jack Luck, Sid Laing, Gordon Hertz, Bert Jerard, Leo Goar, George Moens, Ollie Olsen, Raley Peterson, Larry Jensen, Jens Terjeson, Elmer Pahl, and Homer Beal.

In 1911, anticipating a big crowd, thirty dozen chairs and 1000 cots were purchased. People in Pendleton were asked to volunteer space for cots in their homes during the three days of the show. The board made arrangements for camping grounds and sought to place cots in various lodge halls. Obviously this was the forerunner of the Chamber of Commerce Home Stay program, where local residents open up their homes to our visitors.

CRANBERRY–APPLE CRISP

This is a nice light addition to any brunch or salad luncheon.

6–8 servings

3   cups peeled and chopped apples, Granny Smith or Jonathan's

2   cups fresh cranberries

2   tablespoons all-purpose flour

1   cup granulated sugar

3   packages (1.23 ounces each) instant oatmeal with cinnamon and spice

¾   cup chopped pecans

½   cup all-purpose flour

½   cup firmly packed brown sugar

½   cup butter or margarine, melted

Garnish with a few whole pecans and cranberries, (optional)

✳ Combine all apples and cranberries with 2 tablespoons of flour, tossing to coat. Add 1 cup sugar, mixing well. Place mixture in a 2-quart baking dish.

✳ Combine oatmeal, chopped pecans, ½ cup flour, and brown sugar. Add melted butter or margarine and mix well. Spoon mixture over fruit. Bake uncovered at 350° for 45 minutes.

The 1911 version of the Pendleton Round-Up traffic jam

1975 PENDLETON ROUND-UP COURT COFFEE CAKE (NO PAIN, PLENTY GAIN)

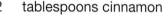

The court members found this in the Sweet Potato Queens Cookbook and adopted it as their own.

12 servings

1	package (24) frozen bread rolls	2	tablespoons cinnamon
1	3.5-ounce package instant butterscotch pudding mix (4 serving-size)	¼	cup butter, melted
		½	cup chopped pecan pieces
1	cup dark brown sugar		

✱ Put half of the frozen rolls in a greased Bundt pan. Then put one-half package of the pudding mix, ½ cup dark brown sugar, 1 tablespoon cinnamon, 2 tablespoons of the melted butter and ¼ cup of chopped pecan over the rolls.

✱ Repeat with the remaining ingredients as above. Cover pan loosely with foil that has been sprayed with vegetable cooking oil. Put a clean towel over that and let sit out overnight. The dough will thaw and rise (if it rises over the top-poke it down).

✱ Next morning bake in preheated oven (350°) for 30 minutes. When done, turn upside down on a serving plate and enjoy.

1975 Round-Up Court Michele Evans, Ann Lorenzen, Queen Lori Anderson, Susan Fitterer, and Jan Terjeson

The 1975 Pendleton Round-Up Court has been getting together for an annual reunion for about 20 years. "We just wanted the fun and friendships we had on the court to continue. We started out at each other's homes, then for girls' weekends at various spots in the Pacific Northwest, including the 'Working Girls Hotel' in Pendleton! We aren't known to be a group that does much cooking when we gather together, but Susan gave us a series of "Sweet Potato Queens" books, and one was a hilarious cookbook. She made us this recipe "No-Pain, Plenty-Gain" Coffee Cake, which we now request every year."...

Queen Lori Anderson Johnson, Princesses Susan Fitterer Kingham, Jan Terjeson Hoffman, Ann Lorenzen Hulden, and Princess-in-waiting Nancy Bittner.

PENDLETON HOUSE
BED AND BREAKFAST ORANGE CAKE

Just the thing to serve with scrambled eggs.

8–10 servings

1½ cups chopped walnuts
1 cup all-purpose flour
1 tablespoon baking powder
4 large eggs
1½ cups granulated sugar

½ cup orange juice
1 tablespoon finely grated orange zest
½ cup olive oil
Powdered sugar

★ Spray 9-inch diameter springform pan with nonstick olive oil spray. Place parchment paper round in the bottom of pan and spray the paper.

★ Grind walnuts in food processor until finely ground but not powdery. Combine ground walnuts, flour, and baking powder. Set aside.

★ Using a mixer, beat eggs in a large bowl until frothy, about 2 minutes. Gradually add sugar, beating until thick and a pale yellow, about 4 minutes. Gradually add walnut and flour mixture.

★ Add orange juice, orange zest, and olive oil, and beat until blended. Transfer to prepared pan. Place on a cookie sheet and bake at 350° until tester comes out clean, about 1 hour. Cool cake completely in pan on rack.

★ Release pan sides. Carefully invert cake onto platter and remove parchment paper. Sprinkle powdered sugar on top of cake and serve.

CHUTE

3

Breads, Rolls, Muffins, & Biscuits

This picture says "We're ready for Round-Up!" like no other. It's the end of harvest and Round-Up is next!

Pictured here is a crew at the Hager Field in 1980. From left to right and up and down: Don Stewart, Jim Lieuallen, Marilyn Lieuallen, Mary Kay Lieuallen, Michael Middlestead, J.T. Lieuallen, Marty Lieuallen, Rich Lieuallen, Marla Lieuallen, Sheldon Lieuallen, Joe Lieuallen, Roger Flory, Phillip Morrison, Shawn Lieuallen, Linda Lieuallen.

DUNLAP BREAD

Shelley Swanson Dunlap received this recipe from her mother, 1941 Round-Up Princess Helen Proebstel Swanson, and she's made it for so long that it's become her signature bread.

3 loaves of bread

2 cups warm water	3⅓ cups all-purpose flour
1 tablespoon active dry yeast	Vegetable oil, for bowl and top of dough
1 tablespoon granulated sugar	Cornmeal for dusting loaves
1 tablespoon salt	¼ cup butter, melted for drizzling on loaves
¾ cup wheat bran, raw	
1½ cups whole wheat flour	

✴ Mix water, yeast, and sugar and let set for 5 minutes. Add salt, raw wheat bran, wheat flour, and 1 cup white flour. Mix 300 strokes. Very slowly add 2 cups white flour until you can knead dough. Turn dough onto lightly floured (⅓ cup) surface. Knead for 15 minutes. Place in oiled bowl, with oil brushed on top of dough. Cover and let rise 1 hour.

✴ Divide dough into 3 pieces. Roll each about 8-10 inches long. Brush with oil and roll in cornmeal. Place on cookie sheet, slit each loaf down the center length. Cover and let rise until double in bulk. Spoon a little melted butter down center of each loaf. Bake in 350-375° oven for 30 minutes or until done.

This bread is good sliced and spread with butter mixed with mashed garlic, wrapped in foil and heated until warm.

*Princess
Helen Proebstel Swanson
in 1941*

One of my fondest memories of Round-Up is as a child of about 10 getting to go to the night show on Main Street. My father and mother, Fred and Sharon Livingston, and my brothers Clayton and F.J. and I met two other families, the Rileys and the Alfords in Pendleton for dinner. We kids, ten of us in all, were so excited to get to stay up late and go to the show that we barely let our parents eat dinner before we rushed them out of the door. I remember a cool fall evening, eating our fill of cotton candy and other treats, listening to the music, watching our parents dance and joining in when the feeling moved us. By the end of the evening show, we were exhausted and asleep almost as soon as the car doors closed. The next day after the pancake breakfast in the park, we were glued to our seats watching the Saturday performance. It was a wonderful trip and little did I know that years later I would have the honor of representing the Pendleton Round-Up as its Queen in 1979. That too was a wonderful experience and I have many memories of that year...*Rilla Livingston*

NEW ENGLAND
OATMEAL–MOLASSES BREAD

This recipe makes four loaves of substantial bread, and is especially good for toasting and for French toast with real maple syrup. Dr. George Nelson, former Round-Up director, brought this recipe with him from Vermont and has been making it for over thirty years.

4 loaves of bread

3	packets active dry yeast	2	teaspoons salt
1	cup lukewarm water	2	teaspoons cinnamon
4	cups old-fashioned rolled oats	1	teaspoon nutmeg
2	tablespoons shortening	4	cups boiling water
1	cup molasses	11	cups all-purpose flour

✱ In a small bowl, dissolve yeast in 1 cup lukewarm water.

✱ In a large bowl, mix with a spoon: oats, shortening, molasses, salt, cinnamon, and nutmeg. Add 4 cups boiling water, mix thoroughly, and let set 15-20 minutes. Add yeast solution and mix, add 4 cups flour and stir to even consistency, add 4 more cups flour and mix well, add 2½ cups more flour, just to distribute flour.

✱ Knead dough on floured (last ½ cup) surface. Knead until blended and dough is smooth. Place in greased bowl and invert immediately. Cover with towel. Let rise until doubled, about 1 hour and 15 minutes.

✱ Punch down and knead again 3-4 times, turn over and cut into 4 sections. Roll each piece to ½ inch thick and the width of bread pan. Roll up, beginning with short side, forming a loaf, pinching edges and ends. Place in 4 greased 9x5x3-inch pans edge side down. Let rise again, about 1 hour and 15 minutes.

✱ Place loaves in a cold oven (not preheated). Turn on oven to 325° and bake for 25 minutes, turn the loaves around and bake another 20 minutes, a total of 45 minutes.

✱ Remove loaves from oven, leave in pan on cooling racks covered with a towel for 5-10 minutes, then turn out of pan. Brush tops with melted butter or margarine for a soft crust, or simply let cool.

EASTERN OREGON RANCH BREAD

Moist, flavorful bread, also great toasted. And here's your chance to get your own sourdough starter.

3 loaves of bread

Sourdough has been in our family for generations. My father made sourdough pancakes or biscuits over the campfire when we would camp out during the cattle drive to the mountains each spring. The grandchildren now ask, "Grandma, will you mix up the sourdough?" Sourdough waffles are a family tradition for Christmas morning breakfast...*Rilla and Sharon Livingston*

SOURDOUGH STARTER (SHOULD BE MADE AT LEAST 3-5 DAYS BEFORE MAKING BREAD)

1	packet active dry yeast	2	tablespoons sugar
2½	cups warm milk	2	cups all-purpose flour

✱ Stir yeast, milk, and sugar together until yeast is dissolved. Stir in flour gradually until a smooth batter forms.

✱ Let stand, loosely covered in a warm place 3-5 days. Stir down batter occasionally.

BREAD

3	teaspoons salt	2	cups milk
1	packet active dry yeast	½	cup shortening (can be butter, margarine, or oil)
3	cups all-purpose flour		
½	cup sugar	3	eggs (beaten slightly with fork)
1	cup mashed potatoes (can use instant)	2	cups sourdough starter
		4	cups all-purpose flour

✱ Mix the salt, yeast, 3 cups flour, sugar, potatoes, milk, shortening, eggs, and sourdough starter together until well blended.

✱ Add the 4 cups of flour (add ½ cup at a time).

✱ Put on floured surface and knead well until it is not sticky to the hands (add a little more flour if necessary).

✱ Place in a greased bowl. Lightly oil the top of the sponge and let rise until doubled in bulk.

✱ Punch down and knead again. Let rest 15 minutes.

✱ Knead lightly again and divide into 3 loaves. Place loaves into 3 greased 9x5x3-inch loaf pans.

✱ Bake at 375° for 30 minutes, or until golden brown.

SEPT. 15 - 18, 2004

This bread was baked every Saturday, especially during Round-Up. Family and friends would drift into the Culham House at 113 SE 10th for hot fresh bread. The favorite of the kids was to cut the heels from the loaves while still hot and pad them with loads of butter. The other favorite was "puffs" made from the dough, the Culham family version of fry bread. Mary Jane Culham would pull off golf-ball sized pieces of dough and fry them in melted shortening. Hot out of the pan, the puffs would be smothered in butter and syrup or peanut butter and syrup...*Carl R. Culham*

CULHAM FAMILY BREAD

If you double this recipe, you'll need a very large bowl to mix it in, but it will be the only baking you'll have to do during Round-Up.

3–4 loaves

½	cup margarine		1	package dry yeast
2¾	cups hot water		⅓	cup hot water
1	cup powdered milk		1	teaspoon granulated sugar
½	cup granulated sugar		10-12	cups all-purpose flour
1	tablespoon salt			

✱ Melt margarine and mix with the hot water, powdered milk, sugar, and salt.

✱ Dissolve yeast in ⅓ cup hot water with a teaspoon of sugar. The yeast will swell and become foamy.

✱ Measure flour into a large bowl. Make a well in the middle of flour and add the liquids. Mix well then knead well. Place in greased bowl and let rise until it's doubled in size.

✱ Punch dough to knock down, knead it down, and let rise again. Divide into 3 or 4 parts, knead each well, and put into 3-4 well greased loaf pans. Let rise, then bake at 350° for 30-40 minutes. The loaves will sound hollow when thumped.

RUSTIC RYE BREAD

Great for ham sandwiches.

two 8-inch round loaves

2	tablespoons active dry yeast	⅔	cup brown sugar
1	cup warm water	3½	tablespoons dark molasses
1	cup all-purpose flour	3	tablespoons melted butter
1	teaspoon granulated sugar	1	tablespoon grated orange rind
1	cup warm water	1	teaspoon salt
3½	cups (or more) all-purpose flour	1	teaspoon vinegar
1½	cups rye flour		Pinch of whole anise

✷ Soften yeast in 1 cup warm water.

✷ Combine 1 cup flour and 1 teaspoon sugar. Add yeast mixture. Let stand until foamy. Stir in remaining warm water. Transfer all into large bowl. Add the flours, brown sugar, molasses, melted butter, orange rind, salt, vinegar, and anise and stir until well combined. Knead until satiny, 25-30 minutes, (can use bread hook). Let rise until doubled, about 1 hour.

✷ Turn dough out and knead until no longer sticky, about 10 minutes. Let rise 30 minutes. Divide into two 8-inch round loaves. Let rise 30 minutes.

✷ Bake at 350° for 25-30 minutes or until loaves are lightly browned.

On August 15, 1940, a fire broke out in the old grandstand during a softball game in the Round-Up arena. The grandstand and all of the Round-Up's freight wagons, stage coaches, buggies, bandwagons, and a sleigh, all stored under the grandstand, were destroyed. Earlier that year, in April, three barns and a shed had burned. With less than a month left until the show, the directors worked "36 hours a day" and 23 days later, a 3,000 seat concrete grandstand was ready. People came together. Some gave a day's wages and contributions came from all over the Northwest, including some offers of old horse-drawn parade vehicles. Opening day was bigger and better than ever. Volunteers are the backbone of Round-Up and always have been.

Both cowgirls and cowboys competed in the Round-Up arena until 1929. The colorful era of the cowgirl at the Round-Up ended in tragedy that year when Bonnie McCarroll died as a result of injuries from a bucking accident. Round-Up directors banned women from bucking events as a result. Bonnie, 32, rode with her stirrups hobble-tied beneath the horse's belly. Most cowgirls rode bucking horses this way. The horse fell on her and dragged her around the arena. Today, cowgirls have returned to competing at the Round-Up as barrel racers.

ENGLISH MUFFIN LOAVES

Excellent toasted!

2 loaves

5½-6	cups all-purpose flour	¼	teaspoon baking soda
2	packets active dry yeast	2	cups milk
1	tablespoon granulated sugar	½	cup water
2	teaspoons salt		Cornmeal (for dusting)

✸ Combine 3 cups flour, yeast, sugar, salt, and baking soda. Heat milk and water until very warm (120°-130°). Add to dry ingredients, beat well (can use mixer). Then stir in enough more flour to make a stiff batter.

✸ Spoon into two 8½x4½-inch pans that have been greased and sprinkled with cornmeal. Sprinkle top with cornmeal. Cover and let rise in warm place for 45 minutes.

✸ Bake at 400° for 25 minutes. Remove from pans immediately and cool. To serve: slice and toast.

KICKED-UP CHEESE BREAD

Great cheese bread with a Cowboy Punch!

16 servings

1	loaf sourdough French bread	1	cup grated sharp Cheddar cheese
6	tablespoons butter		
1	medium Walla Walla sweet onion, chopped	1½	cups mayonnaise
			Garlic salt (to taste)
		1	cup grated Parmesan cheese

✸ Slice bread in half lengthwise. Butter each half of the loaf.

✸ Mix onion, Cheddar cheese, and mayonnaise together and spread on each half of the loaf. Sprinkle both halves with the garlic salt. Generously top the bread with grated Parmesan cheese.

✸ Place the bread on a baking sheet and bake at 425° for 15-20 minutes, until the bread is browned around the edges.

✸ Slice and serve warm.

INDIAN FRY BREAD

Best when eaten warm, right out of the fryer.

6–8 servings

4	cups all-purpose flour	2	cups water
3	tablespoons baking powder		Powdered sugar (optional)
2	tablespoons powdered milk		Honey (optional)
2	teaspoons salt		Huckleberry jam (optional)
1	tablespoon shortening		

✴ Sift all dry ingredients together. Mix in shortening. Add water slowly. Knead until soft. Cover with a towel and let rest for about 10 minutes. Flatten and shape into size wanted and deep fry. Drain and serve.

Indian fry bread can be served plain, sprinkled with powdered sugar, drizzled with honey or the traditional way is with huckleberry jam.

This recipe is from the Indian Cookbook-Earth Company 1974

To many attending the Round-Up, the smell of hot, golden crispy fry bread with butter and huckleberry jam just says "Round-Up" to them.

Food has played an important role in Round-Up celebrations over the decades, and each family and organization has added its own spin. The participation of the Umatilla, Cayuse, and Walla Walla tribes, dating back to the very first rodeo, makes the Pendleton gathering a unique event and adds to the diversity of food associated with Round-Up.

Fry bread appears to have been produced in some form by North American native peoples after European contact. It has many wonderful uses, such as a replacement for bread as a sandwich or using it instead of a tortilla for a taco. Served with butter and huckleberry jam is the all-time Round-Up favorite.

There are as many recipes for fry bread as there are people who make it. Some guard their own versions and don't want to share their recipes. However, they welcome Round-Up fans to their teepees in the village where they happily serve it to visitors. In Roy Raley Park, Native American vendors sell fry bread to guests and let them choose the jam, jelly, or honey that they want to smother on the soft bread.

Mary Hines, respected tribal matriarch, believes that the secret to fry bread is in the kneading ... half an hour at the least.

"Chief Clarence Burke and Frank Tubbs cementing the relationship between the Cowboys and the Indians of Round-Up."

More than once, the Round-Up directors were encouraged to bring their Wild West Show to another venue. It was suggested in 1931 by the District of Columbia's bi-centennial committee that the Round-Up be transplanted to the nation's capital for the event. Round-Up President Henry Collins said, "To set the real Round-Up down in Washington, it would be necessary to take the whole city of Pendleton, people and all, back there, too. For the Round-Up is not just a Wild West show. It is the product of active, intelligent, and general community spirit."

WHOLE WHEAT FRY BREAD

Making fry bread more healthy.

6–8 servings

2	cups whole wheat flour	1	teaspoon salt
2	cups all-purpose flour	¼	cup vegetable oil
4	tablespoons baking powder	1	cup warm water

✳ Mix together whole wheat flour, white flour, baking powder, and salt. Add vegetable oil a little at a time, only enough to make the mixture look like cornmeal.

✳ Slowly add 1 cup warm water, only adding enough to make the dough stick together. Roll into fist sized balls. Cover the bowl with a towel for about 10 minutes.

✳ Pat dough out with your hands to the size of large pancakes.

✳ Fry in hot vegetable oil until golden brown on both sides (about 375°).

To make an Indian Taco: put beans, shredded lettuce, tomato, and cheese on top of fry bread.

No Knead Crescent Rolls

A versatile roll and an easy-to-make roll for the first time roll maker.

3 dozen

1	cup milk	½	cup cold water
½	cup granulated sugar	3	eggs, well beaten
½	cup vegetable oil	2	packets active dry yeast
1	teaspoon salt	5	cups all-purpose flour

✷ Scald the milk. Add sugar, oil, salt, and cold water to scalded milk. Mix in the well beaten eggs and the dry yeast. Gradually add the flour, mixing well. No kneading is necessary. Can be mixed in electric mixer.

✷ Put dough in greased bowl and cover with waxed paper and a towel and let rise until it doubles in bulk.

✷ Divide dough into three equal parts and roll into pie shapes about ½-inch thick on floured board. Cut each pie shape into quarters and each quarter into thirds. Begin at large end and roll into rolls. Place on greased baking sheet and let rise until doubled.

✷ Bake at 375° for 13-15 minutes.

This roll dough can also be made into round sandwich buns.

Cinnamon Rolls

Great for large family gatherings and every Round-Up morning!

30 rolls

1	batch of Round-Up Ropin' Roll Dough (page 68)	2	cups brown sugar
1	cup butter, melted	1	tablespoon cinnamon
		2	tablespoons corn syrup

✷ Mix butter, brown sugar, cinnamon, and corn syrup in saucepan and cook until all of the butter and sugar are melted and blended together.

✷ Divide above dough in half and roll out into a rectangle about ⅓-inch thick. When the butter and sugar mixture is cool, pour onto the rectangle and roll up. Cut each half into 15 slices. Put into 2 greased 9x12-inch pans. Let rise for 30 minutes.

✷ Bake at 350° for 20 minutes. Remove from oven and turn over on waxed paper.

May drizzle with frosting.

To scald milk, place milk in a heavy-bottomed pan on low heat. Stir occasionally until milk is just hot with steam and small bubbles appear around the edges; do not boil. Remove from the heat.

For quick and easy breadsticks, split a hot dog bun down the middle and cut each half lengthwise. Butter each strip. Sprinkle with garlic salt or garlic powder. Place on a cookie sheet and broil until toasted.

Place aluminum foil under the napkin in your roll basket and the rolls will stay hot longer.

To glaze the tops of rolls, brush with a mixture of 1 tablespoon sugar and ¼ cup milk before baking.

For a soft, well-browned but not shiny crust, before baking, brush the loaf with a tablespoon of melted butter.

For a crisp, shiny crust, bake the bread for 20 minutes, then remove from the oven and brush with an egg white that has been beaten with 1 tablespoon of water. Return the bread to the oven to finish baking.

ROUND-UP ROPIN' ROLL DOUGH

Also basic roll dough for Cinnamon and Golden Crown rolls.

2½–3 dozen rolls

1½	cups milk	1½	teaspoons salt
½	cup granulated sugar	¼	cup butter or shortening, melted
2	packets active dry yeast		
2	eggs, beaten	5½	cups all-purpose flour

★ Scald the milk. Add sugar and cool to lukewarm; then add yeast and let sit 5 minutes to activate yeast.

★ In a large mixing bowl, mix the 2 beaten eggs, salt, and melted butter or shortening. Blend in the yeast mixture to egg mixture. Add 3 cups of flour, beat well with mixer, then slowly add remaining flour to make a soft dough. Turn onto lightly floured board; knead until smooth and satiny and no longer sticky, 5-8 minutes. Place in oiled bowl and let rise to double in size. Punch down and let rise again.

★ Make into rolls, place in greased pans, and let rise for 30 minutes. Bake in 375° oven for 15-20 minutes

This dough doubles well.

GOLDEN CROWN ROLLS

A little different take on cinnamon rolls, this recipe makes a beautiful cinnamon ring.

4½ dozen

½	cup butter, melted	¾	cup finely chopped walnuts
1	cup granulated sugar	1	batch of Round-Up Ropin' Roll Dough
¼	teaspoon cinnamon		

★ Roll balls into a little smaller than golf ball size. Roll each ball in melted butter then into mixture of sugar and cinnamon and chopped nuts. Arrange in a well greased 9-inch angel food cake pan and sprinkle with remaining sugar-nut mixture. Cover and rise until doubled.

★ Bake in 375° oven for 15 minutes, then decrease heat to between 350-325°. Bake for 30-40 minutes or until golden brown.

★ When done, cool in pan for 5 minutes, then turn upside down on serving plate and leave the pan around the rolls until cooled. This will keep the rolls together in a ring.

LET 'ER ROLL CINNAMON ROLLS

A cinnamon roll recipe that was used by Wilma Tucker, who was a cook for some of the ranches in the surrounding area.

24 cinnamon rolls

2	packages dry yeast		2	teaspoons salt
½	cup warm water		3	eggs, beaten
½	cup granulated sugar		½	cup vegetable oil, or melted margarine or butter
2	cups milk, scalded and cooled			
8	cups all-purpose flour			

FILLING

½	cup melted margarine or butter		1	cup brown sugar
			1	tablespoon cinnamon

✱ Soften yeast in the warm water. Add sugar and warm milk, stirring until sugar is dissolved.

✱ Add 3 cups of the flour and salt, mix well. Set aside until it begins to bubble. About 45-60 minutes, depending how warm your kitchen is.

✱ Add eggs and oil and the rest of the flour (5 cups). Knead until smooth and satiny. Place in lightly oiled bowl, cover and let rise until doubled, about 1½-2 hours.

✱ While dough is rising, mix the melted margarine/butter, brown sugar, and cinnamon together.

✱ Divide the dough into 2 parts. Roll each part into a rectangle about 18x8-inches and ¼-inch thick. Spread with ½ filling mixture. Roll like a jelly roll, cut into 1½-inch slices. Follow same instructions for 2nd half of dough and place into two greased pans. Let rise until doubled in size.

✱ Bake at 350° for 35 minutes. Frost if desired.

Use dental floss to cut cinnamon rolls into slices. Slide floss under cinnamon roll, bring around the roll up to the top and over and through making a nice even slice.

I received this recipe, written by my grandmother, Wilma McBean Tucker, in the late 1980's. It was from my Aunt Gladys McBean Springston's recipe file. They were both terrific cooks! My grandmother was a cook for some of the ranches in the surrounding area...*Peggy Morris Bronson*

Volunteers always have turned out for the work days, and potluck buffets have helped to lighten the weekend of work.

Fritz Hill

RUM NUT ROLLS

Frozen bread dough needs to be thawed ahead of time-2½ to 4 hours.

12 rolls

1	pound loaf frozen bread dough (thawed)	½	teaspoon rum extract
½	cup brown sugar	¼	cup chopped nuts
¼	cup softened butter or margarine	2	tablespoons melted butter or margarine
1	tablespoon milk	½	cup brown sugar
2	teaspoons all-purpose flour	½	teaspoon rum extract

✷ Thaw bread dough, 2¼-4 hours

✷ Mix ½ cup brown sugar, ¼ cup butter or margarine, milk, flour, and rum extract. Bring to a slow boil. Pour into greased 7x10-inch cake pan. Sprinkle nuts over mixture.

✷ On lightly floured board, roll out dough to a 12x14-inch rectangle. Brush dough with 1 tablespoon melted butter or margarine.

✷ Mix brown sugar and rum extract; spread over dough.

✷ Beginning with the 14-inch side, roll dough up tightly. Cut into 1-inch pieces.

✷ Place cut side down in pan. Brush with remaining 1 tablespoon butter or margarine.

✷ Let rise until dough reaches top of pan.

✷ Bake at 350° for 20-25 minutes. Turn out immediately.

COCONUT BREAD

This bread is a hit for those whose sweet tooth is seriously sweet!

2 loaves

BREAD

5	eggs	2	cups all-purpose flour
2	cups granulated sugar	1	teaspoon salt
1	cup vegetable oil	1⅓	teaspoons baking powder
½	cup milk	1	cup flaked coconut

TOPPING

1	cup granulated sugar	½	cup margarine or butter
½	cup water	1	teaspoon coconut extract

✶ Beat eggs, sugar, oil, and milk together until thoroughly mixed.

✶ Combine flour, salt, and baking powder in a separate bowl. Add flour mixture to egg mixture and beat for about 1½ minutes. Add coconut. Pour into 2 greased and floured loaf pans. Bake 1 hour at 350°.

✶ About 15 minutes before the bread is done, combine topping ingredients (sugar, water, butter, and extract) in a small saucepan and bring to boil.

✶ Remove bread from the oven, and while still hot, using a meat fork, pierce holes through bread over the entire surface. Pour hot topping over bread and allow topping to soak into the loaves.

✶ Loosen edges of bread from loaf pans and place on cooling racks.

To store, wrap in foil. This bread will keep up to 2 weeks in the refrigerator.

This recipe has been a standby (and secret) recipe for years, and was contributed to the cookbook by Rachel Getman, who with her husband, Gary, serve as the scouts for the annual Round-Up / Happy Canyon Wagon Train that takes place in the Blue Mountains every June. Wagons Ho! They get to holler that every day.

The Main Street Free Show is a program of downtown hospitality and entertainment put together by a group of businessmen in 1950 not connected to Round-Up or Happy Canyon, but who wanted to contribute. Later, they took the name "Main Street Cowboys," and their daily free show continues today, billed as "The Greatest Free Show in the West."

BANDIT BANANA BREAD

Lock this one up or bandits will run right off with it.

1 loaf or 12 mini-muffins

2	cups bread flour		¼	cup butter
½	teaspoon baking powder		1	egg
½	teaspoon baking soda		⅔	cup mashed bananas
¼	teaspoon salt		3	tablespoons sour milk or buttermilk
¾	cup granulated sugar		½	cup broken nuts

✱ Sift flour before measuring. Resift measured flour with baking powder, baking soda, and salt.

✱ In another bowl cream until light, the sugar and butter, and beat until light and fluffy. Stir in the egg and mashed bananas.

✱ Stir banana mixture into flour mixture in three parts, mixing alternately with sour milk or buttermilk in three parts. Add nuts.

✱ Pour batter into greased 8½x4½-inch loaf pan. Bake at 350° for 45-60 minutes.

Pour batter into mini-sized muffin tins sprayed with vegetable spray. Use an ice cream scoop and fill half full. Bake 12-13 minutes at 350°.

This recipe can be doubled, as it freezes well. Flavor improves when it is used the next day, if it lasts that long.

Main Street Cowboys Finley Graybeal, Claude Sigman, Sprague Carter, Jr., Arlo Fjelland, Dan Bell, Chuck Hoover, and Gene Perkins help celebrate the opening of Sigman's new parking lot next to the Union Depot (April 6, 1956).

WHOLE WHEAT BANANA NUT BREAD

Very light and tender.

1 loaf

½ cup butter or margarine, melted

1 cup granulated sugar

2 eggs, lightly beaten

1 cup mashed bananas

1 cup all-purpose flour

1 cup whole wheat flour

½ teaspoon salt

1 teaspoon baking soda

⅓ cup hot water

½ cup chopped nuts of your choice

✱ Beat together butter or margarine and sugar. Mix in eggs and bananas, blending until smooth.

✱ Stir together all-purpose flour, whole wheat flour, salt, and baking soda. Add to banana mixture alternately with hot water. Fold in nuts.

✱ Pour into greased 9x5-inch loaf pan. Bake at 325° for 1 hour and 10 minutes.

Good served with butter or cream cheese.

CORN CAKES

Float these little corn cakes on top of steaming bowls of chili.

18 cakes

1½ cups water

¼ teaspoon salt

⅛ teaspoon garlic salt

½ cup hominy grits or cornmeal

½ cup shredded Cheddar cheese

✱ Boil water, salt, and garlic salt in a saucepan. Slowly add hominy grits or cornmeal, stirring constantly. Cook about 5-8 minutes, stirring constantly, until mixture is very thick. Add cheese; stir until melted.

✱ Drop by rounded teaspoonfuls on an ungreased baking sheet. Cool completely. Spoonfuls of mixture can be stored on baking sheet in refrigerator overnight.

✱ Using your hands, shape each spoonful of dough into a ball; flatten between palms. Return to baking sheet. Bake at 400° for 10 minutes.

2003 Happy Canyon Princess Talia Minthorn

My husband Ike and I own the Sankey Rodeo Company. We have been bringing bucking horses and bulls to the Round-Up for many years and have loved every minute of it. One of my greatest memories was getting to see Montie Montana perform in the 1990's, a half a century after his first performance at the Round-Up. WOW! In 2005 our son Wade made the "short go" in the bareback riding, the first year he entered there. That was exciting. We also look forward every year to the saddle bronc riding, Pendleton's signature event. To see our ranch-raised horses being competed on, on the grass with the world's best cowboys is a thrill! Let 'er Buck!...
Roberta Sankey

Montie Montana entertains the Round-Up crowd in 1997.

SANKEY RANCH CORNBREAD

Wonderfully moist!

15 squares

⅔	cup butter	2¾	tablespoons baking powder
1⅓	cups granulated sugar	1⅓	teaspoons salt
2	eggs	2⅓	cups all-purpose flour
2	cups milk	1	cup cornmeal

✳ Mix butter, granulated sugar, eggs, and milk together.

✳ Mix baking powder, salt, flour, and cornmeal together.

✳ Mix both mixtures together and pour into a greased 9x13-inch pan. Bake at 400° for 25 minutes or until done in middle.

'STIR-UP' CORN BREAD SUPREME

My friends rave when I serve this corn bread ..Lynn Whitacre Walker, 1961 Round-Up Court.

10 servings

½	cup butter	½	cup mild Cheddar cheese
½	cup granulated sugar	1	7-ounce can green chiles
4	eggs	1	cup all-purpose flour
1	16½-ounce can creamed corn	1	cup yellow cornmeal
½	cup grated Monterey Jack cheese	4	teaspoons baking powder
		½	teaspoon salt

✳ Cream the butter and granulated sugar. Add the eggs, one at a time, beating after each addition. Stir in the creamed corn and the cheeses, add green chiles.

✳ Sift the flour, cornmeal, baking powder, and salt together and stir into batter mixture. Pour into lightly buttered 9x13-inch pan. Bake at 350° for 30 minutes or until bread is lightly browned.

ORANGE MUFFINS

Great treat for breakfast before heading out to the festivities at the Round-Up Grounds!

36 miniature muffins

1	cup granulated sugar	1	teaspoon salt
½	cup fresh orange juice	1	teaspoon nutmeg
½	cup butter, room temperature	¾	cup sour cream or yogurt
1	cup granulated sugar	1	teaspoon grated orange rind
2	cups sifted all-purpose flour (measure after sifting)	½	cup raisins
1	teaspoon baking soda	½	cup chopped nuts
			Crystallized ginger (optional)

✳ Mix together granulated sugar and orange juice; set aside for dipping after muffins are cooked.

✳ Cream together butter and granulated sugar until smooth.

✳ In separate bowl, mix together flour, baking soda, salt, and nutmeg. Add sour cream or yogurt to butter-sugar egg mixture alternately with dry ingredients, stirring just until mixed. Add orange rind, raisins, nuts, and optional crystallized ginger. Put batter into well-greased miniature muffin tins. Bake at 375° for 12-15 minutes.

✳ Remove muffins from pans and while warm, dip them into the sugar-orange mixture. Cool muffins on wire rack.

If you zest the orange before you juice it, you can use the same orange.

Planning meals for Round-Up visitors is a way of life for Helen Cook. Her husband Don has worked at the Round-Up nearly all his life, was on the board for eight years and spent a two-year term as president. Helen was chaperone for the Round-Up court during the years that Don was court director.

A home economics major in college, Helen learned early on how to tempt a hungry group with her home cooking. These orange muffins have been on her breakfast table many times.

Pickin' Up

BRAN FLAX SEED MUFFINS

These are a meal in themselves and are perfect for grabbing as you head out the door. Take two — they're even good for you!

24–30 regular sized muffins

1½	cups whole wheat pastry flour	1½	cups shredded carrots
¾	cup flaxseed meal	2	apples, cored and shredded (no need to peel)
¾	cup oat bran	½	cup raisins or dried cranberries
1	cup packed brown sugar	1	cup chopped nuts
2	teaspoons baking powder	¾	cup milk
1	teaspoon baking soda	2	eggs, beaten
½	teaspoon salt	1	teaspoon vanilla
2	teaspoons cinnamon		

✶ Mix together flour, flaxseed meal, oat bran, brown sugar, baking powder, baking soda, salt, and cinnamon. Stir in carrots, apples, raisins or cranberries, and nuts.

✶ Combine milk, beaten eggs, and vanilla. Pour liquid ingredients into dry ingredients, and stir just until moistened. Do not over mix. Fill muffin cups ¾ full. Bake at 350° for 20 minutes.

CHUCK WAGON SOURDOUGH BISCUITS

SUPER easy — only two ingredients! Just use equal parts of each, depending on how many biscuits your wranglers are going to eat.

12 biscuits

2	cups self-rising flour, ONLY	2	cups sour cream

✶ Mix equal parts of self-rising flour and sour cream with a spoon.

✶ Flour your hands and roll out the size biscuits you want. Put on a greased baking sheet. Bake at 425° for 12-15 minutes.

Freeze biscuits on cookie sheet before baking. When frozen, store in plastic storage bags. Cook from the frozen state.

COWBOY CHEDDAR CHEESE BISCUITS

Good for a quick lunch with a salad and a cup of soup.

16 biscuits

2	cups all-purpose flour
1	tablespoon granulated sugar
2½	teaspoons baking powder
1	teaspoon pepper
½	teaspoon baking soda
½	teaspoon salt
⅓	cup (6 tablespoons) chilled unsalted butter, cut into ½-inch pieces

1¼	cups grated extra sharp Cheddar cheese
1	cup cold buttermilk
1	tablespoon stone ground or dill mustard
1	egg beaten (for glaze)
1	tablespoon milk (for glaze)

✳ Combine flour, sugar, baking powder, pepper, baking soda, and salt in a food processor and blend. Add butter pieces one at a time using the on/off switch until the mixture looks like fine meal. Place mixture into a large bowl and stir in cheese.

✳ Stir in buttermilk ¼ cup at a time using just enough to bind the dough. Stir in the mustard. Turn the dough out onto a floured surface and knead gently until combined, about 10 turns. Pat out dough to ¾-inch thickness. Using a 3-inch cookie cutter, cut into biscuits. (If too much buttermilk has been used and the dough is too sticky to handle, make drop biscuits, using two spoons to drop dough.)

✳ Place the biscuits onto an ungreased cookie sheet. Combine egg and milk together; and brush the top of the biscuits with the glaze. Bake for about 18 minutes at 400°.

Serve warm with dill butter.

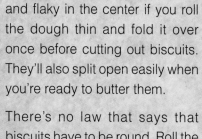

Biscuits will be crisp on the outside and flaky in the center if you roll the dough thin and fold it over once before cutting out biscuits. They'll also split open easily when you're ready to butter them.

There's no law that says that biscuits have to be round. Roll the dough into a rectangle and cut out square shapes so you don't have to keep re-rolling it.

To re-freshen and heat biscuits, put them in a well-dampened paper bag, twist it closed, and put it in a 300° oven for several minutes.

If you want soft-sided biscuits, bake them in a pan with sides and put the biscuits close together. If you want crusty biscuits, bake them on a cookie sheet and place them apart from each other.

Berle Nash with Pam and Dan Duso

Baking powder biscuits were a daily treat at our farm breakfast table. Covered with jam or gravy, the biscuits fed both family and hired hands.

One of my favorite memories of the Pendleton Round-Up is when I served as princess on the Round-Up court in 1935. This is a picture of my horse, Old Buck, who enjoyed the Round-Up as much as I did. Each day, my horse Old Buck and I raced from the east chute across the arena where Buck leaped the rail and reared up on his hind legs as the spectators screamed and cheered. What a wonderful experience — that summer of 1935...*Maxine Conley Stuart*

TENDERFOOT BUTTERMILK BISCUITS

Perfect biscuits for your homemade jam or jelly.

12–15 rolls

½	cup butter or margarine		½	teaspoon salt
2	cups all-purpose flour		1	tablespoon granulated sugar
2	teaspoons baking powder		¾	cup buttermilk
¼	teaspoon baking soda			

✱ Melt ¼ cup (4 tablespoons) butter or margarine in an 8x8 or 9x9-inch pan. Set aside.

✱ Sift dry ingredients together (all-purpose flour, baking powder, baking soda, salt, and sugar). Cut in remaining ¼ cup (4 tablespoons) butter or margarine with pastry blender or two knives until mixture resembles coarse cornmeal.

✱ Make well in dry ingredients. Add buttermilk all at once. Stir only to moisten and dough is free of sides of bowl. Knead gently 10-12 folds. Use light hand. Do not over-knead or dough will be tough.

✱ Roll or pat dough out at least 1-inch thick. Cut with cutter dipped in flour. Place biscuits in pan with melted butter or margarine, turning to coat both sides. Place close together in pan. Bake at 450° about 12-15 minutes.

1936 World Champion Saddle Bronc Rider Stub Bartlemay of Arlington, Oregon at the Pendleton Round-Up

Maxine Conley Stuart

CHUTE

Salads &
Salad Dressings

ANGEL HAIR PASTA

The trick to this salad is chopping everything very finely. And it's definitely a plus to make it a day ahead to meld the flavors.

12 servings

½ pound angel hair pasta or vermicelli (Italian style) spaghetti, broken into small pieces

¾ pound shrimp, finely chopped

1 cup finely diced celery

½ cup finely diced sweet pickles

⅓ cup finely chopped fresh green onions

¼ cup finely chopped green pepper

Salt

1½ cups mayonnaise-type salad dressing

✷ Cook vermicelli or angel hair pasta according to instructions; drain and cool. Add shrimp, celery, sweet pickles, green onions, green pepper to the pasta and mix. Mix in the salt and salad dressing.

You can add 4 or 5 hard-boiled eggs, chopped, if you like a little more protein.

*Jennie Lazinka's legacy continues today with
Patti, Janice, Maureen, Annie, Susan, Mary, and Joan.*

Grandma Jennie Lazinka was an awesome cook. Growing up, the first thing on the Round-Up performance day agenda was to go to Grandma's house for a huge buffet lunch, a table set for a mob! Grandma took great pride in making sure everyone went to the Round-Up grounds well fed and ready for the performance. When Patti and Janice Healy were on the court, Grandma never attended the rodeo, but sat at home and listened to her faithful KUMA with Ted Smith. She assured us that she would know more than all of us as to what happened during the day's show when it was over. Her daughters, Kathryn, Jean, Judy, and Mary Lou were all part of Round Up royalty. Little did she know that the Currin Boys (little then, big hats and all) and the Healy girls would carry on the Lazinka tradition of "ranch raised," and loved the "manes and tails" in the corral and out of the rodeo arena!!...*Susan Healy Hisler and Annie Hisler Weygandt (Pendleton Round-Up Princess 2000), grand & great granddaughters of Jennie Lazinka.*

Confederated tribes of the Umatilla Indian Reservation member David Liberty has long been a stacker of rocks and at one time spent a lot of time balancing rocks and boulders along I-84 between Boardman and Arlington. But alas, law enforcement made him stop. They thought it was causing too many "rubber-neckers" and there would surely be accidents. Huh. We love them.

CHINESE CABBAGE SALAD

An easy salad to assemble, this will awaken your Asian taste buds!

6 servings

DRESSING

1 packet soup seasoning from 3-ounce package oriental noodle soup

1 teaspoon granulated sugar

½ teaspoon salt

½ teaspoon black pepper

3 tablespoons vinegar

½ cup vegetable oil

SALAD

1 10-ounce package shredded cabbage

½ green pepper, chopped

4 green onions, sliced

1 cup frozen peas (uncooked)

1 3-ounce package oriental soup noodles, uncooked and crushed

½ cup toasted slivered almonds

2 tablespoons sunflower seeds

✴ Mix the noodle soup seasoning, sugar, salt, black pepper, vinegar, and oil together. Cover and let stand at least 2 hours. Refrigerate.

✴ Mix together the cabbage, bell pepper, green onion, and frozen peas in serving dish.

✴ Add the dressing and broken oriental soup noodles, almonds and sunflower seeds to the vegetables just before serving.

Add 4-6 boneless chicken breasts, cooked and cut in chunks, for a whole meal deal.

ASIAN SALAD

The cilantro gives this traditional salad a great flavor. Use as much of each ingredient as you like — the quantities listed are only a suggestion.

8-10 servings

CREAMY SOY DRESSING

3	tablespoons white wine vinegar
3	tablespoons granulated sugar
1	tablespoon soy sauce
1	clove garlic, peeled and minced
½	teaspoon Asian sesame seed oil
½	teaspoon powdered ginger
¼	teaspoon cayenne (optional)
1	cup mayonnaise

SALAD

1	head Napa cabbage, sliced and torn
1½	cups snap peas
½	cup slivered almonds
½	cup chopped green onions
½	cup sliced radishes
½	cup fresh chopped cilantro

✱ For Creamy Soy Dressing mix vinegar, sugar, soy sauce, garlic, sesame seed oil, ginger, and cayenne until sugar has dissolved. Add mayonnaise, stir and set aside.

✱ Mix vegetables together. The amounts can vary depending on your own tastes.

✱ When ready to serve, pour the Creamy Soy Dressing over the vegetables and toss.

We always have guests at our house during Round-Up, and it's always interesting. As part of the publicity crew, Wes was asked one year to have a Japanese film crew to our home. They cooked! It was interesting trying to understand their needs for spices and cooking utensils. I think they needed bowls of all sizes and many of them. I had six! It was a great evening, though, with lots of laughs...*Millie Grilley*

Representatives from sister city Haramachi City, Japan (now Minamisoma City) have been frequent visitors to the Round-Up City, and in 2005 they sent a contingency of Samarai warriors. The guests took part in the Westward Ho! Parade and Happy Canyon and made friends everywhere they went.

Paul Cimmiyotti

My father, Paul Cimmiyotti, lived and breathed Round Up. Every year, he worked very hard to entertain people from all over the world at Cimmiyotti's Restaurant. My mother helped him by greeting people at the door and our whole family worked during that very important week. He was honored to be chosen to be on the board of directors, the Grand Marshal of the Westward Ho! Parade, and inducted into the Hall of Fame. He had three daughters on the Round-Up courts, and those were the fondest memories of his life.

Of course, there is also the story of Larry Mahan riding a pony into Cimmiyotti's during Round-Up!...
Cyd Cimmiyotti

SPAGHETTI SALAD

A pasta salad with a new look!

10 servings

1	pound spaghetti or linguine	2	tomatoes, thinly sliced
½	red onion, thinly sliced	¼	cup salad seasoning (Schillings makes a Salad Supreme Seasoning)
½	bell pepper, thinly sliced		
½-1	cucumber, thinly sliced	1	cup Italian dressing

✶ Cook spaghetti or linguine and drain. Rinse in cold water. Combine red onion, bell pepper, cucumber, tomatoes, salad seasoning, and Italian dressing. Add the spaghetti or linguine. If more seasoning is needed, add to taste. Refrigerate overnight.

RODEO SALAD

Crisp and tasty! This can be the "mane" event!

8–10 servings

1	pound hamburger, browned and drained	1	12-ounce package taco flavored corn chips, slightly crushed
1	15.5-ounce can red kidney beans, drained well		
1	1.25-ounce package dry taco seasoning	½	pound Cheddar cheese, shredded
½	large red onion, chopped	1	head iceberg lettuce, shredded
1	3-ounce can sliced olives	2	tomatoes, chopped
	Dash hot sauce	¼	cup Catalina dressing

✶ Mix together hamburger, kidney beans, taco seasoning, red onion, olives and hot sauce. Set aside.

✶ Just before serving, add corn chips, cheese, lettuce, and tomatoes.

✶ Drizzle with dressing. Toss and serve.

TACO SALAD

Quick and tasty!

15 servings

2	pounds lean ground beef	5	green onions, chopped
1	15-ounce can chili beans, drained	1	green pepper, chopped
1½	tablespoons chili powder	1-2	cups grated Cheddar cheese
1	teaspoon garlic powder		Sliced green olives
1	teaspoon salt	1	head iceberg lettuce, shredded
2	tomatoes, or more, chopped	1	12-ounce package tortilla chips, crumbled
2	stalks celery, or more, chopped		Italian dressing

✴ Brown and drain the ground beef. Add beans, chili powder, garlic powder, and salt to the browned meat.

✴ Add to the meat mixture tomatoes, celery, green onions, green pepper, Cheddar cheese, and olives.

✴ Just before serving, add lettuce and tortilla chips, and toss with the Italian dressing.

MEXICAN RICE CHICKEN SALAD

This salad may be served cold or at room temperature.

6–8 servings

3	cups cooked white rice	½	fresh lime or lemon
1	red or green bell pepper, chopped	3-4	avocados, chopped and coated with juice from ½ fresh lime or lemon
1	medium size onion, chopped		Minced garlic
1	8-ounce package frozen green peas		Red salsa
3-4	cooked chicken breasts, chopped		Taco chips

✴ Mix together the hot/warm rice, bell pepper, onion, frozen peas, chicken, avocados, and garlic in a salad bowl. Spread the salsa on top and serve with the sour cream and corn chips.

After the evening performance of the Omak Stampede, the 1975 Round-Up Court and their families snacked again on left-overs from lunch. This Taco Salad was a favorite of everyone and more was served the following day after they rode in the parade... *Annette Fitterer*

Dicy Strom Graham submitted this salad because the peas always remind her of visiting the pea cannery in Pendleton when she was a girl. She would eat handfuls of peas or take a package home for dinner.

JACKIE'S SHRIMP BULGUR SALAD

This recipe is from Jackie Hales Purchase, 1947 Round-Up Queen, and was a favorite at the lunch gatherings at Kathreen Purchase's home.

8 servings

1	bouillon cube	¼	cup chopped green onions
2	cups hot water	½	cup diced celery
1	cup cracked bulgur wheat	¼	cup stuffed green olives, sliced
¼	cup granulated sugar	1	tomato, chopped
¼	cup vinegar	1	6-ounce can shrimp, drained
¼	cup ketchup		
½	cup vegetable oil	3	tablespoons mayonnaise
2	tablespoons chopped green pepper	1	teaspoon salt

Kathi Purchase, Heather Hales, Judy Purchase, and Jack Purchase ready for the 1963 Round-Up.

✶ Dissolve bouillon cube in hot water. Add bulgur wheat and cover, bring to a boil, reduce heat and simmer 30 minutes. Drain and cool.

✶ Combine sugar, vinegar, ketchup and vegetable oil to make dressing. Add bulgur mixture and allow to marinate for at least 1 hour.

✶ Add green pepper, onions, celery, olives, tomato, shrimp, mayonnaise and salt to bulgur mixture. Toss and serve.

Keeping cold foods cold for a picnic or party is always dicey. Make your own ice table using those big plastic bins that fit under your bed. Take a couple of them, plop them on a table and cover the bottoms with a couple bags of ice, settle your salads and whatever you're wanting to keep cold, and voila! Instant portable refrigerator. Or you can rent a real table for big bucks from a rental company.

SEAFOOD BREAD SALAD

This is an oldie but a goodie — you'll like it!!

10–12 servings

1	loaf sliced, sandwich bread	2	6-ounce cans shrimp, drained
6	hard-boiled eggs, diced	1	cup celery, finely chopped
1	large onion, chopped	3	cups mayonnaise
2	6-ounce cans crab, drained		Salt to taste

✶ Cut all crusts from bread. Butter lightly each slice of bread; cut each slice into 16-20 cubes. Add eggs and onion; mix thoroughly. Refrigerate overnight. The next morning, add shrimp, crab, celery, and mayonnaise; salt lightly, and mix well. Refrigerate for 3-4 hours. Serve.

WILTED LETTUCE SALAD

This is a salad of a different era, dating back to 1910. We include it here because it was the recipe of the first Pendleton Round-Up Queen.

6 servings

1	head iceberg or garden lettuce	2	tablespoons water
4	slices bacon, fried and chopped (and the grease!)	2	tablespoons granulated sugar
½	cup vinegar	½	cup chopped onions
		2	hard-boiled eggs, chopped

✹ Fry bacon until crispy. Crumble when cooled. Return to skillet. Add vinegar, water, sugar, and onions to skillet. Heat to boil and pour over lettuce that has been torn into bite-sized pieces.

✹ Add hard-boiled eggs for garnish.

1910 Round-Up Queen Bertha Anger Estes and Princess Genevieve Clark Trombley

COPPER PENNIES

Tried and true ... a favorite of everyone's.

12–16 servings

2	pounds carrots, sliced and cooked	1	cup granulated sugar
1	large onion, thinly sliced	½	cup vinegar
1	green pepper, thinly sliced	½	cup vegetable oil
1	10.75-ounce can tomato soup	1	teaspoon Worcestershire sauce
		½	teaspoon salt

✹ Prepare carrots, onion, and peppers and put in bowl.

✹ In a medium saucepan, combine soup, sugar, vinegar, oil, Worcestershire sauce, and salt. Bring to a boil. Turn off heat and let cool. Pour over vegetables. Refrigerate overnight.

In September of 1963, Bertha Anger Estes, queen of the 1910 Round-Up, rode in an honored position in the Westward Ho! Parade. Genevieve Clark Trombley, one of Queen Bertha's attendants, was asked to accompany her. They were life-long friends, and the only two remaining members of the 1910 court. Their cart was driven by Buck Lieuallen, one-time Pendleton mayor and State Representative, who took an active interest in Round-Up activities. Queen Bertha, wearing the dark jacket, is on the far side of the buggy.

Queen Bertha married Walla Walla farmer Roxie Estes, and the Pendleton belle was soon living out in the wheat country and cooking for large harvest crews with few conveniences. Genevieve married B. F. Trombley, Pendleton auto dealer, and the families had frequent gatherings at the Estes ranch. Bertha became a wonderful cook and was noted for bountiful harvest tables. Salads were not always a favorite menu item with the harvest hands, but Bertha often served wilted lettuce, which met with their approval. The lettuce and onions came from her garden, and a huge bowl of "Farmer Salad" was quickly consumed by the harvest crew. This recipe from the past might be a favorite with your "crew."...*Jayne Frink*

It was long hours in the kitchen for the members of the Pendleton Presbyterian Church, who served meals for long lines of Round-Up visitors. The church attracted large crowds, since the visitors would walk up from the Round-Up grounds to Happy Canyon, which used to be at 320 SW Emigrant Avenue. Visitors would just drop by the church on their way past.

PRESBYTERIAN CHURCH CHICKEN SALAD

This salad has been served for many years at Pendleton's First Presbyterian Women's May Luncheon. Your Round-Up guests will love it! So will you.

20 servings

3 cups chicken, cooked and cubed	1 teaspoon curry powder
3 cups cooked macaroni	1½ teaspoons salt
3 tablespoons lemon juice	¼ cup light cream
1 cup seedless grapes, cut in half	1 cup mayonnaise or salad dressing
1 cup salted cashew pieces	2 hard-boiled eggs, chopped
1½ cups diced celery	Green and red pepper for garnish
1 teaspoon dry mustard	

✷ Combine cooked chicken, macaroni, and lemon juice and chill overnight.

✷ The next morning, add the grapes, cashews, and celery; mix well.

✷ Make a dressing with the mustard, curry powder, salt, and cream. Add the mayonnaise or salad dressing and mix well. Add eggs to salad and mix in the dressing.

✷ Garnish with green and red pepper.

Pineapple tidbits can be substituted for the grapes.

Country Church

MARINATED VEGETABLE SALAD

This recipe serves a lot of people, can be made days before, and is gorgeous!

18–20 servings

2 6-ounce jars marinated artichoke hearts or bottoms, including marinade

1 head cauliflower, cut into florets

1 bunch broccoli, cut into florets

1 pound fresh mushrooms, sliced

2 zucchini, sliced with peel left on

6 carrots, cooked until tender-crisp and sliced like pennies

1 yellow crookneck squash, cut in strips

1 green pepper, cut in chunks

1 red pepper, cut in chunks

½ pound cherry tomatoes

1 cup diagonal-cut celery

2 7-ounce packages Italian dressing mix, prepared as directed on package

✱ Combine artichokes, cauliflower, broccoli, mushrooms, zucchini, carrots, squash, peppers, tomatoes, and celery with dressing and chill at least 2 hours, preferably overnight. Stir every once in a while to mix the marinade throughout. Drain and serve. Use as salad, or put out in a bowl for appetizers.

MARINATED BROCCOLI SALAD

This traditional salad has been around for a long time, and turns up at every event during Round-Up. We never seem to get enough of it.

6 servings

SALAD

2 bunches broccoli, cut in small florets

½ medium red or Walla Walla sweet onion, chopped

½ cup raisins

5-7 strips of bacon, cut and fried

½ cup chopped cashews

DRESSING

1 cup mayonnaise

¼ cup granulated sugar

2 tablespoons raspberry vinegar (or plain white vinegar)

✱ Toss broccoli, onion, and raisins together and set aside.

✱ Drizzle dressing on salad. Add bacon and cashews last.

Parents of the 1975 court still have get-togethers with the girls and their families. Marinated Vegetable Salad is always a hit with everyone.

Chief Clarence Burke

"How I Met My Husband at The Pendleton Round-Up"

Years ago, the Portland Oregon Journal had special trains from Portland to Pendleton for Round-Up, and in 1954, loving cowboys, I headed east to Cowboy Country. I went to a cocktail gathering on the train, and my future husband noticed me, but I didn't notice him. But lo and behold, our seats at the rodeo were right next to each other, and we visited so much that the man sitting on the other side of me said "Girly, this time next year, the two of you will be married."

It didn't take that long. After the Round-Up, we went to Happy Canyon, and danced afterwards and had a glorious time. The next day was the big parade and by then we were a twosome. It was like having ten dates in two or three days. It was just like a dream time. Six months later, we were married...*Phyllis Rice*

U.S Senator Gordon Smith of Pendleton

Layered Vegetable Salad

A pretty wonderful salad that can be made as much as four days ahead, and it just keeps getting better.

16 servings

DRESSING

1½ cups mayonnaise
1½ cups sour cream
1 teaspoon Worcestershire sauce
Salt and black pepper

SALAD

2 bunches fresh spinach, chopped
10 hard-boiled eggs, sliced
1 pound bacon, fried and crumbled
1 medium head iceberg lettuce, shredded
1 cup chopped green onions
1 8-ounce package frozen peas, cooked
1½ cups grated Swiss cheese

- Mix mayonnaise, sour cream, Worcestershire sauce, salt, and pepper.
- In a large glass bowl or pan, layer the spinach, eggs, bacon, lettuce, onions, and peas, in that order. Cover with the dressing. Sprinkle the Swiss cheese over the top. Cover and refrigerate for at least 12 hours.

Broccoli-Cauliflower Salad

Not your typical broccoli salad. Very colorful in a glass bowl.

6 servings

1 cup broccoli florets
1 cup cauliflower florets
4 hard-boiled eggs, sliced
1 cup shredded Cheddar cheese
6 slices bacon, cooked and crumbled
1 cup mayonnaise
½ cup granulated sugar
2 tablespoons white vinegar

- In medium bowl layer broccoli, cauliflower, eggs, Cheddar cheese, and bacon.
- In separate bowl whisk together mayonnaise, granulated sugar, and vinegar for dressing. Drizzle dressing over top of salad before serving.

ROBERTA SANKEY'S CORN SALAD

This salad has a lovely light taste, and the amount of vinegar may be why.

20 servings.

¼	cup olive oil	3	15-ounce cans black beans, drained well
¾	cup white vinegar	4	15-ounce cans corn
3	tablespoons chopped jalapeños, not fresh	3	cups cooked white rice
2	tablespoons lime juice	¾	cup chopped red onion
1	tablespoon ground cumin	¼	cup chopped green onion
2	teaspoons salt	2	chopped tomatoes
¼	cup balsamic vinegar		

✴ Combine olive oil, vinegar, jalapeños, lime juice, cumin, salt, and balsamic vinegar for dressing.

✴ Mix black beans, corn, white rice, red onion, and green onion. Marinate in the dressing for 24 hours, then add the chopped tomatoes.

24-HOUR CABBAGE SALAD

This dressing will keep for several days in the refrigerator, and the salad is great for a picnic.

12 servings

SALAD

1	head cabbage, chopped fine		Sliced ripe or stuffed olives
1	onion, chopped		
1	green pepper, chopped	1	cup granulated sugar

DRESSING

1	cup vinegar	1	teaspoon salt
½	cup vegetable oil	1	tablespoon prepared mustard
1	teaspoon celery seed		

✴ Mix together cabbage, onion, green pepper, and olives. Cover with sugar and let stand while preparing dressing.

✴ Combine vinegar, vegetable oil, celery seed, salt, and prepared mustard in a saucepan; boil 3 minutes. Set aside to cool. When cool, pour over cabbage mixture and stir well.

The Sankeys are long-time stock contractors for the Pendleton Round-Up and Roberta has shared this recipe with others. Bess Linger of Linger Rodeo Company of Miles City Montana served this salad at a branding one year and everyone was blown away by its spiciness.

SALADS & SALAD DRESSINGS

1981 was the last big Round-Up party held in the Indian Village at the Round-Up Grounds. Fifteen couples hosted the party and there were some 400 guests that attended. Kessler's catered the dinner and of course it was wonderful. This was a great way to start the Round-Up season.

The swinging doors will open wide
To let you enter there.
Enjoy the friends you find inside
And throw away each care.

The Indian Village at the
Round-Up grounds
Is the place where we will meet.
To share in friendly, tasty rounds
Of drinks and food to eat.

So mark your calendars one and all,
Friday, August 28th will be fine.
Come join us in our Round-Up call
From six to half past nine.

Hosts: Cecil and Betty Holmes, Joe and Pat Standerfer, George and LaVelle Bonbright, Tom and Betty Branstetter, Ben and Carmen Christensen, Andy and Thelma Echanis, Jerry and Donna Myrick, Fred and Betty Price, John and Gwen Carr, Don and JoAnne Webb, Herb and Margaret McLaughlin, Kenny and Karen Coppinger, Janet and Orville Ellinger, Leonard and Rose Anna King, Pete and Pat Wallace

LAYERED CURRY–GINGER OVERNIGHT SALAD

This is a nice crunchy salad that men find irresistible!

12 servings

6 cups chopped iceberg lettuce	4 cups cubed, cooked chicken
1 10-ounce package frozen small peas or two 8-ounce packages frozen pea pods	2 cups mayonnaise
	1 tablespoon curry powder
½ pound bean sprouts	2 tablespoons granulated sugar
1 8-ounce can sliced water chestnuts, drained	½ teaspoon ground ginger
	Tomatoes
½ cup sliced green onion	Spanish peanuts
1 medium cucumber, chopped	

✳ In a 9x12-inch rectangle pan, layer the lettuce, pea pods, bean sprouts, water chestnuts, green onion, cucumber, and chicken.

✳ Combine the mayonnaise, curry powder, sugar, and ground ginger. Spread over the layered vegetables. Refrigerate 24 hours. Garnish with tomatoes and Spanish peanuts.

For a vegetarian salad, substitute the chicken with 4 cups of fresh mushrooms.

92

BOB'S POTATO SALAD

This is just an old-fashioned kind of potato salad, the way Bob's grandmother made it. Probably the way yours did too.

10–12 servings

DRESSING

½ cup mayonnaise

½ cup mayonnaise-like salad dressing

4 tablespoons vegetable oil

2 teaspoons white wine vinegar

1 teaspoon salt

½ teaspoon black pepper

1 teaspoon prepared mustard

½ teaspoon granulated sugar

SALAD

6 cups cooked potatoes, peeled and cubed

½ cup chopped celery

½ cup chopped green pepper

¼ cup chopped red pepper

¼ cup chopped onion

6 hard-boiled eggs, chopped

Paprika

Parsley flakes

✹ Combine mayonnaise, salad dressing, vegetable oil, vinegar, salt, black pepper, mustard, sugar; stir well. Set aside.

✹ Combine potatoes, celery, peppers, onion, and eggs. Toss to mix.

✹ Add dressing to potato mixture until moist enough to your liking, and mix well. Sprinkle with paprika or parsley flakes. Cover and refrigerate until ready to serve.

Save one of the eggs to slice and decorate the top with.

From the *East Oregonian*, August 6, 1910

J.R. Raley has been elected president of the coming frontier show by the committee last night. Will Ingram is business manager; J.W. Gwinn, secretary; and Roy Ritner, Treasurer. Paul Sperry will be parade manager, and Mark Moorhouse, exhibition manager.

I have enjoyed being a pennant bearer for the Round-Up Court and riding with them in all of the parades. My mother is my biggest supporter in everything I do; along with my Grammy and Papa who live in Steptoe, Washington, and make the three hour drive to be here for me. My Grammy and I have had lots of fun cooking. She's shown me so much. A lot of things you can't get from a cookbook. Huckleberry Champagne Salad is a family favorite and very yummy! She always makes this for family gatherings and potlucks and there are never any leftovers! Everyone asks for the recipe...
Crystal Mitchell

LAYERED POTATO SALAD

A very pretty salad when layered in a clear glass bowl with fairly straight sides.

12 servings

5	pounds small red potatoes (choose potatoes all close to the same size so they cook evenly)
2	cups sour cream
2	cups mayonnaise

2	heaping tablespoons horseradish
2	teaspoons whole celery seed
1	teaspoon salt
2	medium onions, minced
2	bunches parsley, minced

✳ Bring a large pot of water to a boil. Place the red potatoes in the rapidly boiling water. Boil for about 20 minutes until a fork easily pierces a potato. Allow to cool until the potatoes are room temperature. Slice into ¼-inch slices.

✳ Mix sour cream, mayonnaise, horseradish, celery seed, and salt. Place a layer of sour cream mixture in bottom of bowl. Top with a layer of potato slices. Top the potato slices with another layer of sour cream mixture, sprinkle with a layer of onions and parsley. Repeat with another layer of potato slices until ingredients are used, ending with onions and parsley.

HUCKLEBERRY CHAMPAGNE SALAD

There's really no Champagne in this salad - it's just so light that it feels as if there is!

20 servings

1	8-ounce package cream cheese, softened to room temperature
½	cup granulated sugar
1	12-ounce non dairy whipped topping

1	20-ounce can pineapple tidbits, drained
2	cups fresh, or frozen and thawed, huckleberries
2-3	bananas, sliced
½	cup sliced almonds

✳ Whip cream cheese and add sugar. Fold in whipped topping. Add pineapple, huckleberries, bananas, and almonds.

STRAWBERRY SALAD

The different fruits make for a great combination — it almost tastes like dessert!

8-10 servings

1	6-ounce strawberry gelatin	1½	cups crushed pineapple, drained
2	cups boiling water	1	slightly mashed banana
¾	cup cold water		Sour cream to cover salad
2	cups frozen, unsweetened whole strawberries, cut in half		

✱ Dissolve the strawberry gelatin in 2 cups boiling water. Stir to dissolve. Add cold water and the frozen strawberries. Mix well and add the crushed pineapple and banana. Pour one-half of the salad mixture into a 9x12-inch dish and place in the refrigerator to set.

✱ Spread the set gelatin with sour cream and add the remaining half of salad mixture and return to the refrigerator to set.

APPLE PECAN BLUE CHEESE SALAD

What a great combination!

6 servings

RASPBERRY VINAIGRETTE DRESSING

¾	cup raspberry vinegar	Zest of 1 small orange
¾	cup olive oil	Salt and black pepper
1½	teaspoons granulated sugar	

SALAD

1	Rome or Pippin apple, cored and cut into thin wedges	2	ounces Blue cheese
1	bag mixed salad greens	½	cup toasted pecan halves
			Raspberries for garnish

✱ Combine vinegar, olive oil, sugar, orange zest, salt, and black pepper in a jar with a tight fitting lid and shake well. Set aside.

✱ Toss apple, salad greens, Blue cheese, and pecans with enough vinaigrette dressing just to coat. Garnish with raspberries and serve immediately.

The year 1988, our daughter Sandi was on the Round-Up court, and we hosted the Round-Up and Happy Canyon courts, their parents, Round-Up and Happy Canyon directors and their wives, Governor Neil Goldschmidt and his entourage during Chief Joseph Days in Joseph, between rodeo performances on Saturday at our home. Just as we got home from the afternoon rodeo performance, the Forest Service called, stating that there was a fire in the woods where Dave was building road and that he should go there to move his dozers and other equipment before it burned. So David, Terry Simpson, and Craig Willis took off to move the equipment. There went my party helpers! But we managed. The worst thing was that when we uncovered the food tables for the guests, some of the cinders from the fire, 15-20 miles away, drifted onto the food and the strawberry salad looked like ash, but the guests were all really nice about it...*Darlene Turner*

Hermiston, Oregon watermelons are the quintessential summertime treat. More than 600 acres of watermelons are harvested every summer from the fertile high desert of Eastern Oregon. The climate of warm days and cool nights combine to produce the highest sugar content and best tasting watermelons available anywhere, and they are very plentiful during the days of the Pendleton Round-Up.

Chief Jesse Jones

WATERMELON SWEET ONION SALAD

This salad showcases the local onions and watermelon we have in Eastern Oregon.

10–12 servings

DRESSING

¼	cup red wine vinegar	2	tablespoons chopped, fresh mint
½	cup olive oil		
	Salt and black pepper	1	sweet onion, halved and thinly sliced

SALAD

1	5-pound seedless watermelon, cubed in bite-sized pieces	½	cup pitted Kalamata olives (optional)
4	ounces crumbled feta cheese		Whole mint sprigs for garnish

✱ Place vinegar in a small bowl, and slowly whisk in the olive oil. Whisk in salt and black pepper to taste, and the mint. Place the sliced onion in a medium bowl and pour the dressing over; toss to coat. Let sit for at least 10 minutes or up to 1 hour.

✱ In a large bowl, add the watermelon, onion, feta cheese, and olives. Gently toss with dressing and onions until melon is evenly coated. Garnish with mint sprigs.

RED HOT PINEAPPLE SALAD

A variation on an Ambrosia salad, this will perk up your taste buds!

6 servings

½	cup red hots (candy)	1	8 or 9-ounce carton frozen non-dairy whipped topping
1	20-ounce can crushed pineapple	1	cup miniature marshmallows
		½	cup coconut, if desired

✱ Mix red hots and pineapple; let soak overnight.

✱ The next morning add the thawed whipped topping, marshmallows, and coconut to the pineapple mixture. Keep refrigerated until ready to serve.

TROPICAL CHICKEN SALAD

A colorful, cool and refreshing salad for a warm day.

6–8 servings

POPPY SEED DRESSING

3	cups granulated sugar	2	teaspoons dry mustard
1¼	cups white vinegar	1	tablespoon poppy seeds
3⅓	cups vegetable oil	¼	cup dried onion flakes

SALAD

1	head iceberg lettuce, shredded	12	ounces cooked chicken breast or turkey, diced
1	large head Romaine, torn in small pieces	1	11-ounce can Mandarin oranges, drained
1	carrot, peeled and shredded	1	pint fresh strawberries, hulled and sliced
¼	cup shredded red cabbage	3	ounces pecan pieces
1	16-ounce can pineapple tidbits, drained	1	cup fresh blueberries

✳ Mix sugar, vinegar, oil, and mustard, together in blender. Add poppy seeds and onion flakes. Blend. Store in refrigerator until ready to use. Dressing will keep for up to 3 weeks.

✳ Combine lettuce and romaine with carrot and red cabbage. Arrange on 8 or 10 large chilled plates. Top with pineapple, chicken, and oranges. Garnish with strawberry slices, blueberries and pecan pieces. Serve with Poppy Seed Dressing.

Nita and Grey

On May 18, 1980, Mt. St. Helens blew, and who knew if there would even be a Rose Festival Parade. But it rained, and our royal Pendleton Round-Up court headed west with their horses. While the court and parents were off being entertained by Mr. and Mrs. Mort Bishop of the Pendleton Woolen Mills, our horses were making the most of their "digs" at the Portland Meadows Race Track. This included daughter Nita's grey horse rolling in all the manure he could find, and instead of being grey, he was green! So while everyone else left, out came the brushes, soap, and water, and by the time we had him cleaned up, he'd had it and didn't want to get in the trailer. After a whole lot of maneuvering, we were on our way, with Grey's head hanging out the back window. If we were late, the court couldn't ride.

We arrived just in time to see the court putting on each horse a beautiful blanket of roses given to us by the Rose Parade officials to go behind the saddles. All the horses were acting kind of skittish — don't know if it was the ash or Mt. St. Helens rumbling gently in the background. It was a good thing our court were real cowgirls and came from good rodeo family stock. We got ready in time, and although it was close, it was one wild and crazy "Let 'er Buck" experience. Several of the parents have since passed away, and our girls are close to being 50 years old. Our family intends to be in Pendleton for the 100th. We are scattered across the United States...*Betty Nichols, mother of Nita*

Oregon grows 99 percent of the hazelnuts, or filberts in the United States, and is our most important nut crop. There are more than 3.1 million hazelnut trees in Oregon, grown on 28,500 acres, mostly in western Oregon. Most of Oregon's hazelnuts are grown in the Willamette Valley from Eugene, north to Vancouver, Wash. Some are also grown in British Columbia.

The United States produces only about 3 percent of the world's hazelnuts. Ninety-seven percent of the world's hazelnuts are grown in Turkey, Spain and Italy, where they were domesticated from wild trees many centuries ago.

ORANGE HAZELNUT SALAD

This delightfully light salad complements any meal.

4 servings

ORANGE VINAIGRETTE DRESSING

1	teaspoon grated orange peel	½	teaspoon granulated sugar
2	tablespoons fresh orange juice	¼	teaspoon salt
2	teaspoons white wine vinegar	3	tablespoons olive oil

SALAD

4	cups mixed salad greens	½	cup soft goat cheese
½	cup toasted hazelnuts (see note)		

★ Combine orange peel, orange juice, vinegar, sugar, and salt in small bowl. Whisk in olive oil.

★ In large bowl, toss greens with vinaigrette. Arrange on plates and sprinkle with toasted hazelnuts and crumbled goat cheese.

To toast hazelnuts, spread the shelled nuts in a shallow pan and roast in a 250° oven for 20-30 minutes, stirring from time to time. To remove skins, wrap in a terrycloth towel and rub vigorously.

Today's Mounted Band at Happy Canyon

98

PERFECT PICNIC SALAD

This salad takes the worry out of having to refrigerate it, not always possible when you're on a picnic!

4 servings

LEMON-MUSTARD DRESSING

2	tablespoons vegetable oil	¼	teaspoon salt
2	tablespoons lemon juice	¼	teaspoon black pepper
1	teaspoon Dijon mustard		

SALAD

1	cup fresh seedless grapes, red or green	¼	cup minced green onions
1	15-ounce can small white beans, drained	2	tablespoons chopped fresh parsley
½	cup diced celery		Lettuce leaves

✱ Combine vegetable oil, lemon juice, mustard, salt, and black pepper; mix well and set aside.

✱ Combine grapes, beans, celery, green onions, and parsley; mix well. Serve on lettuce leaves with the Lemon-Mustard Dressing.

Round-Up Mounted Band at the Westward Ho! Parade

The Pendleton Cowboy Mounted Band was formed in 1985 to reprise the original Pendleton Round-Up Mounted Band of 1911. It was the 75th Anniversary of the Pendleton Round-Up and the band was to be a historical re-enactment that was to last one year. But it keeps going and going and going…The 40 band members, outriders, and flag bearers have played each year since then in parades and rodeos in Oregon, Washington, Idaho, Montana, and Nevada.

Although the Band is known for its riding and playing and joyousness, the members also enjoy member-made meals with our families several times each year. Its cooks prepare a wide variety of appetizers, meats, salads and desserts; summer fare for hungry horsemen. Of course its most solemn moments are toasted with a few sips of Pendleton Whisky, neat....*Gary Zimmerman*

Casey Currin

FRESH SPINACH SALAD

It's the dressing that makes this salad special; the ingredients can be altered to fit your druthers.

12–16 servings

DRESSING

1	cup vegetable oil	1	tablespoon salt
¼	cup red wine vinegar	⅓	cup ketchup
1	tablespoon Worcestershire sauce	1	tablespoon minced onion
		½	cup sugar

SALAD

1	bunch fresh spinach	1	cup sliced mushrooms
½	pound bacon (or more), fried and diced	1	4-ounce can sliced water chestnuts, drained
2	hard-boiled eggs, sliced or diced	¼	cup chopped red onion
1	cup bean sprouts, fresh or canned	½	cup sliced or slivered almonds (or other nuts)

✱ Mix oil, wine vinegar, Worcestershire sauce, salt, ketchup, onion, and sugar and shake well.

✱ Wash and cut up spinach. Add the bacon, eggs, bean sprouts, mushrooms, water chestnuts, red onions, and almonds and toss well.

✱ Add just enough dressing to coat right before serving, as spinach tends to lose its zip quickly.

Dungeness Crab and Asparagus Salad with Orange Mustard Dressing

This salad was developed by Suzie Barhyte for Barhyte Specialty Foods and is one of the most elegant salads we've seen.

6 servings

- 2 pounds asparagus, trimmed
- ½ cup chopped fresh chives or green onions
- 3 navel oranges
- 1 pound Dungeness crabmeat
- Juice of 1 orange
- ⅓ cup sweet and hot stone ground mustard
- 1 teaspoon grated orange peel
- Salt and black pepper
- Chives or green onions for garnish

★ In a large pot of boiling salted water, cook the asparagus for about 3 minutes until crisp tender. Cool immediately by immersing in a bowl of ice water.

★ Cut top 6 inches from asparagus and set aside. Slice remaining asparagus into ¼-inch thick rounds. Transfer slices to large bowl and mix in ½ cup chives.

★ Remove peel and white pith from oranges. Cut between membranes to remove orange segments and drain off any juices. Place orange segments in bowl with asparagus and chives. Gently mix in crabmeat.

★ Whisk together orange juice, mustard, and grated orange peel. Season with salt and pepper to taste. Pour over salad and gently mix in.

★ Arrange the 6-inch asparagus spears on 6 plates. Mound the salad in the center and sprinkle with chives or green onion.

Volunteers help out all year long, hauling dirt, building fence, building bull corrals, assembling and painting chute gates, whitewashing barns, organizing souvenir booth, feeding the volunteers, replacing seats, removing rock, spreading gravel, planting. There's always plenty to do. Scores of hard working men, women, and children turn out.

Bob Thompson and Steve Mohrland

Salad greens prepared ahead of time tend to lose their nutritive value and may arrive at your destination looking like the cowboy who was dragged in by the steer. To prepare lettuce for the road, separate the leaves, wash them thoroughly, and dry them by wrapping them lightly in a terrycloth towel and storing in the refrigerator.

CITRUS TOSS–UP SALAD

This dressing can be used on a number of different salads too.

8 servings

SALAD DRESSING

1	cup vegetable oil	1	teaspoon salt
⅓	cup tarragon vinegar	½	teaspoon celery seed
¼	cup granulated sugar	2	tablespoons grated onion

SALAD

1-2	heads Romaine lettuce, torn in small pieces	1	6-ounce can water chestnuts, drained
1	11-ounce can Mandarin oranges, drained	2	tablespoons toasted sesame seeds
1	small red onion, sliced thinly	2	tablespoons sliced almonds (optional)

✶ Mix vegetable oil, tarragon vinegar, granulated sugar, salt, celery seed, and grated onion in a jar. Shake well and set aside.

✶ Layer the romaine lettuce, Mandarin oranges, red onion, and water chestnuts in a large bowl and refrigerate until serving time. Drizzle light coating of dressing over the salad at serving time and sprinkle the top with sesame seeds and almonds. Do not toss.

Rainbow Finger Gelatin Salad

Check your refrigerator to make sure it's level!!!

10–12 servings

Never freeze a gelatin salad.

1	3-ounce package red gelatin	1	envelope unflavored gelatin
1	envelope unflavored gelatin	1	cup boiling water
1	cup boiling water	1	3-ounce package yellow gelatin
	Mayonnaise	1	envelope unflavored gelatin
2	envelopes unflavored gelatin	1	cup boiling water
½	cup tap water	1	3-ounce package green gelatin
1	can sweetened condensed milk	1	envelope unflavored gelatin
1½	cups boiling water	1	cup boiling water
1	3-ounce package orange gelatin		

★ Mix red gelatin with 1 envelope of unflavored gelatin, add 1 cup boiling water. (Make sure all of the gelatin dissolves.) Pour in a 9x13-inch pan that has been greased with mayonnaise. Put in refrigerator for 25 minutes.

★ Mix 2 envelopes of unflavored gelatin with ½ cup tap water, add 1 can sweetened condensed milk, then add 1½ cups boiling water. This makes the white layer for each of the three sections.

★ After the red layer sets, pour 1+ cup of the white mixture on top of it. The white mixture should be warm but not hot or it will melt the first layer. Let this layer set in the refrigerator for 20 minutes.

★ While the white layer is chilling make the orange layer (same as for the red layer) so it can cool, thus being ready to pour at the end of the 20 minutes.

★ Repeat for the white, yellow, white and green gelatin layers remembering to chill each layer for 20 minutes in the refrigerator. Gelatin mixtures should be warm enough to adhere to the previous layer but cool enough not to melt the layers.

★ Cut the molded gelatin into 1½-inch squares, then diagonally into triangles. Arrange on large serving platter.

Preparation time is about 2½ hours. This is quite labor intensive, but it sure makes you a hero with the kids.

I have a friend from South Dakota who remembers that Jell-O dishes at community events were a big status sign because it meant that the family had a refrigerator! ...*Polly Helm*

CRANBERRY SALAD

You don't need to wait until the holidays to fix this salad. It's a crowd pleaser.

10–12 servings.

1	regular bag fresh cranberries, washed, and chopped in blender or food processor	1	11-ounce can Mandarin oranges, drained (reserve juice)
½	cup granulated sugar	1	cup crushed pineapple
2	cups orange juice	1	cup halved, red seedless grapes
1	6-ounce package cherry or strawberry flavored gelatin	1	cup pecan pieces (optional)
			Frozen non-dairy whipped topping

✱ The day before serving, chop cranberries, and add granulated sugar. Mix and let sit for a couple of hours, until sugar dissolves.

✱ Heat orange juice until it boils. Stir and dissolve flavored gelatin in orange juice. Add Mandarin oranges, pineapple, grapes, and pecan pieces to dissolved gelatin. Stir in reserved Mandarin orange juice and cranberries. Pour into 9x13-inch glass dish, cover and refrigerate overnight.

✱ Serve with frozen non-dairy whipped topping as garnish.

Sonny Hanson's boys Clayton & Chase, with Denton Ward, behind the scenes at the Pendleton Round-Up during the National Anthem.

PATRIOTIC SALAD

You can't help but think of the cannon going off to signal the start of each day's rodeo at the Round-Up Grounds, and the grand entry that follows it. Gives you a little shiver.

16-24 servings

1   3-ounce package strawberry gelatin
1   envelope unflavored gelatin
½   cup cold water
1   cup half-and-half
¾   cup granulated sugar
1   teaspoon vanilla

2   cups sour cream
1   3-ounce package black raspberry gelatin
1   cup boiling water
1   16-ounce can blueberries, drained, save juice

✶   Dissolve strawberry gelatin as directed on package. Place in 9x12-inch clear glass dish. Chill until firm.

✶   Soak unflavored gelatin in cold water. Combine half-and-half with sugar and stir over low heat. Add unflavored gelatin and stir until dissolved. Cool. Add vanilla and sour cream to mixture. Cool completely and pour over strawberry mixture. Place in refrigerator until firm.

✶   In separate bowl, mix black raspberry gelatin with 1 cup boiling water, let cool. Blend in blueberries and juice. Layer over strawberry mixture. Chill 6 hours.

Each layer must be set firm before adding the next one.

This salad is reminiscent of the patriotic opening of each round-up performance. Five flags, led by the American flag, the Canadian flag, and the Oregon flag are brought into the arena by flag bearers traveling at a breathtaking pace, followed by the Queen and Court. Most attendees wouldn't miss the Grand Opening, and being in their seats by 1:15 pm and no later! is very important to see this heart-stopping spectacle.

We knew a couple on their honeymoon who came for Round-Up and a year later came back with their three month old baby...
Grace Lund

Betty Branstetter

CURRY DRESSING

This dressing is good on salads, but especially good in sandwiches, using non-fat or low-fat mayonnaise. It's also good for a dipping sauce. The beauty of it is that you can make it really low calorie and it's still wonderful.

2 cups

2	cups mayonnaise	¼	teaspoon salt
2	tablespoons curry powder	⅛	teaspoon cayenne
1	tablespoon Worcestershire sauce	¼	teaspoon hot pepper sauce
3	tablespoons salsa	1	tablespoon chopped onion
		½	teaspoon chopped garlic

★ Mix together the mayonnaise, curry powder, Worcestershire sauce, salsa, salt, cayenne, hot pepper sauce, onion, and garlic and refrigerate for 24 hours for the best flavor.

FRUIT SALAD DRESSING

This dressing will keep even bananas fresh for several hours.

1 cup

⅓	cup frozen limeade or lemonade concentrate, thawed	⅓	cup vegetable oil
⅓	cup honey	1	teaspoon poppy seed or celery seed

★ Blend the limeade, honey, oil, poppy seed, mixing well. Refrigerate unused portion.

CHUTE

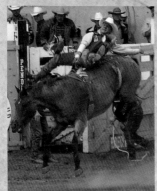

Soups & Stews

Gathered in their western finery are (front row): Walter Holt, Bruce Holt, Coach Murry, an Irwin brother, Jack Olsen; (back row): Herb Thompson, (unidentified), Roy Raley, and Roy Ritner. We believe this photo was taken in the late 1920's or early 1930's.

MEATBALL MINESTRONE

If we have the occasional cold Round-Up, this is a hearty soup to warm the cockles.

10-12 servings

SOUP

2	packages au jus gravy mix	1	cup sliced celery
8	cups water	1	teaspoon dried oregano
1	medium onion, thinly sliced	1	teaspoon dried basil
1	28-ounce can whole tomatoes, shredded into small pieces, including juice	1	15-ounce can kidney beans
		1	15-ounce can garbanzo beans
2	cups tomato juice	1	cup dried noodles
1	cup sliced carrots		Parmesan cheese

MEATBALLS

1	10-ounce package frozen chopped spinach, thawed	½	teaspoon garlic salt
1½	pounds lean ground beef	½	teaspoon salt
⅓	cup fine dry bread crumbs	¼	teaspoon black pepper
1	egg	2	tablespoons vegetable oil

✴ In a large pot, mix au jus mix and water. Bring to a boil and add onion, tomatoes, tomato juice, carrots, celery, oregano, and basil. Simmer, covered.

✴ To make the meatballs, press out as much water as possible from the spinach. Mix the spinach with the ground beef, bread crumbs, egg, salt, and pepper. Shape into ½-inch balls and brown in hot vegetable oil.

✴ When the meatballs are well browned and the carrots and celery are tender, add the meatballs, beans, and noodles. Cook until the noodles are tender. Serve steaming in bowls and sprinkle with Parmesan cheese.

Years ago, women competed right along with men for the money and the trophies, and they could be just as tough as the cowboys. In 1914, Bertha Blancett, wife of cowboy Del Blancett, came within 12 points of winning the All-Around Title.

1995 Round-Up Princess Marty Perkins

The unique Westward Ho! Parade is held Friday morning of Round-Up week. Beginning with a big bang at 10 a.m. the Westward Ho! Parade, is unique in that no motorized vehicles are allowed in the line of the march. You will see most of the Indians who are camped at the Round-Up grounds, dressed in their tribal finery from grandmother to the tiniest tot. All types of early transportation are featured, from mules with a jerk line to oxen-drawn covered wagons, old-time log skidders, Mormon carts, buggies, surreys, and much more. Riding groups and music furnished by numerous marching bands from surrounding communities participate. The Westward Ho! Parade pays tribute to the early days in the West and to the pioneers whose descendants are participating in the Round-Up.

SOUTHWESTERN SPICED CHICKEN BLACK BEAN STEW

There's a jazzy kick to this with great texture.

8-10 servings

3 slices thick-sliced bacon	2 15-ounce cans black beans, drained and rinsed
2 tablespoons olive oil	1 chipotle chile or 2 chiles in adobo sauce
6 boneless, skinless chicken thighs or 2 chicken breasts	2 cups chicken broth
1 large onion, diced	2-4 tablespoons fresh lime juice
1 red bell pepper, cored, seeded, and diced	¼ cup chopped fresh cilantro
2 cloves garlic, minced	Salt and pepper
2 teaspoons chili powder	Chopped cilantro
1 teaspoon ground cumin	Lime wedges
1 12-ounce strong dark beer or stout	Sour cream
	Tortilla chips

✱ Fry bacon until crisp. Remove from skillet and crumble. Add olive oil to bacon fat in skillet.

✱ Cut chicken into bite-sized pieces and add to skillet with onion and red pepper. Season with salt and sauté until chicken is no longer pink. Add bacon, garlic, chili powder, and cumin. Cook 2-3 minutes. Pour all into a large soup kettle. Add beer, beans, chipotles and chicken broth. Bring to boil. Reduce heat, simmer 30-50 minutes. Add lime juice and cilantro. Season with salt and pepper.

Charles "Boots" Mathews, an outrider for the 10-up mule hitch on Jenny. Mules pull this freight wagon every year for the Westward Ho! Parade.

ROUND-UP MULLIGAN

This was Ethel Temple Cresswell's recipe, and she got it from Roy Rittner in the early 1900's. Ethel used to triple the recipe and have it on the back of the stove for anyone working or visiting Round-Up. This makes a wonderful meal topped with Cheddar cheese and served with good sour dough bread...Charlotte Cresswell

10–12 servings

2	stewing hens (the 21st century calls for 2 cut-up chickens)
2	beef knuckles
2	onions, chopped
2	tablespoons parsley
2	teaspoons salt
½	teaspoon black pepper
2	15-ounce cans HOT chili (meat and beans)

1	15-ounce can red kidney beans, undrained
2	14.5-ounce cans green beans, drained
2	15.25-ounce cans vacuum packed corn (again, regular canned corn works today)
2	4-ounce cans sliced mushrooms
1	15-ounce can green peas
1	teaspoon chili powder

✶ In large pot, simmer chicken, beef knuckles, onions, parsley, salt and pepper until chicken is tender, about 1 hour. Let meat cool in broth, then remove fat. Remove meat from bones and cut in pieces. Discard beef knuckles.

✶ In large pot, add the chili, beans, corn, mushrooms, and peas. Add chicken and enough of the broth to just cover. Add chili powder and heat gently.

If you can make the broth a day ahead and refrigerate, the fat is easily removed because it hardens on the top.

Save the extra tasty broth for another recipe. Or you may like to use it to add to your Mulligan the next day if it needs a bit of thinning.

I was a young girl back in the 1920's, and one of the things I enjoyed doing was taking tickets at the Round-Up. It was even more fun when the tickets were all taken and the show started. We would close the gates and go to the grandstand. We could choose any seats that were empty, so we had a great view...*Kathryn Furnish Ramey*, oldest living court member

This is the story of how I met my lifetime friend, Kathryn Ramey, at the Round-Up. She is over 90 years old and just happens to be the oldest surviving Round-Up court member!

We were leaving the South Grandstand after the Saturday Round-Up in 1994. I saw a lady fall down on the concrete steps in front of me. I hurried to help her to her feet, made sure she was okay, and gave her a hug. She said her name was Kathryn and she was very grateful. She said that she was shaken up and would probably have some bad bruises but she would be okay. I told her my name was Ronda and I worked for a doctor in Hermiston.

To my surprise, Kathryn and her husband, Mike Ramey, walked into my place of work a couple of weeks later with a gift and thank you card. Kathryn said she had a hard time finding me. But there she was to say thank you for the assistance and much needed hug. We have been friends ever since. I hope I get to help her celebrate her 100th birthday in 2012...*Ronda Meagher*

LENTIL SOUP

Wonderful with crackers, biscuits, or hard rolls and a fruit salad.

4-6 servings

2	tablespoons vegetable oil	2	14-ounce cans chicken broth
1	large onion, finely chopped	1	15-ounce can diced tomatoes, undrained
1	small green pepper, finely chopped	1	cup water
1	carrot, finely chopped or shredded	¾	cup dried lentils, rinsed
1	large garlic clove, finely minced	¼	cup champagne and honey mustard

✸ In a Dutch oven or large soup pot, cook onions in oil to caramelize. Add pepper, carrot, garlic, chicken broth, tomatoes, water, and lentils. Simmer, covered for 1 hour or until lentils and vegetables are tender. Stir in mustard immediately before serving.

Most any kind of flavored mustard can be used, including dill, with great results.

TACO SOUP

1½	pounds ground beef	1	teaspoon chili powder
1	medium onion, diced	1	teaspoon garlic powder
1	46-ounce can tomato juice	1	3-ounce can sliced olives
1	15-ounce can black beans, drained	1	16-ounce can diced tomatoes
1	15-ounce can white beans, drained	1	15-ounce can whole corn
2	14 ounce cans chicken broth		Salt and black pepper
1	1.25-ounce package taco seasoning		Cheddar cheese
			Sour cream
			Diced green pepper

✸ Brown the meat and onion in a large skillet, drain off fat. Place in a large pot. Add the tomato juice, beans, broth, taco seasoning, chili powder, garlic powder, olives, tomatoes, corn, salt, and pepper and simmer for 20-30 minutes.

✸ Garnish with grated Cheddar cheese, sour cream, and diced green pepper.

MULTI-BEAN SOUP

The hardest part of this recipe is chopping the onions.

6 servings

2 cups diced onions

2 tablespoons vegetable oil

1 tablespoon chili powder

1 16-ounce can black beans

1 16-ounce can pinto beans

1 16-ounce can kidney beans

1 28-ounce can peeled and diced tomatoes with juice

1 7-ounce can chopped green chiles

1 quart reduced sodium chicken broth

¼ cup chopped cilantro

Cheddar cheese

Sour cream

Chopped green onions

✳ In a large heavy pan (about 5 quarts), cook onions in oil for 4-5 minutes on medium heat. Add the chili powder and cook for 1 minute.

✳ Drain beans. Stir in tomatoes with juice, beans, chiles, and broth. Bring to a boil, reduce heat, and simmer for 30 minutes while stirring occasionally.

✳ Stir in the cilantro and serve. You may garnish with cheese, sour cream, and/or green onions.

Queen Paulette Rice discussing what should be in the trailer with brother Paul L. Rice, Jr. Paulette's official Queen mount Poncho doesn't care, just loves his grass.

113

In 1966, a greeter's committee started work early in the year with motels and other tourist businesses. The Wally Byam Club came early with 500 trailers and continues on a smaller scale today.

Margaret Troedson and Creagh Hawes

CHILLY DAY CHILI

This recipe gives you a choice between canned beans or you can make your own from scratch!

6–8 servings

BASE

2	16-ounce cans chili beans or Chili Beans (below)	2	tablespoons chili powder
1	pound ground beef	2	teaspoons salt
1	cup chopped onion	1	12-ounce can tomato juice
1	cup chopped celery	1	10-ounce can concentrated beef broth
2	cloves garlic, minced	1	28-ounce can whole tomatoes
3	tablespoons all-purpose flour		

✻ Prepare the chili beans, if using, or heat canned beans and keep warm.

✻ Brown the ground beef in a large skillet until no longer pink. Drain all but 2 tablespoons of drippings from the skillet. Add onion, celery, and garlic to the beef. Sauté until the onion is tender.

✻ In a small bowl, combine flour, chili powder, and salt. Sprinkle the flour mixture over the browned beef and stir until coated. Gradually stir in the tomato juice and beef broth. Pour the beef mixture into the pot of warm beans. Chop the tomatoes and stir them into the beef mixture. Bring to a boil and reduce heat. Cover and simmer for 15 minutes.

IF YOU'RE MAKING YOUR OWN CHILI BEANS:

1½	cups dried pinto or red beans	½	cup chopped onion
3	cups water	1	tablespoon chili powder
1	teaspoon salt	2	tablespoons taco sauce
1	tablespoon vegetable oil		

✻ Sort and rinse the beans. Place in a large saucepan and cover with water to about 3 inches above the beans. Soak for 8 hours or overnight, or quick-soak by bringing the beans and water to a boil for 2 minutes before letting stand for 1 hour. Drain the soaked beans and discard the water.

CHILLY DAY CHILI - CONTINUED

- Combine the soaked beans, 3 cups water, and salt in a large saucepan. In a small skillet, heat oil. Add onion and sauté until tender. Stir chili powder and taco sauce into the onion.
- Pour the onion mixture into the beans and bring to a boil. Reduce heat, cover, and simmer until beans are tender, 1-1½ hours. Add hot water, if necessary, to keep beans covered during cooking. Keep warm until ready to use.

During Round-Up you never know when extra people may show up. You could have planned a small party and all of a sudden your house is full or you could have planned no party and all of a sudden your house is full. It's a good idea to keep extra nuts and snack items on hand for such occasions. Also, sandwich making materials along with crisp vegetables to make it stretch further or sliced for munchies.

Quick Chicken Chili

Here is a quick and easy version of the ever-popular white chili.

4-6 servings

1 tablespoon vegetable oil
4 boneless, skinless chicken breasts, cut into ½-inch chunks
1 medium onion, chopped
2 cloves garlic, minced
1 14.5-ounce jar salsa
3 15-ounce cans small white beans, undrained
3 tablespoons mesquite-flavored cooking sauce/marinade
⅓ cup chopped cilantro
Monterey Jack cheese, grated
Cilantro for garnish

- Heat oil in Dutch oven or large pot, add chicken chunks and sauté over medium heat, stirring frequently until chicken loses its pink color. Add onion and garlic, sauté and stir until onion is clear and chicken is browned.
- Reduce heat to low, add salsa, white beans, cooking sauce and cilantro. Simmer 3-5 minutes, stirring occasionally.
- Ladle into bowls, top with grated cheese and chopped cilantro.

1941 Princesses June Kirkpatrick, Helen Proebstel, and Mary Hassell, and 1944 Queen Janet Thompson at the 75th Pendleton Round-Up in 1985

When planning a party for a large crowd, choose recipes that you feel great about serving, that can be done ahead and then easily brought out as the party gets into full swing. Make sure you have two or more appetizers out when your guests arrive, along with easy-to-serve drinks. Beer and soft drinks on ice along with wine work great. Pitchers of mixed drinks that the guests can serve themselves take whole bunches of stress off you.

Suzie Barhyte

WHITE CHICKEN CHILI

This is a great recipe to start in the slow cooker in the morning, let it cook while you're at the rodeo, and impress your famished guests (well, not TOO famished, because there's lots of great food at the Round-Up grounds!) when you get home.

6–8 servings

3 boneless, skinless chicken breasts, cooked and shredded or chunked

3 15-ounce cans small white beans (Great White Northern), drained

1 10-ounce can diced tomatoes with green chiles, undrained

1 4-ounce can chopped green chiles

1 14.5-ounce can chicken broth

2 teaspoons ground cumin

1 teaspoon dried oregano

1 teaspoon cayenne pepper

1 teaspoon salt

1 medium onion, chopped

1 tablespoon minced garlic

1 tablespoon vegetable oil

1 16-ounce carton sour cream

3 cups grated Monterey Jack cheese

Cilantro

✱ Into a crockpot, put the chicken, beans, tomatoes, green chiles, chicken broth, cumin, oregano, cayenne, and salt.

✱ In a small pan, sauté the onion and garlic in the vegetable oil, and add to the crockpot. Simmer all day.

✱ Serve with sour cream and cheese. Sprinkle cilantro on top.

Chicken breasts on the bone with skin have more flavor than boneless, skinless breasts. Bake (or boil) for 1 hour, then take the meat off the bone and shred. Throw away the skin and bones.

Canned chicken meat does not do well in the crockpot.

If you like, you can add the sour cream and the cheese to the crockpot in the morning, but with so many people not eating dairy these days, it's just another way we show our guests we care.

To cook on top of the stove, throw everything into a stock-pot and simmer for an hour or two.

CHICKEN AND CORN FIESTA CHOWDER

This is a stick-to-your-ribs kind of soup.

8–10 servings

1 tablespoon butter or margarine	2 cups chicken breast, cooked and cubed (canned chicken works great)
1 cup chopped onion	
1 clove garlic, minced	1½ cups shredded Monterey Jack cheese
2 15-ounce cans creamed corn	Sliced green onions
1 15-ounce can whole kernel corn	Black olives
1 cup chicken broth or stock	Sour cream
2 cups milk	Salsa
1 4-ounce can diced green chiles	Diced avocado
1 teaspoon ground cumin	Crumbled tortilla chips
1 teaspoon white pepper	
¼ teaspoon hot sauce	

✳ In a large, heavy pot, melt butter and sauté onion over medium heat until translucent, about 6 minutes. Add garlic and cook 2 minutes longer. Do not allow onion and garlic to brown.

✳ Purée both corns and chicken stock in a blender or food processor. The mixture should not be completely smooth, but should still have some texture. Add corn mixture to pot, and simmer gently over medium heat for 10 minutes.

✳ Stir in milk, green chiles, cumin, white pepper, and hot sauce. Add chicken and cheese, stir until cheese melts. Ladle into soup bowls.

✳ Serve immediately with your choice of garnishes. It's good without garnishes as well.

1961 Round-Up Court Lynn Whitacre, Jan Thompson, Queen Mary Lou Lazinka, Marilyn Foster, and Carla Myers

When Johnny Bauer was Round-Up President, he assigned to Bob Stangier the task of providing a Friday night dinner to entertain dignitaries and directors, but with one stipulation: it had to be self-sufficient. No money would be coming from the Round-Up. After having it catered for the first couple of years at the expense of Bob and his brother Jack Stangier, the Round-Up directors moved the party to the Pendleton Country Club in 1961 where they could cook the dinner themselves and save a little money. Steaks were grilled on Dan Bell's barbecue, Bob brought in coleslaw from Kentucky Fried Chicken, and his three kids washed and hand-wrapped the potatoes, which were baked on-site. The Buckle Club, as it came to be called, a tribute to the silver belt buckles given to directors (their only "pay"), has come a long way from those days, but still is held every Friday evening for Round-Up directors, Happy Canyon directors, their guests, and attending dignitaries. And everyone pays for dinner.

CIOPPINO

This hearty fish stew is easily and quickly prepared. Serve with a salad and garlic bread.

4–5 servings

The Pendleton Round-Up is a true feat of sport in the most traditional sense of rodeo due to its traditional events, old-time wooden bucking chutes and one-of-a-kind green grass arena bordered by a dirt track. It has resisted the modern-day notion of advertising in the arena in favor of a family friendly atmosphere.

1	pound red snapper or halibut (or ½ pound each or 1 pound of scallops or prawns)	1	teaspoon thyme
1	tablespoon vegetable oil	1	teaspoon marjoram
1	cup chopped onion	1	teaspoon oregano
2	cloves garlic, finely minced	1	bay leaf
1	8-ounce can tomato sauce	¼	teaspoon black pepper
2	16-ounce cans tomatoes	¼	cup chopped parsley or 1 tablespoon dried parsley flakes
½	cup water or dry white wine	1	dozen steamer clams (scrubbed)
1	teaspoon basil	1	cup shrimp meat

✶ Cut fish into ½-inch chunks and set aside.

✶ Heat oil in a large kettle and sauté onions and garlic until onions are tender but not brown. Add tomato sauce, tomatoes, wine, basil, thyme, marjoram, oregano, bay leaf, pepper, and parsley. Let simmer 20-30 minutes until as thick as desired, stirring occasionally. At this point, the soup base can be refrigerated to serve later, before adding the fish, clams and shrimp.

✶ When ready to serve, add fish and scrubbed steamer clams. Cook until clams open, about 10 minutes. Just before serving, add shrimp meat.

1998 Round-Up Princess Casey Seeger

NORTHWEST SEAFOOD STEW

A little twist on preparing the catch of the day.

6 servings

1	pound halibut	2	16-ounce cans chopped tomatoes
½	pound sole	1	8-ounce can tomato sauce
½	pound red snapper	1	cup water
¼	pound large raw shrimp	3	potatoes, diced
6	slices bacon, diced	1½	teaspoons salt
¾	cup chopped onion	⅛	teaspoon black pepper
1	clove garlic, minced	¼	teaspoon oregano
¾	cup chopped celery	¼	teaspoon basil
¼	cup chopped green pepper	1	teaspoon chopped parsley

✴ Cut the halibut, sole, and red snapper into bite-sized pieces. Peel the shrimp. Fry bacon in a large saucepan. Add onion, garlic, celery, and green pepper. Sauté until the vegetables are translucent.

✴ Add the tomatoes, tomato sauce, water, potatoes, salt, pepper, oregano, and basil. Cover and simmer for 15 minutes. Add the fish and shrimp. Cover and continue cooking for 5-8 minutes or until the shrimp turns pink and the fish flakes when tested with a fork.

✴ Garnish with chopped parsley.

Just in case you get one of your soups too salty, don't panic. Just add cut raw potatoes to the soup, and throw them away once they are cooked and have absorbed the salt. Your soup is saved!

Brittney Bean

119

The Pendleton Round-Up has hosted an Indian Encampment of more than 300 teepees, housing families that have participated in the week-long festivities for generations. The Round-Up has a 94-year partnership with the Happy Canyon Indian Pageant and Night Show, where the epic drama of the Old West unfolds nightly with a live cast and original score. Indian participation has been a strong attraction since 1910, and their presence delights visitors from all over the world. Pottery, leather goods, beadwork, jewelry, and many more authentic hand crafted items are offered for sale next to the Indian Encampment and along the Umatilla River Parkway.

CLAM CHOWDER

Very easy, lovely consistency.

12 servings

3	slices bacon	½	cup all-purpose flour
1	cup chopped onions	½	quart cream
1	cup chopped celery	½	quart milk
2	cups diced potatoes	1½	teaspoons salt
2	6-ounce cans minced clams	¼	teaspoon black pepper
½	cup butter		

✸ Fry bacon pieces, crumble and set aside. Place the vegetables in a saucepan. Drain clam juice and pour juice over the vegetables. Add enough water to barely cover the bottom of the pan and simmer, covered, over medium heat until the vegetables are tender.

✸ In the meantime, melt the butter in another large pot. Add the flour and blend, stirring constantly with a wire whisk. Add the cream and milk and stir until smooth and thick. Add the undrained vegetables, bacon, and clams. Heat through and season with salt and pepper to taste.

If you prefer a thicker chowder, substitute heavy cream for the milk.

ZUCCHINI GARDEN CHOWDER

One of the best things to do with zucchini!

6–8 servings

2	tablespoons butter	¼	teaspoon black pepper
2	medium zucchini, sliced	24	ounces chicken broth
1	medium onion, chopped	1	teaspoon lemon juice
2½	tablespoons butter	2	15-ounce cans whole kernel corn, undrained
½	cup all-purpose flour		
1	tablespoon dried parsley or 2 tablespoons minced fresh parsley	1	28-ounce can stewed tomatoes
		2	cups half-and-half
1	teaspoon dried basil	2	cups grated Cheddar cheese
1	teaspoon salt	¼	cup grated Parmesan cheese

✱ Melt 2 tablespoons of butter in a medium skillet and sauté zucchini and onion.

✱ In a large pot, melt the remaining butter and stir in the flour, parsley, basil, salt, and pepper. Slowly pour in the chicken broth and heat through. Add half-and-half, corn, tomatoes, and sautéed vegetables. Add cheeses. Cover and simmer for 5 minutes.

1976 Happy Canyon President Bob Hawes presents Hall of Fame Inductee plaque to his father-in-law Joseph P. Brennan, M.D.

In 1969, the Pendleton Round-Up and Happy Canyon Hall of Fame became the first of its kind to have been started by an individual rodeo. Its first home was in the Round-Up Pavilion. In 1976, work started on a home for it under the South Grandstand where it stayed until 2006. The museum then moved from its cramped quarters to a new $1.2 million two-story building across the street.

Ten men, including Round-Up founder Roy Raley, and five horses were the first selections to the Hall of Fame. Each year several more outstanding participants or animals are added to the list of those who have made the Pendleton Round-Up the "Granddaddy" of all rodeos.

In 1931, they came up with the Greeter Girls, a cowgirl cavalcade on horseback, to meet the trains. Director George Strand chose former Round-Up Queen Kathleen McClintock to lead the greeters. The Cowgirl Cavalcade, with 188 members and assorted entertainers, greeted trains with a 10-minute show.

*Cowgirl
Kathleen McClintock,
lead Greeter Girl*

Roasted Yellow Pepper Soup and Roasted Tomato Soup with Serrano Cream

This is quite involved, but very dramatic and very tasty.

6 servings

FOR THE PEPPER SOUP

3	tablespoons finely chopped shallot
½	teaspoon dried thyme, crumbled
1	tablespoon unsalted butter
	Salt and black pepper

6	yellow peppers, roasted and coarsely chopped
1½	cups low-salt chicken broth
¼	cup heavy cream
	Fresh lemon juice

FOR THE TOMATO SOUP

3	pounds plum tomatoes, quartered lengthwise
3	large cloves garlic
3	tablespoons finely chopped shallot
½	dried crumbled oregano

	Salt and black pepper
1	tablespoon unsalted butter
1½	cups low-salt chicken broth
¼	cup heavy cream
	Fresh lemon juice

FOR THE SERRANO CREAM

3	fresh Serrano chiles or jalapeños, seeded and chopped fine
1	large garlic clove, minced and mashed

½	teaspoon salt
½	cup crème fraîche or sour cream

✶ Make the pepper soup: in a heavy saucepan cook the shallot, thyme, and salt and pepper to taste in the butter over moderately low heat. Stir until the shallot is soft. Add the bell peppers and 1½ cups of the broth. Simmer the mixture, covered, for 12-15 minutes, or until the peppers are soft.

✶ In a blender, purée the soup in batches until it is very smooth. Force through a fine sieve set over a pan. Whisk in the cream, additional broth, lemon juice, and salt and pepper to taste.

ROASTED YELLOW PEPPER SOUP - CONTINUED

★ Make the tomato soup: Spread the tomatoes, skin side down, in one layer in two foil-lined jelly-roll pans. Add garlic to one of the pans. Bake the tomatoes and the garlic in a 350* oven for 45 minutes to an hour, or until tomatoes are very soft and their skin is dark brown. Let the tomatoes and the garlic cool in the pans on racks.

★ In a heavy saucepan cook the shallot, oregano, salt, and pepper to taste in the butter over moderately low heat. Stir until the shallot is soft. Add the tomatoes, garlic (skins discarded), and 1½ cups of the broth. Simmer the mixture, covered, for 15 minutes.

★ In a blender, purée the soup in batches until it is very smooth. Force through a clean fine sieve set over the pan, and whisk in the cream, additional broth if necessary, lemon juice, and salt and pepper to taste.

★ Make the Serrano cream: In a blender, blend together the chiles, garlic paste, and the crème fraîche until the mixture is combined well. (Don't over-blend the mixture or the cream may curdle.) Force the mixture through a fine sieve set over a small bowl.

★ To serve the soup, ladle ½ cup of each soup into two glass measuring cups. Pour the soups simultaneously into a shallow soup bowl from opposite sides of the bowl and drizzle some of the Serrano cream over each serving.

In Pendleton, we only have two seasons. Before Round-Up ...and .... After Round-Up.

The John and Polly Johnson family's three daughters, carrying on the Round-Up tradition. Court members Natalie, 1997; Emily, 2004; and Liz, 2001.

123

There are so many ways to fix asparagus, we find it to be an incredibly versatile vegetable. Try sautéing it in a little olive oil and just before serving, sprinkle a little orange zest over it. Or toss the asparagus with olive oil and grill until just charred on the outside, sprinkle with a little kosher salt, and serve. Our grandmothers undoubtedly served it with melted butter or mayonnaise, but we know better these days. Oh sure.

ASPARAGUS SOUP

Yummo!

8 servings

1½	pounds asparagus	10	spearmint leaves
1	large white onion, diced	1	quart heavy cream
3	cloves garlic, chopped	8	ounces Asiago cheese, grated
1	tablespoon olive oil	8	ounces Blue cheese, crumbled
1	32-ounce box low sodium beef broth		Black pepper
			Truffle oil (optional)

✳ Blanche asparagus. Set aside eight 4-inch spears for garnish. Chop remaining asparagus into pieces.

✳ Add diced onion and chopped garlic to soup pot. Sauté in olive oil until onion is translucent. Transfer onion and garlic to a blender, add asparagus, beef broth, and mint leaves. Purée.

✳ Return mixture to soup pot. Add cream. Bring to simmer. Slowly add both cheeses to soup, stirring occasionally. Add pepper to taste. Serve in soup bowls, drizzle 5-6 small drops truffle oil and float asparagus spears for garnish.

Local Gourmet Cook and Round-Up Director Billy Lorenzen (the asparagus soup is his recipe) and Happy Canyon costumer and designer Verneda Wagner.

CHUTE

Potatoes, Rice, & Beans

After the show was over, volunteers, helpers, and friends would gather around a pickup for a Tailgate Party. There would be lots of people passing by, stopping and joining in the fun. Everyone would be hot, tired, and thirsty after helping with the show and would enjoy snacks and cocktails on the tailgate of a pickup. You can tell by the picture it was GREAT FUN.

CHUCK WAGON POTATOES

No cowboy missed a meal when this dish was served up.

8 servings

5	pounds red potatoes	1½	cups soft margarine
1	large onion, diced		Salt and freshly ground black pepper
½	cup chopped garlic		
1½	cups precooked chopped bacon	1	cup grated Cheddar cheese
		½	cup chopped chives

✱ Wash potatoes and cut them into bite-sized pieces. Place potatoes, onions, garlic, and bacon in roasting pan. Mix with margarine and add salt and pepper to taste. Cover and cook in 400° oven for 1 hour.

✱ Remove cover and return to oven for 20-25 minutes or until brown. Top with grated cheese and chives.

MAKE AHEAD MASHED POTATOES

Make these early and get out of the kitchen!

12–16 servings

8	large russet potatoes	⅛	teaspoon black pepper
1	8-ounce package cream cheese	1	tablespoon butter
1	cup sour cream	½	cup minced onion
2	teaspoons salt	½	cup minced celery
¼	teaspoon garlic powder	1	tablespoon parsley
		¼	cup butter or margarine

✱ Cook potatoes until tender, then peel. Mash with sour cream, cream cheese, salt, garlic powder, pepper, and butter.

✱ Sauté onion, celery, parsley, and butter and add to mashed potatoes. Put in 2½-quart baking dish. Refrigerate overnight.

✱ Bake covered at 350° for 45 minutes.

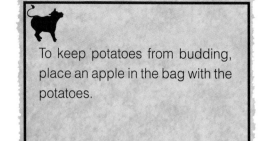

To keep potatoes from budding, place an apple in the bag with the potatoes.

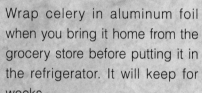

Wrap celery in aluminum foil when you bring it home from the grocery store before putting it in the refrigerator. It will keep for weeks.

I truly enjoyed the years I served on the Round-Up Board of Directors. My responsibility was to assist and help in the Indian Village and the Indian peoples. They never failed to do the very best for the Round-Up festivities. These potatoes are a favorite of mine...
Jack Howland

On Labor Day weekend we have the Walla Walla Fair and Frontier Days Rodeo. It's a very long day with the parade being in the morning and the rodeo not starting until evening. To say "thank you" to all who supported us through the year, my parents, Richard and Sally, and I decided to have a barbecue after the parade for the Round-Up and Happy Canyon courts and their families, all the directors and families (about 120 people). Harold Thompson, John and Cathy Thompson, Bruce and Betty Jane Bugbee, and my brother Steve were also hosts. We served chicken, tri-tip, jack rabbit scalloped potatoes, salads, vegetables from the garden, and Southern peach cobbler. Everyone enjoyed themselves so much it became a 10-year event.

My father Richard Allen served as a Round-Up director, 1995-1999, and I was a Round-Up princess in 1993...*Sally Allen*

JACK RABBIT QUICK AND EASY SCALLOPED POTATOES

Make this ahead and freeze it until company comes.

12–16 servings

2	pounds frozen hash browns	1	10.5-ounce can cream of chicken soup
½	cup melted butter		
1½	teaspoons salt	1	pint sour cream
¼	teaspoon black pepper	2	cups grated Cheddar cheese
1	1-ounce envelope dry onion soup mix	2	cups crushed cornflakes
		¼	cup butter, melted

✷ Thaw potatoes.

✷ Combine butter, salt, pepper, soup mix, soup, sour cream, and cheese and mix well. Gently stir in potatoes. Put into large lightly greased casserole dish or in 2 small casserole dishes.

✷ Mix crushed cornflakes and butter and sprinkle on top of potato mixture. Bake uncovered at 350° for 45-50 minutes.

BAKED CINNAMON "SWEEK" POTATOES

These potatoes are a favorite of Hall of Famer and Round-Up volunteer, Jack Sweek, inspired by his wife, Gene. They especially like it with pork or venison.

2 servings

1	large sweet potato	½	teaspoon brown sugar
½	cup apple, diced	2	teaspoons butter
½	teaspoon cinnamon		

* Cook sweet potato in oven at 350° until knife inserts easily. Remove and make a slit in top of potato. Place apples in slit. Sprinkle with brown sugar and cinnamon and dot with butter.

* Return to oven until butter is melted.

COCONUT RICE

This is a specialty of Hamley's Steakhouse and they serve it with their Maple-Glazed Salmon.

6 servings

2	cups short grain "cal rose" rice	3	tablespoons toasted coconut shavings (see note)
1½	cups water		Salt and black pepper
1	8-ounce can coconut milk		
2	tablespoons butter		

* Put rice, water, and ¾ can coconut milk in a rice steamer and cook.

* When rice is nearly ready (starting to go dry in the steamer), add the rest of the coconut milk, butter, coconut shavings, salt, and pepper.

* When rice is finished, fluff the rice and serve with salmon.

Toast coconut shavings on a bare baking sheet in a 250° oven just until they start to turn golden brown.

Tessie Williams, elder of the Confederated Tribes of Umatilla Indian Reservation, is close to a living legend at Round-Up and Happy Canyon. An inductee into the Hall of Fame for her many contributions, Tessie has hosted a full dinner in her teepee at the grounds on Thursday of Round-Up for the Round-Up and Happy Canyon royalty, chaperones, and directors. The menu typically consists of fry bread, huckleberry jam, salads, salmon, and corn on the cob. Tessie presented her handmade gifts to the guests, often beaded necklaces, medallions, and yarn bags.

Tessie Williams

In 1975, the Round-Up court and their families attended the Omak, Washington Stampede. They were guests of Princess Susan Fitterer's grandparents, Frank and Norris Fitterer. Before the show, they were served dinner in true Western fashion — baked turkey breasts, wonderful salads, and wild rice casserole. The meal was finished off by a special cake celebrating Susan's parents' 25th anniversary...*Annette Fitterer*

1975 Round-Up Court:
Ann Lorenzen, Michele Evans,
Queen Lori Anderson,
Jan Terjeson, Susan Fitterer

WILD RICE CASSEROLE

This will fill up your hungriest cowboy!

12–16 servings

1 cup wild rice, cooked	2-3 tablespoons butter
1 cup long grain rice, cooked	2 6-ounce cans mushrooms
2 large onions, chopped	2 10.75-ounce cans cream of mushroom soup
2 cups diced celery	8 ounces sliced almonds
1 green pepper, chopped	

✷ Sauté onion, celery, and pepper in butter. Add canned mushrooms, chopped, and include the juice of one can. Add mushroom soup and almonds, and mix all together with both rices.

✷ Bake at 350° for 1 hour.

If you skip the soup and use fresh mushrooms, this makes a nice rice pilaf.

PATIO BEANS

An easy dish for a cowboy's cookout!

10 servings

1 24-ounce can vegetarian baked beans	½ cup brown sugar
1 16-ounce can kidney or black beans	1 teaspoon vinegar
	Dash of Worcestershire sauce
1 16-ounce can white or garbanzo beans	¾ cup cubed sharp Cheddar cheese
½ cup ketchup	2 tablespoons bacon bits

✷ Drain most of the liquid from the cans of beans and combine them in a large baking dish.

✷ In a medium-sized saucepan, combine ketchup, brown sugar, vinegar, and Worcestershire sauce. Simmer for 5 minutes. Combine the ketchup mixture with the beans, add the cheese and bacon bits, and mix well. Bake at 350° for 45 minutes.

Use your favorite kinds of beans for this recipe. Use soy-based bacon bits to make this an easy dish for vegetarians.

ZUCCHINI RICE CASSEROLE

You can freeze this before baking. Just let it thaw for an hour before baking.

12–16 servings

1½ pounds zucchini (or more)	1 10.5-ounce can creamed soup
1½ cups shredded sharp Cheddar cheese	1¼ cups water
¾ cup long-grain rice, uncooked	Salt and black pepper to taste
1 cup sliced mushrooms	1 teaspoon Worcestershire sauce

✱ In 9x13-inch pan, spray with cooking spray and arrange one-third of the zucchini, cut in ¼-inch slices. Top with one-third cheese, one-half the rice and one-third of the mushrooms.

✱ Make another layer of the same. Make last layer of zucchini and mushrooms.

✱ Combine soup, water, salt, pepper, and Worcestershire sauce. Mix and pour over layers then top with remaining one-third cheese. Cover and bake at 325° for 1½ hours until rice is tender and bubbling. Remove and let stand for 10-15 minutes before serving.

CROCKPOT BEANS

Guaranteed to get people to ask you for the recipe!

6–8 servings

1 pound bacon	1 16-ounce can kidney beans
1 pound ground beef	1 cup brown sugar
1 16-ounce can baked beans	1 cup ketchup
1 16-ounce can pork and beans	½ teaspoon liquid smoke

✱ In a large skillet, brown the ground beef. Fry up the bacon and cut up into 1-inch pieces.

✱ Place ground beef, bacon, beans, brown sugar, ketchup, and liquid smoke into a large crockpot and cook on high all day.

This recipe may be refrigerated after cooking and re-heated and will taste just as delicious the second time!

People don't always lock their cars in Pendleton, but we must do it during zucchini season. An unlocked car is just an invitation for your neighbors to sneak a few of the prolific vegetables in the front seat, and run.

2001 Queen Tiah DeGrofft

We moved to Colorado 23 years ago, but I come back to Pendleton every year for the Round-Up, and now I bring my grandchildren, who are scattered from Oregon to Colorado. My husband Patrick passed away, but I still keep all the good thoughts and memories in my heart. Happy Canyon, the rodeo, main street, shopping, barbecues, old friends, the Cowboy Breakfast, the parades...Round-Up has always been a part of my life... Nettie Murphy

SEVEN BEAN PLUS

Great to fix in a roaster.

16–20 servings

2	pounds ground beef	1	16-ounce chili beans
1	large onion, chopped	1	16-ounce can pork and beans
½	teaspoon garlic salt	½	cup brown sugar
¼	teaspoon garlic powder	¼	cup molasses
1	teaspoon salt	3	tablespoons prepared mustard
½	teaspoon black pepper	1	26-ounce can tomatoes
1	15-ounce can butter beans	1	15-ounce can tomato sauce
1	26-ounce can lima beans	2	cups water
1	16-ounce can green beans	1	bay leaf
1	16-ounce can kidney beans	4	beef bullion cubes
1	16-ounce can garbanzo beans	½	cup ketchup

✷ Fry the ground beef and onion together.

✷ Drain the fat and add the garlic salt, garlic powder, salt, and pepper.

✷ Drain the beans and combine with the meat mixture in a roasting pan. Add the brown sugar, molasses, mustard, tomatoes, tomato sauce, water, bay leaf, beef bullion cubes, and ketchup. Add more water later if necessary.

✷ Bake at 325° for 1 hour and 30 minutes.

"Pioneers" on the June 2007 Pendleton Round-Up and Happy Canyon Wagon Train

BBQ BAKED BEANS

Always a great side dish

16–20 servings

1	16-ounce can red kidney beans	½	cup vinegar
1	16-ounce can butter beans	¾	cup brown sugar
1	16-ounce can green lima beans	1	teaspoon garlic salt
2	12-ounce cans baked beans	½	teaspoon dry mustard
½	pound bacon, diced	1	cup ketchup
1	large onion, chopped		

✳ Drain kidney beans, butter beans, and lima beans.

✳ Fry the bacon in a medium skillet and remove to plate.

✳ Sauté the onions in the bacon drippings. Add vinegar, sugar, garlic salt, dry mustard, and ketchup to the pan and mix well. Add the bacon and cook for 20 minutes.

✳ Mix the sauce with the drained beans and baked beans. Cover the dish and place in refrigerator for 24 hours.

✳ Place the beans in an oven-safe pot and bake at 350° for 1 hour or more.

Julie Tubbs, Scott Duff, Barry Roesch, Jim Lieuallen, Steve Johnson, and Sally Hopper

In 1961, local service clubs partnered with the Round-Up for a family barbecue, and 2,500 pounds of beef was consumed. You could count on needing a ton of prime beef, a few milk cans of barbecue sauce, a wagonload of coleslaw, 4,000 buns, gallons of coffee, and tubs of beans, which provided dinner for the crowd after the Wednesday show, with entertainment at the popular barbecue provided by musicians and pony rides. Some 4,000 people are served. Until 1985, the 75th anniversary, the barbecue was staged in the arena, and then moved to Roy Raley Park. It rained that week. All week.

John Bauer, former R-Up director, came into the R-Up office during the 75th anniversary, told the staff he'd been president during the 50th anniversary, it had rained that whole week, and it was raining now, and he would suggest (very quietly, he said), not to even mention it when the 100th anniversary comes up.

Mary Esther Alford was a 1945 Round-Up Court princess. After the Saturday mid-show parade, she got off her horse and into the family car and her mother drove her straight to college in southern California. She was two weeks late starting her freshman year because of Round-Up. Coming back to college after attending a concert in Los Angeles, she was on a bus and felt someone staring at her from across the aisle. She looked over and a young soldier asked her if she was from Pendleton. When she nodded, he pulled a picture of her and her horse from his wallet which had been cut out of a newspaper. He asked for her to sign it and write down her phone number. Feeling like a celebrity, she happily signed her name. Ah, but she did not leave her phone number. These beans are her favorites.

JEAN'S BEANS

Prepare and serve warm from a crockpot to keep warm.

12–16 servings

½	pound bacon	1	16-ounce can lima or butter beans, drained
2	large onions, sliced	1	16-ounce can garbanzo beans, drained
2	cloves garlic, minced		
½	cup vinegar	1	28-ounce can kidney beans, drained
1	teaspoon dry mustard		
1	cup brown sugar	2	28-ounce cans pork and beans

✱ Cut up the bacon into 1-inch pieces and fry in a large frying pan. Add the onion and garlic and cook until soft. Add the vinegar, dry mustard, and brown sugar and simmer for 20 minutes.

✱ Add the lima beans, garbanzo beans, and kidney beans to the sauce and place into a casserole dish along with pork and beans. Bake for 1 hour at 350°.

BEST IN THE WEST BBQ BAKED BEANS

This may also be cooked in a crockpot after browning beef, bacon, and onion.

20–24 servings

1	pound ground beef	4	tablespoons molasses
1	pound bacon, chopped	1	teaspoon chili powder
1	medium onion, chopped	¾	teaspoon pepper
½	cup ketchup	2	16-ounce cans butter beans, drained
½	cup barbecue sauce		
1	teaspoon salt	2	16-ounce cans red kidney beans, drained
4	tablespoons prepared mustard		
		2	16-ounce cans pork and beans

✱ Brown the ground beef, bacon, and onion. Drain the fat and add ketchup, barbecue sauce, salt, mustard, molasses, chili powder, and pepper. Stir well. Add the beans and mix thoroughly.

✱ Bake for 1 hour in a large casserole dish at 350°.

DRUNKEN BAKED BEANS

You're liable to find Pendleton Whisky just about everywhere and it adds a zing to these beans.

6–8 servings

6	slices bacon	2	tablespoons horseradish
1	large onion, sliced	2	21-ounce cans pork and beans
½	cup molasses	½	cup Pendleton Whisky

✶ Sauté bacon and onion until bacon is cooked but not crisp, about 10-15 minutes. Add molasses and horseradish.

✶ Open the cans of pork and beans and set aside the liquid (you can add some back in later if it seems too dry). Add the bacon and Pendleton Whisky. Pour into a crockpot or baking dish with a lid.

✶ Bake in the oven at 250° for 7-8 hours or a crockpot all day.

✶ Add reserved liquid from the beans and more whisky to taste if necessary.

My dear friend Vivian (Mrs. Manny) Silk gave me this recipe long ago. I have made it nearly every teepee raising party and the Fourth of July. Vivian was a "casual" chef and used recipes that were ever-changing, so don't be afraid to add or subtract your own choice of ingredients...*Margaret Troedson*

Annual Teepee-Raising Party

*This poem was written by my great grandfather Zebdal Lewis after he attended the first Round-Up in 1910. He was 21 years old. He lived in Adams for a few years where he met and married Stella Lieuallen. Years later (around the late 1930's through the early 1940's) when they lived in Walla Walla, Stella's brothers, Ravella and Paul Lieuallen would borrow Zeb's horses, Punch and Judy, for the two lead horses in the stagecoach races...*Michele Allen Henson*

THE ROUND-UP OR BUST

Talk about your talkabouts
And your worlds of seven wonders
I know sumpthins comin' off
That beats them all to thunder.

It beats all your circuses
And your operas great and grand.
Nothing but the U.S Army
Against it could make a stand.

There'll be Indians by the hundreds
The braves, their families and papooses.
And no doubt they'll be astraddle
The spotted and marked Cayuses.

Next out comes Buffalo Vernon
A doin' stunts with his long rope
And the way he keeps them comin'
Makes your heart jump in your throat.

But the stunt that brands them all
Is Bull doggin' long horned steers
And the man with the nerve to do it
Would just box a lion's ears

The steer comes a runnin' out
Two men after 'em just a yellin'
Right up to the grandstand
They're a comin' just a hellin'

Vernon rides up and grabs him
By his shiny horns so long
And he then proceeds to doggin'
Before that excited throng

Maybe he can't ride that outlaw
For it's a two to one bet
That he's throwed a lot more would-be's
Than has ever rode him yet

It sure is a royal battle
As you watch it from your seat
You get the spirit of the contest
And you wonder which will beat

The man seems glued to the saddle
But his legs work free and loose
And the hair flies from the horse's hide
Like the feathers from a goose

At last the man has conquered
For the horse ceases to ride
He dismounts. His face is all-beaming
He's sure he's rode well for that prize

And I can't begin to tell you
In this letter here of mine
All the things that come of yearly
For I haven't got the time

But take this from an old ranger
That the Round-Up is sure great
I know what I am sayin', stranger
And I am givin' you this straight

Bring everybody with you
Not just your kids and wife
Fetch 'em all that can travel
They'll have the high time of their life

Well, boys, I must be hikin'
I bid you all adieu,
But I am goin' to the Round-Up
If it is the last thing that I do

Written by Zebdal Lewis, 1910

C H U T E

Vegetables

During World War II, the Umatilla County Mounted Patrol was activated to patrol the area in case of airplane crashes or other accidents. Here they gather at the Round-Up grounds. Note the old bucking chutes and announcer's stand in the background. And look at the empty North Hill!

Some of the members of the group include Bud McIntyre, Cy Proebstel, Doc Glenn, Ralph Tachella, Walter Holt, Sr., Dr. William Stram, Laurence Lieuallen, and Ravella Lieuallen.

BEER BATTERED ASPARAGUS

This can be served as an appetizer as well. No need to garnish — they go too fast!

6 servings

1	cup all-purpose flour
1	teaspoon salt
1	tablespoon finely grated lemon peel
¼	teaspoon black pepper

1	cup beer (A lager works best but you can use a pale ale. Do not measure foam.)
4	cups vegetable oil
1	pound medium asparagus

✳ Whisk together flour, salt, lemon peel, and pepper in a bowl until combined. Add the beer, whisking until smooth but do not over-beat batter.

✳ Heat oil to 375° in a deep-fat fryer or a 3 to 4-quart Dutch oven. If using a Dutch oven use about 3 inches of oil in the pan. Dip trimmed and thoroughly dry asparagus into batter to coat. Working in batches of 10 spears, drag one at a time gently against rim of bowl to remove excess batter. Drop spears one at a time in the hot oil. Make sure to cook no more than 10 spears at a time as it will overcrowd the pan. Stir gently to keep spears from sticking to each other. Cook for 2-3 minutes until golden brown. With a slotted spoon transfer fried spears to a paper-towel lined baking sheet. Keep the asparagus warm in a 200° oven while cooking all the spears.

✳ Serve with a buttermilk dip or dressing or your favorite onion ring dip.

In the early 80's, Pendleton Round-Up Court Chaperones Doug and Heather Corey saw a sculpture of a court member riding in a divided skirt, made by Shirley Warner Dickerson of Walla Walla, a former Round-Up court member (1950) and sculptor. That inspired them to approach Shirley about sewing leather outfits for the 1985 court, in celebration of the Round-Up's 75th anniversary. The pattern used was from the 1929 court, shown here. Shirley used between four and five deer hides to make one outfit. "She had to work around the bullet holes," laughed her husband.

Both black and white queen outfits are on display at the Round-Up and Happy Canyon Hall of Fame, and except that one is much newer than the other, you'd be hard pressed to tell which was which.

1929 Court, Allegra McCormmack, Kathryn Furnish, Queen Kathleen McClintock, Dena Lieuallen, Adelyn McIntyre. Kathryn Furnish Ramey is the oldest living court member.

1985 Court, Tina Simpson, Jody Gugin, Shannon VanDorn, Queen Andrea Beck, Ellen Kilkenny

JIMMY NAUGHTON'S
GRILLED BROCCOLI AND PECANS

Be forewarned: if you put these on the table before dinner, your guests will eat them as appetizers. Oh, go ahead!

1	pound broccoli	½	cup olive oil
1	cup pecan halves	1	tablespoon kosher salt

✳ Trim broccoli into bite-sized pieces and place in a gallon zip lock bag with the pecan halves. Cover generously with olive oil and sparingly with kosher salt. Let stand in the refrigerator for a minimum of 30 minutes or as long as overnight.

✳ Cook over a very hot grill. Using a vegetable grilling pan (similar to a frying pan except this one has holes in the bottom) stir frequently.

✳ When the broccoli is tender and the pecans are nicely toasted and dark, about 5-10 minutes, pull from the grill and serve with thinly sliced grilled London Broil.

STETSON HOUSE OF PRIME
GREEN BEANS

The specialty of the house, these green beans never go off the menu.

4-6 servings

4	strips bacon, cut into 1-inch pieces	¾	teaspoon black pepper
			Pinch white pepper
1	1.1-ounce envelope au jus mix	2	14.5-ounce cans whole green beans, drained, or 1 pound fresh green beans, trimmed
3	cups water		
1	tablespoon garlic powder		

✳ In large saucepan, fry the bacon until crisp. Remove to a paper towel to drain, reserving drippings. When bacon is cool, crumble and set aside.

✳ Add au jus mix, water, garlic powder, and peppers to the bacon drippings. Stir well and bring to a boil. Add green beans and heat for 3-4 minutes if using canned green beans (which Stetsons does). If using fresh green beans, bring to a boil and cook until tender, 8-10 minutes. Serve topped with crumbled bacon.

When you are cooking green beans, fresh, canned or frozen, add 1 cap full of oil to them. This makes such a difference. They'll taste like beans fresh from the garden.

MY GRANDMOTHER'S SCALLOPED CORN

This comfort food makes a beautiful sauce with a wonderful texture.

8 servings

3	tablespoons all-purpose flour	½	cup chopped onion
1	teaspoon salt	1	cup milk
¼	teaspoon paprika	2	cups canned whole kernel corn, drained
¼	teaspoon dry mustard	1	egg yolk
	Cayenne pepper	⅔	cup buttered bread crumbs
3	tablespoons butter		

✴ Generously butter a 1½-quart baking dish. Mix the flour, salt, paprika, mustard, and cayenne pepper together, set aside.

✴ Melt the butter in a skillet, add the onions and cook until soft. Stir in the flour mixture and cook, stirring and smoothing for 2-3 minutes. Add the milk, stirring constantly, and bring it to a boil. Stir in the drained corn and egg yolk. Spoon into the baking dish and cover with crumbs. Bake in 400° oven for 25 minutes until the crumbs are brown and the center is cooked.

Insert a toothpick into the center and when it comes out clean, corn is ready. Or if the baking dish is too deep for a toothpick, use a piece of uncooked spaghetti.

The connection between the city of Pendleton and Pendleton Woolen Mills has been a love affair going back now for over 100 years. Since 1909, Pendleton Woolen Mills has thrived under the guidance and management of the Bishop family, and today the company owns and operates seven facilities, manages 75 retail stores, and publishes direct mail catalogs. The family thread has continued its presence every September at the Pendleton Round-Up.

Don Hawkins, Easton Corey, George Corey, Steve Corey, Mort Bishop II

Kids and Round-Up ... well, there are a couple of schools of thought on this. There are those who take the kids everywhere, and then there are those who ship the kids off to Grandma's for the week. You've heard that old saw: Kids really take the "G" out of Gourmet? There are those who think that kids really take the "R" out of Round-Up.

Whichever your school of thought, you'll see kids everywhere and all of them with a cowboy hat. Let 'er Buck!, you little cuties.

Kate Hill, daughter of Steve and Jane Hill

GULLIVER'S CORN

This is served at all special occasions of the Currin family.

6 servings

2   10-ounce packages frozen corn
1   cup heavy cream, whipped
1   cup milk
1   tablespoon salt
¼   teaspoon Accent
6   teaspoons (or less) granulated sugar
    Pinch white or cayenne pepper
2   tablespoons melted butter
2   tablespoons all-purpose flour

✶   Combine corn, whipped cream, milk, salt, Accent, sugar, and pepper in saucepan and bring to boil. Simmer 5 minutes

✶   Melt butter, add flour to make a roux. Mix well and add to corn. Heat until thickened.

ORANGE BALSAMIC CABBAGE

Cabbage done a different way. Great sauce!

12 servings

½   cup orange marmalade
3   tablespoons balsamic vinegar
3   tablespoons margarine, melted
2   pounds cabbage
1   onion, coarsely chopped
2   tablespoons water
    Finely shredded orange peel

✶   Stir together orange marmalade, balsamic vinegar, and margarine.

✶   Core and cut cabbage into coarse chunks along with the onions and place in 3-quart saucepan with cover. Sprinkle with water. Cover, bring to boil, simmer for 8-10 minutes until cabbage is crisp-tender. Lift cabbage and onions with a slotted spoon and place on a serving platter. Sprinkle with orange peel. Drizzle with some of the sauce, and serve the remaining sauce in a small pitcher.

CHILE RELLENO LOAF

For Chile Relleno fans, don't invite anyone over for this. Eat it all yourself. Then go to the gym tomorrow.

4 servings

1	7-ounce can whole chiles	2	eggs
½	pound Cheddar cheese, grated	½	cup all-purpose flour
½	pound Monterey Jack cheese or Pepper Jack cheese, grated	½	teaspoon salt
½	cup milk	1	8-ounce can tomato sauce
		1	tablespoon chopped olives Cilantro

✱ Remove seeds from the chiles and layer chiles with grated cheeses alternately into loaf pan. Beat eggs well with milk. Mix in flour and salt and pour over the chiles and cheese.

✱ Bake uncovered at 350° for 30-45 minutes. Add olives to tomato sauce and pour over the loaf and bake 10 minutes longer. Let sit at least 10 minutes before unmolding. Garnish with cilantro.

CHILE RELLENO CASSEROLE

Ole! Close to the Loaf, but this one will feed your guests too.

8-10 servings

4	4-ounce cans whole green chiles	1	pound Monterey Jack cheese, grated
1	pound sharp Cheddar cheese, grated	1	15-ounce can evaporated milk
		3	eggs
		1	8-ounce can tomato sauce

✱ In a 9x13-inch buttered dish, layer 2 cans of chiles (remove seeds and open them up to lay out flat to cover bottom of dish). Top with Cheddar cheese. Place the other 2 cans of chiles on top and top with Jack cheese.

✱ Beat eggs, add milk, and blend. Pour over chiles and cheese. Bake at 350° uncovered 35-45 minutes. Remove from oven. Pour tomato sauce over, covering the top. Bake 15 minutes longer.

The story of the Walla Walla Sweet Onions began over a century ago on the Island of Corsica, off the coast of Italy. It was there that a French soldier found a sweet onion seed and brought it to the Walla Walla Valley. This sweet onion developed over generations through the process of carefully hand selecting onions from each year's crop, ensuring exceptional sweetness, jumbo size, and round shape. Today's growers are not just raising sweet onions, they're cultivating a tradition. Walla Walla Sweets are available mid-June through September.

Chef Raymond Burke with a Junior Indian Beauty.

FRENCH FRIED ONION RINGS

Substitute water for the beer if you like (but it won't be as good).

2	large Walla Walla Sweet Onions	½	teaspoon salt
1	egg	1½	teaspoons baking powder
½	cup all-purpose flour	½	cup beer
1	tablespoon cornstarch		Salt

★ Beat egg well. Mix together flour, cornstarch, salt, and baking powder and sift over beaten egg. Mix to a smooth batter. Add beer until batter is a little thicker than heavy cream.

★ Slice onions into medium-thick rings. If desired, steam rings for no more than 2 minutes to soften them up. Coat the onion rings with batter. Heat oil to 375° and drop in rings. Cook to a light golden brown. Remove from oil and salt lightly.

SWEET ONION QUICHE

Very nice served with fruit and bacon.

6 servings

4	large Walla Walla sweet onions, chopped	1	teaspoon salt
3	tablespoons butter	⅛	teaspoon black pepper
1	tablespoon vegetable oil		Nutmeg
¼	cup all-purpose flour	1	cup grated Swiss cheese
2	eggs (or 3 egg yolks)	1	8-inch pie shell, partially baked
½	cup heavy cream	1	tablespoon butter

★ Sauté onions in butter and oil over a very low heat until golden yellow (at least 15 minutes). Sprinkle flour over onions and cook 2-3 minutes longer. Cool slightly.

★ Beat together eggs, cream, salt, pepper, and nutmeg. Stir in half the cheese. Pour into pie shell, sprinkle with remaining cheese and 1 tablespoon butter that has been cut into pea-sized dots. Bake 25-30 minutes at 375° until puffed and golden brown.

CRUNCHY WALLA WALLA ONION RINGS

These are baked instead of fried.

8 servings

2	large Walla Walla Sweet onions (about 2 pounds)	2	slightly beaten eggs
		1½	cups seasoned bread crumbs

✱ Cut onions into ½-inch thick slices. Separate into rings. Coat each ring with egg, then with bread crumbs. Place on buttered baking sheets. Broil 4 inches from heat 5-6 minutes or until golden brown.

WALLA WALLA SWEET ONION RINGS

These are a little labor intensive (standing over a hot stove breading and frying), but a glass of Crazy Aunt Sue's Sangría can see you through and you'll like the results!

8 servings

2	Walla Walla or other sweet onions, sliced about ¼-inch thick and separated into rings.	3	tablespoons onion powder
		3	tablespoons garlic powder
3	cups buttermilk	1½	teaspoons salt
3	cups all-purpose flour	1½	teaspoons black pepper
		4	cups vegetable oil

✱ Place onion rings in a large bowl. Pour in the buttermilk and toss to coat. Soak rings for at least 1 hour, tossing occasionally.

✱ Mix flour, onion powder, garlic powder, salt, and pepper in a large bowl.

✱ Heat vegetable oil to 350°. Shake excess buttermilk off onion rings, and working with a few at a time, coat with dry mixture. Drop in hot oil and fry until golden brown, about 2 minutes. Do not overcrowd pan. Drain on a paper towel lined sheet pan, and keep warm in a 200° oven.

To tell if the oil is heated to the right frying temperature, drop a kernel of corn in the pan and when it pops it's ready for frying.

Since 1983, all of the Round-Up concessions have been handled by local vendors and service clubs. That first year they provided barbecued beef, sausages, enchiladas, hamburgers, tacos, corn dogs, pizza, gyros, souvlakia, and barbecued chicken. Over the years, the fare has included yogurt bars (not a hit), curly fries, lamb and beef kabobs, nachos, onion rings, shrimp kabobs, ice cream cones (a huge hit, even if the weather is cool), Mexican specialties, and elephant ears. Having local groups provide the foods is one of the best reasons to head down to the Round-Up grounds. Excellent food!

Director Wives Ann Cimmiyotti, Katy Hudson, Patsy Moffit, Judy Rew, and Carmen Christensen

We've heard of many ways to avoid any tears when peeling an onion. Maybe one of these will work for you.

1) Wear ski goggles (or eyeglasses).

2) Put the onion in the refrigerator or freezer before you cut it.

3) Chew gum while you're peeling.

4) Keep your eyes shut.

5) Put a spoon in your mouth while peeling and chopping.

6) Put a matchstick in your mouth (don't light it).

7) Peel the onion next to a burning candle.

8) Hold a piece of bread in your mouth.

9) Rub your hands with lemon juice before picking up the onion.

10) Peel it underwater.

11) Have someone else peel your onions.

ONION-STUFFED ONIONS

A nice variation to serve with steaks.

6 servings

6 medium onions
Paprika
4 tablespoons butter or margarine
¼ cup light cream
¼ cup chopped ripe black olives

2 tablespoons chopped pecans
¼ teaspoon salt
¼ cup dry bread crumbs
1 tablespoon melted butter or margarine

✱ Peel onions. Cut a thick slice from top of each and set aside. Using a tablespoon, scoop out center of each onion and set aside. Cook onion shells in boiling, salted water for 25 minutes or until tender. Drain. Brush each with cooking oil and sprinkle generously with paprika.

✱ Coarsely chop the tops and centers of onions and sauté them in 4 tablespoons butter or margarine until tender. Stir in cream, olives, pecans, and salt. Spoon mixture into cooked onion shells.

✱ Combine bread crumbs with 1 tablespoon melted butter and sprinkle over onions. Sprinkle with paprika. Bake in 350° oven for 15 minutes.

C H U T E

The Grand Entrée

MEDITERRANEAN TENDERLOIN OF BEEF

A little taste of Greece at Round-Up puts you in a little romantic mood, but what's new?

4 servings

1	2-pound beef tenderloin, excess fat removed
2	teaspoons whole coriander seeds
½	teaspoon whole black peppercorns
¼	teaspoon coarse salt
2	tablespoons extra virgin olive oil (preferably Greek)
½	cup extra virgin olive oil
2	large shallots, thinly sliced
1	large clove garlic, thinly sliced
½	cup oil packed sun-dried tomatoes, thinly sliced
⅓	cup cured black olives (Calamata), pitted and quartered
⅓	cup chopped flat leaf parsley
½	pound tubular pasta, such as penne or ziti
½	teaspoon salt
¼	teaspoon freshly ground black pepper
⅛	teaspoon red pepper flakes

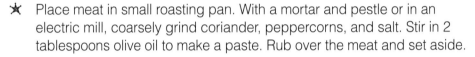

✱ Place meat in small roasting pan. With a mortar and pestle or in an electric mill, coarsely grind coriander, peppercorns, and salt. Stir in 2 tablespoons olive oil to make a paste. Rub over the meat and set aside.

✱ In a medium saucepan, heat 1 tablespoon of the olive oil over low heat. Add the shallots and garlic and cook until soft, but not brown, about 5 minutes. Stir in the sun-dried tomatoes, olives, parsley, and remaining olive oil. Heat, stirring, until warmed through. Cover to keep warm and set aside.

✱ In a 425° oven, roast the meat until medium rare, about 30-40 minutes. The internal temperature should reach 125°. Remove the meat to a carving board, cover loosely with foil and let rest 10 minutes. Strain the roasting juices into the sun-dried tomato sauce.

✱ While the meat is cooking, cook the pasta in a large pot of boiling salted water until tender, but firm, about 12 minutes. Drain, return the pasta to the pot and stir in the sauce. Season with salt, pepper, and red pepper flakes. Cover to keep warm.

✱ To serve, carve the meat against the grain into ¼-inch slices and arrange on a serving platter. Transfer the pasta to a serving bowl and serve the two together. Pour any meat juices from carving over the tenderloin.

From the *East Oregonian*, July 31, 1910:

Pendleton now has a Frontier Celebration Association, and plans are under way to stage the biggest celebration ever held in the northwest. To be held in conjunction with the District Fair, the show will feature exhibitions of bronc riding, steer riding, fancy roping, wild horse races, and other "wild west" events. Shares in the association will be sold for $10 a share to finance the event.

I lived in Pendleton 1965-1975, and enjoyed the Round-Up, Happy Canyon, parades, and Wednesday's Family Barbecue. We always knew we'd have out of town company during that week. Happy times were had then...
Connie Palmer

LONDON BROIL

This is so easy to double, triple, or quadruple and you can feed all your guests steak and not run short on money for Round-Up tickets!

4–6 servings

1½-2 pound top round steak (London Broil cut)

3 tablespoons Worcestershire sauce

3 tablespoons soy sauce

1 tablespoon olive oil

1 tablespoon sherry

2 cloves garlic, minced

1 teaspoon finely chopped fresh ginger (or ¼ teaspoon powdered ginger)

✶ Combine Worcestershire sauce, soy sauce, oil, sherry, garlic, and ginger in plastic re-sealable bag. Mix well. Add steak and marinate for at least 30 minutes and up to 12 hours (refrigerate if marinating for longer than 2 hours).

✶ Broil or grill according to taste. Let set 5 minutes, then slice on the diagonal in ½-inch slices.

ROUND-UP LONDON BROIL

You probably won't have leftovers, but if you do, this makes a dynamite French dip sandwich.

6–8 servings

1	4-pound top sirloin steak, cut 1¾-2 inches thick	2	cloves garlic, crushed
1	cup vegetable oil	2	tablespoons dry mustard
½	cup lemon juice	1	tablespoon coarse ground pepper
¾	cup soy sauce	2¼	teaspoons salt
¼	cup Worcestershire sauce	1½	teaspoons parsley flakes
¼	cup red wine vinegar		

★ Mix oil, lemon juice, soy sauce, Worcestershire sauce, vinegar, garlic, mustard, pepper, salt, and parsley flakes in blender and pour over meat. Marinate in refrigerator 24 hours, turning frequently.

★ Grill on barbecue 20-25 minutes over medium fire or until internal temperature reaches:

Rare:	120-125°
Medium Rare:	130-135°
Medium:	140-145°

★ Slice in strips and serve.

I was born September 11, 1924 in Pendleton, raised and schooled there. Many times I attended the Pendleton Round-Up, Happy Canyon, and the Cowboy Shuffle Dances. I ushered in the grandstand. My father, James A. Isaac, played in the original band...*Joan Isaac Rose*

In 1913, fifty special trains were parked in Pendleton for the show, their Pullman cars providing accommodations for thousands. The entire town turned into a mammoth hotel. Beds and cots were even placed on the flat roofs of downtown stores. Garages and barns became bedrooms. Tents were everywhere. The Oregon National Guard loaned the city a carload of tents. Members of the Commercial Club wore prominent badges that said, "Ask me. I live here." The crowds just kept coming and cots of Pendleton Field were placed in nooks and crannies all over town to accommodate the many guests.

Rose Wall, trick rider and wife of stock contractor

JIMMY NAUGHTON'S
GRILLED LONDON BROIL

We do like our London Broils here in Pendleton, and this one was developed by Jimmy Naughton, co-owner of Zimmerman's Hardware. Jimmy is a frequent participant in barbecue contests and one of our favorite chefs!

8–10 servings

1	2-inch thick cut of top round roast, about 4 pounds	2	teaspoons freshly cracked black pepper
2	teaspoons kosher salt	2	teaspoons granulated garlic
		2	teaspoons brown sugar

✶ Have roast at room temperature.

✶ Mix equal parts salt, pepper, garlic, and brown sugar. Rub a generous amount on both sides of the meat, and grill over a very hot fire for 5 minutes, turn and cook on the other side until rare or medium rare.

✶ Pull from grill and let rest for at least 10 minutes.

✶ Slice across the grain as thinly as possible. Serve with grilled broccoli and pecans (see Vegetable section).

By letting thicker cuts of beef come to room temperature before they are grilled, you are able to cook them more evenly. If the cut is pulled from the fridge and thrown on the grill, the outside will be done but the center will be raw! And if the center is done, the outside will be burnt and dry.

Kosher salt has larger grains, so it doesn't dissolve as readily as table salt; it also has no additives (iodine).

Freshly cracked pepper has a more fresh, full depth of flavor.

Granulated garlic has larger grains so it doesn't dissolve.

Brown sugar holds the other ingredients together. It also caramelizes on the surface of the meat, making for nice grill marks and a savory flavor.

PITCHFORK BARBECUE

This is a horse of a different color. If you choose this method to barbecue your steaks, you will probably not have the best steak you've ever eaten, but you'll have the most fun! A Pitchfork Barbecue makes a great party.

As many as you want to feed

This mostly has to do with the equipment. You will need a 60-quart cast iron kettle to hang over a fire and rigged so you can raise or lower it to control the temperature of the oil. Also needed is an oil or candy thermometer and two or three 3-tine pitchforks with short handles. And of course, you'll need a New York Steak about 1 inch thick for each of your guests.

✱ The day before the party, render out about 50 pounds of beef suet into oil. Skim out the cracklings and discard. The oil is now ready for frying. You'll want to keep it at 350 degrees.

✱ Skewer the steaks onto a pitchfork tine. You should be able to do about three on one pitchfork. Plunge into the hot oil. They will cook in 3 to 5 minutes, depending on whether you want rare, medium-rare, or medium. (Before cooking, let the steaks warm to room temperature to keep the hot oil from cooling off too fast.)

You really can use canola oil if the thought of rendering 50 pounds of fat is too daunting. A commercial oil called Fri Max works well, but remember that the beef tallow imparts a much better flavor. Cholesterol, here we come!

It helps to dip the empty pitchforks into the oil before skewering the steaks, because the steaks will slide off better after being cooked. You'll need tongs to remove the steaks from the pitchfork.

Top Photo:
June Mohrland and Bob Mumm

Bottom Photos:
Reyburn Collis, Patrick Maney, Fred Westersund

The Pitchfork Barbecue has its beginnings with local rancher Bob Mumm, who found this recipe in 1990. But until he built a fire pit in his back yard with the appropriate rigging to raise and lower the kettle, the recipe sat dormant in his cookbook. He experimented many times and found that controlling the oil temperature was very difficult, and went through five or six thermometers, cooking several! More recently, electronic thermometers have been used and the wireless variety is definitely a plus! Fred and Jean (a cousin of Bob) Westersund helped in the testing and Fred built a pit of his own and entertained the Teepee Raising group with a Pitchfork Barbecue.

One of our favorite "testing and tasting" parties was held at Steve and June Mohrland's ranch west of Pendleton where we cooked steaks in the hot oil on pitchforks for 75 guests. We also had a baked bean cook-off and frankly, I don't think we met a baked bean recipe we didn't like. Salads and cookies were also tested and tasted, and we had a good start to compiling the recipes.

THE PLATEAU PENDLETON WHISKY STEAK

This recipe was developed by Brian vonEggers, chef at Plateau Restaurant at Wildhorse Resort and Casino. Pendleton Whisky Steak is a four-step recipe. First, roast the shallots; second, use the shallots in the aïoli; third, prepare the steak; and fourth, deglaze the pan to create a sauce.

4 servings

ROASTED SHALLOT AÏOLI

Aïoli is a garlic mayonnaise. In French ail means garlic and oli means oil. Chef Brian's version substitutes shallots.

½ cup roasted shallots	1 tablespoon chef's salt (mixture of salt, pepper, paprika, and powdered ginger)
Olive oil, black pepper, your choice of fresh herbs	
3 egg yolks	½ cup vegetable oil
½ cup sour cream	½ cup olive oil
1 tablespoon horseradish	

✶ To roast the shallots, peel and trim to the same size and toss with a little olive oil, pepper, and fresh herbs. Place on a piece of aluminum foil, fold the foil into a pillow, and roast in the oven at 325° for 45 minutes. Purée shallots in food processor. Add egg yolks, sour cream, horseradish, and chef's salt. Quickly mix these ingredients. With machine running, slowly drizzle in the oil until it is all incorporated.

STEAK

4 10- to 12-ounce strip loin steaks	2 tablespoons clarified butter or vegetable oil
2 tablespoons black peppercorns	1 tablespoon chopped shallots
1 tablespoon kosher salt	2 cups Pendleton Whisky
	3 tablespoons butter

✶ Trim all excess fat and sinew from meat. Run whole peppercorns through spice mill for fresh cracked pepper flavor and place in shallow dish. Salt the steaks lightly on both sides, then press each side into the cracked pepper to create a pepper crust. Heat pan to high on stove top. When pan is hot, add butter or oil. Sear the steak, flipping after 1½ minutes. Steak should be dark brown on the outside.

THE PLATEAU PENDLETON WHISKEY STEAK - CONTINUED

✴ At this point the whole pan can go into the oven (if pan handle is heat resistant) or turn the heat down and finish cooking to desired steak temperature on stove top. Remove steaks from pan to cutting board, add shallots to pan and sauté briefly, de-glaze pan with Whisky, being careful to add whisky away from open flame. Be prepared when returning to flame for a flare-up.

✴ Reduce heat until almost dry and finish sauce by melting butter into it. (Don't let it simmer after butter has been added or it will separate.)

✴ After steaks have rested 3-5 minutes, slice on bias 4 or 5 slices and fan out. Pour whisky sauce over top. Drizzle the roasted shallot aïoli over steak.

PACIFIC RIM MARINATED BEEF TRI-TIP

This recipe proved to be one of Oregon Beef Council's most popular. It was the recipient of the People's Choice Award at the Oregon Chapter of the American Heart Association's Affair of the Heart.

6 servings

1½-2 pound beef tri-tip	1 tablespoon chopped fresh ginger
4 green onions, sliced	
1 cup soy sauce	4 cloves garlic, crushed
3 tablespoons sesame oil	1 teaspoon toasted sesame seeds
1 tablespoon sugar	

✴ Trim excess fat from meat. Combine remaining ingredients except sesame seeds.

✴ Place meat and marinade in covered glass dish or plastic bag. Refrigerate 6-8 hours or overnight.

✴ Remove meat from marinade. Grill over medium coals, turning occasionally, about 25-30 minutes for rare. Remove from grill. Tent with foil for 10 minutes. Cut cross-grain into thin slices, place on serving platter, and sprinkle with sesame seeds.

From the *East Oregonian*, September 4, 1910:

J.R. Raley, president of the Round-Up Association, has received a letter from former President Theodore Roosevelt, regretting that he must turn down an invitation to attend the big show.

Flint Rasmussen, popular bullfighter, barrel man, clown, and fantastic singer, dancer, and entertainer, performed at the Pendleton Round-Up for the last time in 2005 before signing full time with PBR (Professional Bull Riding). On Saturday, his last performance day of the Round-Up, Flint ran across the arena and threw his hat into the North Grandstand. It landed in the lap of Macey Rae Erice. After the show, Macey and her mother Monica found Flint and took this picture.

BULLFIGHTER'S STUFFED STEAK

This flank steak isn't nearly as difficult as it may look, and it's a real crowd pleaser. Sort of reminds us of a rodeo bullfighter curled up into a tight little ball just before he jumps into the barrel.

6 servings

STEAK

1   flank steak, ¾-inch thick, about 1¼ pounds, butterflied

2   red bell peppers

3   tablespoons chopped parsley

6-8 thin slices prosciutto or other cured ham

24 fresh basil leaves

2   tablespoons grated Parmesan cheese

Freshly ground black pepper to taste

MARINADE

¼   cup olive oil

¼   cup red wine vinegar

2   cloves garlic, chopped

2   tablespoons chopped parsley

¼   teaspoon black pepper

✶   With long end of the steak facing you, run a thin sharp knife through the middle thickness of the meat, leaving about ½-inch at the long opposite end to make a "hinge." Flip meat open to resemble a butterfly.

✶   Combine marinade ingredients, marinate steak for 2 hours at room temp.

✶   Halve peppers lengthwise, remove seeds. Place skin side up on broiler tray, lined with aluminum foil, 4 inches from heat. Broil until skins are charred black. Seal peppers in a plastic or paper bag for 15 minutes to steam. Peel off skins.

✶   After 2 hours, remove steak from marinade and scrape off any excess marinade. Lay meat open on a long piece of aluminum foil on a flat surface. Reserve marinade.

✶   Place the 4 pepper halves on top of steak to cover it. Sprinkle with 1 tablespoon of the parsley. Cover with prosciutto slices. Arrange basil leaves in a single layer over complete surface of prosciutto. Sprinkle the surface with grated Parmesan, the remaining 2 tablespoons parsley, and the black pepper.

BULLFIGHTER'S STUFFED STEAK – CONTINUED

* With the long side of the layered steak facing you, lift it from the foil and roll it tightly away from you. It will only roll about one and half times and should look like a jelly-roll. With pieces of kitchen string, tie the steak at 2 to 3-inch intervals.

* Place steak on its aluminum foil in a shallow baking dish and pour marinade over the top. Bake 30 minutes at 350°, basting twice.

* Remove from oven, let rest for 5-7 minutes before slicing. Slice into ½-inch slices. Serve with sprigs of basil, if you have any left.

In those early days, who could have fully anticipated how many people would show up for Round-Up? And how to feed all these folk? In 1912, a 400-seat temporary cafeteria opened on Main Street near the Umatilla River Bridge, one of many temporary cafes and hot dog stands scattered throughout the city. There was no limit to the merry-making of the crowds at the Round-Up. In the years to follow, hot dog and hamburger stands flourished.

GENE'S ROUND-UP ROAST

This meat is fork tender with an excellent rub flavoring.

10-12 servings

1	5- to 6-pound beef rump roast	½	teaspoon paprika
½	teaspoon celery salt	¼	teaspoon nutmeg
½	teaspoon garlic powder	⅓	cup brown sugar
½	teaspoon onion powder		

* Place roast in center of large sheet of heavy-duty aluminum foil.

* Mix celery salt, garlic powder, onion powder, paprika, and nutmeg and sprinkle evenly over the roast to cover.

* Spoon brown sugar over the top of roast. Fold over top and sides of foil and place in roaster pan. Roast at 300° for 2 hours, then turn temperature down to 250° and roast another 2 hours.

Branding the stock before Round-Up was an annual event. Walter Holt, kneeling, and Jack Olsen, former Round-Up directors, take their turn with the branding irons. Different local families provided calves for the Round-Up, so several branding irons were in the fire, one for each rancher bringing in his calves.

BARBECUED TERIYAKI STEAK

About as easy as grilling gets!

4 servings

4	steaks, 1-inch thick	¼	cup brown sugar
¼	cup soy sauce	2	tablespoons lemon juice
1	tablespoon vegetable oil	¼	teaspoon ground ginger
1	clove garlic, minced (or ⅛ teaspoon garlic powder)		

✶ Blend soy sauce, oil, garlic, brown sugar, lemon juice, and ginger. Pour over 4 steaks. Cover and refrigerate 3-24 hours, turning often. Grill as desired.

BEER POT ROAST

This is also called Flemish Pot Roast, has a wonderful flavor and very tender meat.

8–10 servings

1	4- to 5-pound chuck roast	1	12-ounce can beer
1	tablespoon olive or vegetable oil	1	tablespoon brown sugar
		1	tablespoon white vinegar
4	medium onions, peeled and sliced	1	bay leaf
2	tablespoons butter or margarine	2	cloves garlic, sliced
		1½	teaspoons salt
2	tablespoons all-purpose flour		

✶ Brown both sides of roast in a Dutch oven using the oil.

✶ In a separate pan, brown onions in butter until golden. Sprinkle with the flour and cook 2 minutes. Add the beer, brown sugar, vinegar, bay leaf, garlic, and salt. Mix together and pour over meat and simmer, covered, at least 2 hours or until meat is tender. If you choose to use the oven, roast for 2-3 hours at 350°, covered. Remove from oven and serve, spooning sauce over the meat.

TERIYAKI FLANK STEAK

The oil keeps the juices in while the steak cooks, and the honey adds a dark crust.

6 servings

1	1½- to 2-pound flank steak	2	tablespoons honey
½	cup olive or vegetable oil	½	teaspoon ground ginger
¼	cup soy sauce	4	little green onions, sliced
2	tablespoons garlic powder		Parsley

✻ Mix oil, soy sauce, garlic powder, honey, ginger, and onions and marinate flank steak 24 hours, turning occasionally.

✻ Broil over hot coals 6-8 minutes per side for medium. Slice across the grain into ½-inch strips. Serve on a bed of parsley.

BULGOGI

Bulgogi literally means "fire meat" in Korean (this refers to the cooking technique — over an open flame — rather than the dish's spiciness). The term is also applied to variations such as dak bulgogi (made with chicken) or dweji bulgogi (made with pork), although the seasonings are different.

2-3 servings

1	pound sirloin, sliced into thin strips	2	teaspoons minced garlic
¼	cup soy sauce	1	teaspoon sesame oil
2	tablespoons sugar		Black pepper
2	tablespoons chopped green onion		

✻ Combine all ingredients. Marinate beef 1 hour.

✻ Broil over grill or fry in pan just until the meat loses its pinkness. Bulgogi is traditionally served with white rice.

Good marinades depend on three components: acids, oils, and other flavors. Begin with one part acid (vinegar, mustard, lemon juice) to three parts oil (olive, vegetable, chile). Add some salt and pepper. To make a hot and spicy marinade, whisk in some chili powder, curry powder, or hot pepper sauce. Honey, molasses, or ketchup will produce a sweeter marinade. Fresh herbs and garlic are always good. The sky and your own imagination are the only limits. When you get your own marinade perfected, share it with your Round-Up guests.

SAWTOOTH POT ROAST

Holy Pot Roast, Batman! This recipe was contributed by Adam West, who grew up in Walla Walla, and whose mother was a cowgirl and loved rodeos!

6–8 servings

1	2½- to 3-pound beef or elk chuck roast	4	carrots, cut in 2-inch chunks
2	tablespoons butter	3	stalks celery, cut in 2-inch chunks
2	tablespoons olive oil	1	large onion, peeled and cut in half
	Salt and black pepper		
3	cloves garlic, slivered	6	red potatoes, unpeeled and cut in half
1	large onion, peeled, sliced, and separated into rings	1	16-ounce package frozen peas
1	apple, cored and sliced into rings		Dash of steak sauce

✸ Heat cast iron skillet, adding butter and olive oil. Rub salt and pepper on roast, and knife in the slivered garlic.

✸ Brown roast on all sides. Place onion and apple rings on top of roast. Add about 1-inch water and cover with aluminum foil.

✸ Place in oven at 400°, making sure to keep the liquid level up while roasting.

✸ After 1 hour, add sliced carrots, celery, the 2 onion halves, and the potatoes. Replace foil.

✸ Continue roasting 2 more hours, making sure the water doesn't run dry. About 15 minutes before serving, sprinkle the peas on top and return to oven.

✸ Remove from oven. Sprinkle the steak sauce around and on top; serve directly from the skillet.

As a child Adam West lived on a ranch near Walla Walla, Washington a town just 40 miles northeast of Pendleton. He has many fond memories of the Pendleton Round-Up and still treasures a saddle given to him as a boy that was made in Hamley's Saddle Shop.

THE BEST SOUR CREAM POT ROAST

*These directions are for a slow cooker, but you can also cook it in the oven at 300°
for 3 hours. True comfort food!*

6–8 servings

1	5- to 7-pound beef or elk bottom round roast or small brisket
1	onion, chopped
1	package beef gravy mix
1	cup water
½	cup ketchup

¼	cup dry red wine
2	teaspoons Dijon mustard
1	teaspoon Worcestershire sauce
1	clove garlic, minced
	Salt and freshly ground pepper
½	cup sour cream
2	tablespoons all-purpose flour

✳ Place roast in a crockpot or slow cooker.

✳ Mix together all other ingredients <u>except sour cream and flour</u> and pour
over roast. Cook 4-6 hours.

✳ Add flour to sour cream and whisk smooth. Remove meat from sauce
and strain gravy into a saucepan. Add the sour cream mixture and heat
just to a boil. Slice meat and serve with the gravy. This makes enough
gravy for potatoes too.

From the *East Oregonian*,
September 3, 1910:

Will Switzler, well-known Umatilla
stockman, is here today from
Umatilla. He is assisting Sheriff
Til Taylor, chairman of the horse
committee for the Round-Up.
Switzler said he will bring a
number of wild horses from his
range across the Columbia River
in Washington.

*Mother and Daughter Corrin Graybeal
and Carolyn Thompson were willing
tasters at our testing parties.*

When my husband, Robin, and I were first married, he and his brother ran a large herd of Hereford cattle. Every spring when the baby calves were worked, they would put all the bull parts (testicles) in a bucket and throw them away. One spring Robin asked me to fix a batch of Rocky Mountain Oysters. What? I protested that I had never done that. In fact, I had never seen one. But he was confident that I could handle the job. So I cleaned and soaked them in salt water. I then I rinsed them, dipped them in batter and fried them. No one could bite through them or chew them as I didn't realize the tough outer casing has to be removed before cooking. Not only that, they tasted like the disinfectant they had used on the calves. The next spring they promised they would hold off on the disinfectant until after the "oysters" were in the bucket and I learned how to remove the edible inner part from the tough casing. Here is the process I learned through trial and error. Peeling Rocky Mountain oysters does make for an interesting answer to the question, "So how was your day?"...*Mary Lou Fletcher*

The dish is said to be an acquired taste, but not completely inedible. Many customers who order Rocky Mountain oysters use generous amounts of hot sauce or dipping sauces to enhance (disguise?) the flavor. If you should happen to discover Rocky Mountain oysters on a menu while on vacation, you can no longer claim ignorance as an excuse.

ROCKY MOUNTAIN OYSTERS

Not usually found on restaurant menus, these "prairie oysters" have been a delicacy (or at least a novelty) among cattle ranchers for generations.

Will vary, depending on how many calves you're castrating

As many calf testicles as you can get ahold of
Salt water
1 cup all-purpose flour
¼ cup grated Parmesan cheese
1 teaspoon garlic powder
½ teaspoon onion powder
½ teaspoon salt
¼ teaspoon black pepper
1 egg
1 tablespoon milk
Vegetable oil for frying

★ Clean the testicles and soak them in salt water for 1 hour to remove excess blood. Rinse.

★ Carefully cut a slit halfway around each testicle from long end to long end just deep enough to cut open the casing. Pry open slightly and with the knife tilted almost flat, cut under the inner portion and remove it to a cutting board. Discard the casing.

★ Using a spatula, flatten each fry to about ¼-inch to ⅜-inch thick. I found that 2 or 3 fries could be put together to make a larger one if some were small. Place each fry on a cookie sheet that has been covered with a sheet of waxed paper or plastic wrap.

★ After all the fries are on the cookie sheet, cover with plastic wrap and put in the freezer over night.

★ Take the fries out of the freezer about 30 minutes before cooking to allow them to thaw slightly. Mix together in a small bowl, flour, cheese, garlic powder, onion powder, salt, and pepper.

★ In another bowl beat the egg and milk. Dip each fry into the egg mixture, then the flour, and fry in hot oil until golden brown on both sides. Drain on paper towels. Keep hot in warm oven or serve immediately. These can be served plain or with a dipping sauce if you prefer.

Two dipping sauces that we like are horseradish and sour cream mixed together and a mustard sauce made by mixing half mustard and half mayonnaise.

LLOYD DOSS'S HOT MUSTARD

Served with baked ham, it's the best!!

3 cups

4	ounces dry mustard	3	eggs
1	cup white wine or vinegar	1	cup granulated sugar

✶ In a glass bowl mix together the dry mustard and white wine. Let it sit overnight.

✶ The next morning beat the eggs with the granulated sugar and add to the wine/mustard mixture. Cook in a double boiler, stirring occasionally until thick.

✶ Cool and store in the refrigerator.

PAT'S SWEET HOT MUSTARD

Excellent flavor!

3½ cups

4	ounces dry mustard	1	cup granulated sugar
1	cup vinegar	1	teaspoon salt
2	large eggs	1½	cups mayonnaise

✶ Mix the mustard and vinegar and let sit overnight.

✶ Add eggs, sugar, and salt to mustard mixture. Cook in a double boiler until thick. Let mixture cool, and then add mayonnaise.

My friend Lloyd (Tommy) Doss sang with the Sons of the Pioneers when the group included Ken Curtis, Lloyd Perryman, Shug Fisher, Karl and Hugh Farr. After Lloyd left the Sons, he and his wife, Naomi, made their home at Imnaha, Oregon, where they owned a country store and tavern. Who can forget his incredible voice? Lloyd is also famous for his Hot Mustard recipe, and has given me permission to include it here. He sends his regards and compliments to the people who are working to make the Pendleton Round-Up Centennial Cookbook a success....*Claudine Willis*

1983 Round-Up Princess Sarah Branstetter

Around 1969-70, just one day before the Pendleton Round-Up's Dress Up Parade, my husband Orville and I decided to invite some people to the house after the parade for a party. Because it was such short notice, we chose to invite neighbors only, so after he left for work that morning, I started telephoning our immediate neighbors. When he came home for lunch and asked how many were able to come, I told him that everyone I called was coming — a total of 60 adults plus kids. Laughingly, I asked, Now, what are we going to serve 60+ people? After the reality of feeding all these guests hit us, we decided on barbeque beef on a bun, salad and beans. The only problem was I did not have a great barbeque sauce recipe so he planned on asking around at work (Pendleton Grain Growers) and thankfully, Grace Rosenberg gladly offered her recipe. We had so much fun that we continued having this party (the parade during this time period was in the evening) for about 10 years and Grace's recipe was always a major part of our parties. Grace is gone now but I know she would be happy to share her recipe for the centennial cookbook...*Carolyn Gerberding*

GRACE'S BARBEQUE SAUCE

This sauce can be multiplied easily to make a large batch, canned or frozen for later use.

2-3 cups

1	cup ketchup	1 tablespoon Worcestershire sauce
1	cup water	
2	teaspoons prepared mustard	1 tablespoon vinegar
¼	teaspoon red pepper	2 tablespoons chopped garlic

✷ Combine ketchup, water, mustard, red pepper, Worcestershire sauce, vinegar, and chopped garlic. Cook on high heat until the sauce boils, then turn down to simmer for approximately 1 hour or until sauce thickens.

KEEPIN' IT SIMPLE BBQ SAUCE

Nothin' fancy, but always a favorite at our annual summer barbeque fest...Polly Helm

as much as you make

Equal parts ketchup, mustard, dark molasses, and Worcestershire sauce.

✷ Mix together and use on your favorite meats.

QUICK BARBEQUE SAUCE

Yummy for Ribs. A favorite recipe of Katy Hudson, the wife of Round-Up President Ron Hudson, was made ahead of time to have ready for Round-Up guests.

2 cups

⅓	cup Worcestershire sauce	2 tablespoons brown sugar
1	10.75-ounce can tomato soup	3 tablespoons white vinegar
1	small onion, chopped	

✷ Mix Worcestershire sauce, tomato soup, chopped onion, brown sugar, and white vinegar in a 1-quart saucepan. Simmer until the onions are cooked to your taste.

Steak Marinade

This steak marinade is part of the traditional Saturday night Round-Up dinner at the Krout house. We always have extra steaks on hand when the kids are here for Round-Up as they usually find more friends to bring home for dinner...Marlene Krout

3 cups

1	cup red wine vinegar	1	tablespoon salt
1	cup ketchup	4	teaspoons prepared mustard
½	cup olive oil	1	teaspoon pepper
½	cup soy sauce	1½	teaspoons garlic powder
¼	cup Worcestershire sauce		

✱ Whisk all ingredients together thoroughly. Marinate your choice of steaks for 3-8 hours. Barbecue steaks to desired doneness, basting as the steaks cook.

Indian Dancers, 1911

Blue Cheese Steak Sauce

From a family of cattle ranchers, steak is naturally Past Round-Up Queen Jennifer Raymond Davis' favorite food, especially when it's topped with the family's favorite recipe, Blue Cheese Steak Sauce.

4 servings

½	cup crumbled blue cheese	1	tablespoon lemon juice
¼	cup butter or margarine	1	teaspoon salt
1	teaspoon Worcestershire sauce	½	teaspoon freshly ground black pepper
1	tablespoon prepared mustard		

✱ Cream together blue cheese, butter, Worcestershire sauce, prepared mustard, lemon juice, salt, and pepper, and spread over cooked steak.

In the late 1980's, Safeway started a tradition that became a real Round-Up favorite. For over 20 years, together with the Pendleton Round-Up and Happy Canyon Hall of Fame, they threw a beef ribs barbecue on Thursday evening, following the rodeo. Hundreds of cowboys and cowgirls sat down to a finger-licking good meal of barbecued beef ribs, coleslaw, baked beans, rolls and locally-grown watermelon. Properly attired in big bibs, guests enjoyed the all-you-can-eat meal until they couldn't take another bite. Forty-five hundred pounds of beef ribs were pre-cooked and then finished on barbecue grills in the parking lot. Caterers in the area loaned the barbecues and volunteers served the delicious food. Musicians entertained the crowd with Western music and storytelling. Children enjoyed riding in one of the old Round-Up wagons pulled by a team of horses. On Thursday night of Round-Up, everyone went home full and happy.

The Round-Up has become a tradition in the Dobbs marriage. My husband Grant was a bull rider, but broke his back in Pendleton in 1957 riding bulls. That was the end of his bull riding career and quitting was one of the hardest things he's ever done. We were married in 1984, and I made Round-Up reservations the next year. We have only missed one year since then. Hawthorne School is our Pendleton home. We now come in for the entire week so we can do the PBR as well as Round-Up...*Mabel Dobbs*

For years, the school district has offered the school grounds of several local schools as "trailer parks" and invited every RV to come and park. Hawthorne School has become one of the favorite locations because of its proximity to the Round-Up Grounds.

SCRUMPTIOUSLY GOOD MEATBALLS

This is a great make-ahead recipe. Just put it in a carrier and you're good to go.

6–8 servings

MEATBALLS

2	pounds ground beef	2	eggs
⅔	cup cracker crumbs	½	teaspoon salt
⅔	cup oatmeal (quick or regular)	1½	teaspoons chili powder
½	cup chopped onion	½	teaspoon garlic powder
1	5-ounce can evaporated milk	⅛	teaspoon black pepper

BARBECUE SAUCE

2	cups ketchup	½	teaspoon garlic powder
1	cup brown sugar	1	teaspoon dry mustard
¼	cup finely chopped onion		

✷ Combine ground beef, cracker crumbs, oatmeal, onion, milk, eggs, salt, chili powder, garlic powder, and pepper and shape into about 40 meatballs. Put in 9x13-inch pan. (You can make the meatballs the night before and let them sit in the refrigerator overnight.)

✷ Combine ketchup, brown sugar, onion, garlic powder, and mustard in medium saucepan and stir until brown sugar is dissolved. Pour sauce over meatballs. Cover and bake at 400° for 1 hour, removing the cover the last 10 minutes.

Sandhollow Snowmobile Club Meatballs

These are good when the bulls are bucking or when the snow is flying.

Lots!

The introduction of PBR (Professional Bull Riding) on Monday and Tuesday evenings of Round-Up week brought even more reasons for friends to gather before the show and continue the party that began the week before.

MEATBALLS

3	pounds ground beef	2	tablespoons horseradish sauce
1	pound pork sausage	1	tablespoon garlic salt
3	cups quick cooking oatmeal	1	tablespoon dry mustard
½	cup milk	⅛	teaspoon hot sauce
3	tablespoons Worcestershire sauce		Parsley sprigs for garnish

SAUCE

½	cup granulated sugar	1	teaspoon paprika
¾	cup red wine vinegar	1½	teaspoons salt

✱ Mix ground beef, sausage, oatmeal, milk, Worcestershire sauce, horseradish sauce, garlic salt, mustard, and hot sauce together and shape into finger food sized balls. Place in 9x13-inch baking pan sprayed with non-stick cooking spray.

✱ Mix sugar, vinegar, paprika, and salt in small saucepan and bring to boil. Cover meatballs with sauce, bake at 350° for 30 minutes. Garnish with parsley sprigs.

When you're saving half an avocado, leave the pit in the half you're saving, and spray the cut surface with non-stick cooking spray. This keeps the air from turning the avocado brown.

SOUTH OF THE BORDER TORTE

I have served this South of the Border Torte at Round-Up many times throughout the years. One year I served it to our dinner guests, Sonny and Bess Linger, from Miles City, Montana, the livestock contractors for the Round-Up in the 1980's. Bess was a Texas gal and loved Mexican food. She raved over this dish....Betty Jean Holmes

8–10 servings

1	pound ground beef	1	package taco seasoning
1	medium onion, chopped	8-10	flour tortillas
1	1-pound can stewed tomatoes	1	pound Cheddar cheese, grated
1	8-ounce can tomato sauce	1½	cups sour cream
1	4-ounce can diced green chiles		

✸ Brown beef and onion in frying pan. Add stewed tomatoes, tomato sauce, green chiles, and taco seasoning. Simmer 10 minutes.

✸ Spray a 9x13-inch pan with non-stick cooking spray. Place ¼ of the mixture in bottom of the pan. Place a layer of tortillas on top. Repeat layering until all ingredients are in the pan. Spread with sour cream. Sprinkle grated cheese over the top. Bake at 350° for 25 minutes or until cheese bubbles.

Add another 4-ounce can of diced green chiles on top of the sour cream, before you sprinkle on the cheese.

This can be frozen, but don't add the sour cream and cheese topping until you're ready to bake it.

Arena Pickup Man
Billy and Marlo Ward

CORNED BEEF AND CARROTS
WITH PENDLETON WHISKY GLAZE

Even those who aren't fond of corned beef said they liked this one! But serve it to people who really like corned beef! They'll love it.

6–8 servings

1	2- to 3-pound corned beef	¼	cup Pendleton Whisky
6	large carrots, scraped and cut in bite-sized pieces	⅛	teaspoon nutmeg
½	cup orange marmalade	1	tablespoon horseradish sauce

✱ Cook corned beef brisket according to package directions (stove top or oven, either one). Trim fat off cooked brisket and place on cookie sheet coated with non-stick cooking spray.

✱ Boil marmalade, whisky, and nutmeg in small saucepan until slightly reduced, about 5 minutes, stirring constantly. Mix in horseradish sauce.

✱ Toss carrots with the glaze and place around the corned beef. Brush corned beef with remaining glaze. Bake at 425° for 30 minutes or until carrots are tender.

Local attorneys Steve Hill, Gene Hallman, Brian Dretke, and Dave Gallaher ham it up (pun intended) at the Pendleton Underground's Empire Meat Market. Open year round, the Pendleton Underground has added a world that you won't find in the history books. It has just celebrated its 20th anniversary, having opened in 1989 and has been conducting tours and telling stories since 1989. A once a year event, the Underground Comes to Life, brings together over 75 live actors to re-enact what would have taken place 100 years ago. Card players, dancers, Chinese workers, working girls, and merchants from the past are all there to greet you.

They'd like to put this on for all of our Round-Up guests, but the 75 live actors are busy with Round-Up and Happy Canyon.

Steve Currin was a bulldogger for many years. One year he missed the head of the steer, but was on the ground beside it when it ran past him. He grabbed the tail of the steer and proceeded to work his way up the steer's back while running along beside it. He grabbed onto the horns and threw that steer to the ground. The crowd at the Round-Up exploded with yells and cheers. It was truly a show of "never giving up." Steve has won the bulldogging championship and is now retired from rodeoing. He is an active cattle rancher on Little Butter Creek near Heppner, Oregon and Barbecue Wrap-ups is a family favorite...*Aunt Marlene Currin*

The Ron Currin Family, inductees into the Hall of Fame Toni and Kelli, LisAnne and Steve, Judy and Ron, Sr., Ronny and Toni

BARBECUE WRAP-UPS

This is easy and can be prepared in the foil 1-2 days early.

4 servings

1	pound lean ground beef	1½	cups peeled and sliced potatoes
	Salt and black pepper	8	green pepper rings
4	large onion slices	8	tablespoons barbecue sauce

★ Season ground beef with salt and pepper. Shape into four patties. Place each patty on a square of aluminum foil. Top each patty with a slice of onion, ¼ of the potatoes, 2 green pepper rings, and 2 tablespoons barbecue sauce. Close foil over patty, double-folding edges tightly. Grill on barbecue 25-30 minutes.

BEEF KABOBS

Because you can use whatever vegetables you like (or none!), this is a very versatile recipe.

6-8 servings

3	pounds lean beef round steak or chuck steak, cut into 1-inch cubes	¼	cup Worcestershire sauce
		¼	cup prepared mustard
1	cup vegetable oil	2	cloves garlic, minced
¾	cup soy sauce	1	tablespoon coarsely cracked black pepper
½	cup lemon juice		Assorted vegetables (or not)

★ Mix oil, soy sauce, lemon juice, Worcestershire sauce, mustard, garlic, and pepper in a gallon plastic re-sealable bag. Add beef to the marinade. Refrigerate and marinate 24-36 hours, turning the bag from time to time.

★ Onto skewers, thread the beef alternating with onions, peppers, mushrooms, etc. Broil over hot coals to rare or medium rare, brushing with remaining marinade.

HARVEST ZUCCHINI CASSEROLE

Easy and can be made ahead of time and baked when needed.

1½	pounds sliced zucchini	¼	teaspoon basil
1	pound ground beef	¼	teaspoon black pepper
1	cup chopped onion	2	cups cottage cheese
1	cup instant rice	1	10.5-ounce can cream of chicken soup (or other type of cream soup)
1	teaspoon garlic powder		
1	tablespoon oregano	1	cup grated Cheddar cheese

✶ Cook zucchini in boiling water until barely tender. Drain.

✶ Brown beef with onion. Add rice, garlic powder, oregano, basil, and pepper.

✶ Place ½ of zucchini in bottom of a 2½-quart casserole. Cover with complete mixture of beef and rice. Spoon cottage cheese over all. Add remaining zucchini.

✶ Spread cream soup over all and sprinkle with grated cheese. Bake uncovered at 350° for 35-40 minutes or until bubbly.

You can add raw zucchini, but adjust baking time accordingly.

KALBE (KOREAN STYLE BEEF RIBS)

Korean Style Ribs are cut differently than we here in America are used to, but our grocery store meat cutters can cut them for us. They're cut not with the rib, but against the rib. Make sure that they slice it about ¼-inch thick. You'll have small bones with the meat instead of long pieces of bone...JayMan, also known as Jim Harrison, behind-the-scenes cook at the Round-Up Grounds for the crews.

5	pounds beef ribs	2	cloves garlic, sliced
1	cup Japanese soy sauce	1	cup chopped green onions
¼	cup cold-pressed sesame seed oil	2	tablespoons granulated sugar
		½	teaspoon ground ginger

✶ Place ribs in pan, mix soy sauce, sesame oil, garlic, green onions sugar, and ginger and pour over ribs.

✶ Let the ribs rest in the refrigerator for about 1 hour. Remove and grill on barbecue. Do not overcook as they are thin and will cook very fast.

I have been attending the Pendleton Round-Up every year since 1977, so I celebrated my 32nd consecutive year this year. I look forward to many more years of Round-Up fun, great rodeo, and special memories. This is one of my favorite recipes...*Melanie Heald*

Mike Watkins, Robbi Ebel, and Bev Kopperud take a break during Round-Up 2008 to show Dutch photographer John Van Helvert and his daughter Dominick the surrounding country on horseback.

In the early 1970's, it was a popular thing for 4-6 couples (or more) to get together and host a Round-Up / Happy Canyon party for as many as 200-300 people. Of course all food was prepared and served by the hosts and hostesses. We did not barbecue as often or have catered parties — too expensive then when we all were young and had small children and small budgets. Everything was done or produced at home and "by hand" (invitations, food, decorations). One year, the hosts were Betty Lou and Emile Holeman, Mike and Tricia Boylen, Bruce and Karen Boylen, and Bill and Betty Kilkenny. We made our own handkerchief print aprons and had our names on the top. Red bandana print was used as the theme, and we made a sign on a cotton sheet with red

(continued on next page)

Emile Holeman, Betty and Bill Kilkenny, Mike Boylen, Bruce and Karen Boylen, Tricia Boylen, and Betty Lou Holeman, Round-Up party hosts

SLOPPY JOES

Making friends is one great thing about Round-Up, and you'll make friends with this one.

20-24 servings

3	pounds lean ground beef	¼	cup brown sugar
2	10-ounce cans tomato soup	1	tablespoon chili powder
1	cup water	18-24	buns or rolls
⅓	cup vinegar		

✱ Sauté ground beef in large pan until brown. Drain off fat. Add soup, water, vinegar, brown sugar, and chili powder and simmer, covered, for 30 minutes, stirring occasionally. Serve with buns or rolls.

Store in refrigerator until ready to use, or freeze. If frozen, return to refrigerator the night before use and re-heat when needed.

THE ROUND-UP SPECIAL

If you have leftovers, roll them in flour tortillas for a second dinner.

12-14 servings

3	pounds ground beef	3	15-ounce cans red kidney beans, drained
3	cups chopped onions		
3	packages chili seasoning	¾	cup pitted sliced black olives
3	8-ounce cans tomato sauce	1½	cups shredded sharp Cheddar cheese
2	cups water		Corn chips

✱ In heavy kettle, cook meat until no longer pink, and drain. Add the onions, chili seasoning, tomato sauce, and water. Bring to boil, cover and simmer 15 minutes, stirring occasionally.

✱ In 4-quart casserole about 3½-inches deep, layer the meat mixture with the beans, olives, and cheese.

✱ Bake in a slow 325° oven for 50-60 minutes and serve over corn chips.

You can substitute 1 tablespoon chili powder, 2 teaspoons cumin, and 1 teaspoon oregano if you don't have the chili seasoning packages.

SPICY LASAGNA

With the four cheeses in this lasagna, it's for sure a cheese-lover's delight.

12 servings

1	pound ground beef	2	teaspoons Italian seasoning
½	pound Italian sausage	1	teaspoon oregano
4	ounces pepperoni slices	1	teaspoon dried parsley
1	onion, chopped	1	16-ounce package lasagna noodles
1	28-ounce can tomato sauce (or your favorite pasta sauce)	16	ounces mozzarella cheese
1	16-ounce can tomato sauce	8	ounces Monterey Jack cheese
1	teaspoon garlic powder	8	ounces Cheddar cheese
1	teaspoon black pepper	4	ounces Parmesan cheese
1	teaspoon salt	16	ounces sour cream

✸ Brown ground beef, sausage, and onion. Drain. Add the pepperoni. Add tomato sauce and seasonings. Simmer for 30 minutes.

✸ Cook lasagna noodles according to package directions and drain. Layer the bottom of a 9x13-inch greased baking dish with half the noodles. Next add a layer of the meat mixture.

✸ Grate cheese and mix together. Sprinkle half the cheese on top of meat mixture. Add the rest of the noodles, the rest of the meat mixture, sour cream, and remaining cheeses.

✸ Bake, covered for 30 minutes at 350°. Uncover and bake another 10 minutes.

✸ Let rest 20 minutes before cutting.

You can add a package of chopped spinach (thawed and squeezed dry) if you'd like to add some color. Just spread it between the first layer of cheese and the second layer of noodles.

(continued)

bandana letters welcoming the guests, and cloth letters were glued on the original invitations.

One always kept a list of all party givers the hosts and hostesses had been invited to in previous years (sort of a payback). The parties were held in private homes, yard, barns, or anywhere available. In these earlier years the menus were of foods that could be made early and frozen, to be heated at the appropriate time. A typical menu might consist of Sloppy Joes, Citrus Toss-Up Salad, Fresh Vegetable Mix, and Black Bottom Cupcakes.

Sometimes, open bars were available (Pendleton folk have always liked their mixed drinks) and tubs of ice cold beer and pop were served. Decorations were pretty elaborate, as they are sometimes today. Parties were a wonderful way to see old friends and visit because it was before the Hospitality Tent (and today the Roy Raley Room). Sometimes entertainment was provided. One always wrote a thank-you note to all hosts, etc. As the years went by, these parties have become fewer and smaller...*Betty Lou Holeman*

The Round-Up Polo Party began in 2000. The La Grande Polo Club was also established that year and remains the only official size polo field in Oregon outside of Portland. La Grande Polo Club members and hosts Steve and Melissa Davis (Princess 1968) Joseph along with Scott (Round-Up timer) and Sharon Tullis, Bryant and Rilla Livingston (Queen 1979) Cameron, former director Tim and Nancy Mabry, and former director Bob and Ann Lorenzen Hulden (Princess 1975) offer an enjoyable afternoon of polo and barbecue under the blue eastern Oregon skies. The courts have fun running their horses on the grass and their families get a much needed moment of relaxation before Round-Up gets into full swing.

In addition to Flanken Style Ribs (those cut the opposite direction, resembling a piece of bacon with small slivers of bone), we serve Caesar salad, warm French bread, and fresh sweet Hermiston watermelon. No one leaves hungry from this party.

Sweet 'N Spicy Beef Ribs with Grilled Peaches

This recipe, developed by the Oregon Beef Council, was featured in The Oregonian FOODday Column.

4 servings

BEEF

| 4 | pounds beef back ribs | 4 | peaches, halved and pitted |
| 4 | tablespoons water | | |

SAUCE

12	ounces chili sauce	1½	teaspoons hot pepper sauce
½	cup molasses	1½	teaspoons crushed red pepper pods
½	cup water		
3	tablespoons lemon juice	½	teaspoon cinnamon

✶ Divide ribs into 2 slabs about 3-4 bones each. Place each slab on a double thickness of foil that is twice the length of slab plus 8 inches. Sprinkle each slab with 2 tablespoons of water. Form foil packets around ribs, leaving some air space. Place packets on grill over medium-low coals. Cover cooker and grill 1 hour, turning every 20 minutes.

✶ While ribs are cooking, combine chili sauce, molasses, water, lemon juice, hot pepper sauce, red pepper pods, and cinnamon in a small saucepan. Bring to a boil, reduce heat and simmer 10 minutes, stirring occasionally.

✶ Remove ribs from foil and place directly on grill. Brush both sides with sauce. Continue grilling over low heat 30 minutes, brushing ribs occasionally with sauce.

✶ During the last 10 minutes that ribs are grilling, place peach halves cut side down on grill. Grill 5 minutes. Turn and brush cut side with sauce. Grill 5 additional minutes or until peaches are soft, brushing occasionally with additional sauce.

✶ Thoroughly heat remaining sauce. Serve ribs with peaches and additional sauce.

SPAGHETTI PIE

This is a really easy recipe to double, and you probably will want a second one for the freezer anyway.

6 servings

6 ounces spaghetti
2 eggs, beaten
¼ cup grated Parmesan cheese
2 tablespoons butter
⅓ cup chopped onion
1 cup sour cream

1 pound Italian sausage, casings removed
1 cup water
1 6-ounce can tomato paste
4 ounces mozzarella cheese, sliced or grated

✳ Break spaghetti in half and cook in boiling water until done. Drain. While still warm, combine spaghetti with eggs and Parmesan. Pour into a well-greased 10-inch pie pan and pat mixture up and around sides with a spoon.

✳ Melt butter, add onion, and sauté until limp. Stir in sour cream, and spoon mixture over noodle base.

✳ Cook sausage in skillet until it's no longer pink. Drain. Add tomato paste and water. Mix well and simmer for 10 minutes. Spoon sausage/tomato mixture on top of sour cream mixture, Bake at 350° for 25 minutes. Distribute mozzarella evenly over pie and return to oven for another 10 minutes. Let rest 10 minutes before cutting in wedges.

Kitty Wilkes Canutt was a professional bronc rider and All Around Champion Cowgirl at the 1916 Pendleton Round-Up. It was at this rodeo that she met and married Yakima Canutt, a winner of the title "All Around Cowboy" in 1917, 1919, 1920 and 1923. They were divorced in 1919. Kitty was known as the "Diamond Girl" or "Diamond Kitty", because she had a diamond set in her front tooth, which she would occasionally remove and pawn when she needed rodeo contest entry money.

From the *East Oregonian*,
September 11, 1910:

Prize worth $2,500 will be awarded to the Round-Up by local merchants, and special excursion trains will come from Portland, Spokane, and Heppner. Travel agents Williams McMurray and Jack O'Neill have told the Round-Up committee that Pendleton is "only preparing for half the number of visitors she will be called on to entertain."

SPAGHETTI TORTA

If you don't have a springform pan, a large casserole dish will work just fine.

4–6 servings

1	tablespoon butter	½	cup sliced black olives
3	tablespoons grated Parmesan cheese	¼	cup fresh chopped parsley
½	pound spaghetti	1	tablespoon dried basil
2	eggs, beaten	2	tablespoons dried oregano
3	tablespoons butter	2	tablespoons olive oil
½	pound Italian sausage	½	teaspoon salt
1	cup chopped onion	½	teaspoon black pepper
2	cloves garlic, minced	¼	teaspoon red pepper flakes
¼	pound mushrooms, sliced	1	cup grated fontina, provolone, or mozzarella cheese
1	14.5-ounce can Italian tomatoes		

✱ Butter an 8½-inch springform pan. Coat with Parmesan.

✱ Cook spaghetti, drain. Mix well with 2 beaten eggs and 3 tablespoons butter.

✱ In a large pot, cook sausage, drain. Sauté onions, garlic, and mushrooms in the same pot.

✱ To the meat mixture, add tomatoes, olives, parsley and seasonings. Mix well.

✱ Layer in prepared pan as follows: half the spaghetti, half the meat sauce, half the cheese. Repeat layers, ending with the remaining cheese.

✱ Bake 40 minutes at 375°. Let set for 10 minutes. Remove the sides of the pan and slice into wedges.

If time is short, you can substitute a jar of your favorite spaghetti sauce ... just add a few red pepper flakes for some added zing.

Margaret Gianotti and Suzie Barhyte offer their specialties.

SWEET 'N SPICY PORK TENDERLOIN

This is an unusual ingredient combination, but it really does work! And if you're really in a hurry, you can use bottled minced ginger and garlic.

8 servings

2	tablespoons soy sauce	⅔	cup bottled salsa
2	teaspoons minced ginger	2	tablespoons seedless raspberry jam
2	teaspoons minced garlic	4	tablespoons freshly chopped cilantro
2	teaspoons vegetable oil		
2	1-pound pork tenderloins, each trimmed and cut crosswise into 12 (¾-inch) slices		

✱ Combine soy sauce, ginger, and garlic in small bowl.

✱ Heat oil in a large nonstick skillet over medium-high heat. Flatten each pork piece to ½-inch thickness using your fingertips. Add pork to pan, spoon soy sauce mixture evenly over pork slices. Cook 3 minutes or until browned. Turn pork over, cook 3 minutes or until done. Remove from pan.

✱ Add salsa and jam to pan, cook 30 seconds on medium-high heat, until slightly thick, stirring constantly. Serve pork with salsa mixture and sprinkle with cilantro.

BAR-B-QUED ROAST PORK – IOWA STYLE

Iowa ... Oregon ... we both love this recipe!

8-10 servings

1	6- to 8-pound pork loin roast, well trimmed (bone-in)	1	tablespoon garlic salt
2	tablespoons olive oil	1	teaspoon black pepper

✱ Rub the roast with olive oil, then season it with the garlic salt and pepper. Put in plastic bag for 6-8 hours.

✱ Remove roast from bag and barbecue on the grill on medium high heat and sear all sides until brown, about 7-10 minutes per side.

✱ When roast is well-seared, place on heavy aluminum foil and continue barbecuing until pork is finished, 180° by thermometer. Slice, eat, and enjoy!

Flag bearers race around the arena on very fast horses every day to start the show, and this is how it's supposed to be done. But every now and then, things go awry. In the 2007 show, Tygh Campbell's horse caught his foot in the rail and fell, and Tygh ended up on the ground with the flag still in his grip. The horse quickly recovered and took off with the others, just where he was supposed to go, leaving Tygh on foot. He became quite a hero that day when, from the east end of the arena, he ran, flag held high, around the arena. It's not such a great distance on a fast horse, but it's really a long haul on foot. Good job, Tygh!

The Main Street Cowboy shows on Main Street, beginning early in the week, are billed "the Greatest Free Show in the West" providing family entertainment nightly on four blocks of Main Street.

PORK TENDERLOIN BALSAMICO

This is quite lovely, very easy, and requires almost no prep time. It's especially for your fancy guests.

4-6 servings

4	cloves garlic, minced	2	1½- to 2-pound pork tenderloins
2	tablespoons chopped fresh rosemary	2	tablespoons olive oil
1	tablespoon grated lemon peel	½	cup beef broth
2	teaspoon salt	½	cup balsamic vinegar
2	teaspoon pepper	2	tablespoons butter
		2	tablespoons capers

✶ Combine garlic, rosemary, lemon peel, salt and pepper. Press mixture onto tenderloins.

✶ In large skillet with ovenproof handle, heat oil over medium heat. Add tenderloins and cook, turning frequently, until browned, 8-10 minutes. Transfer to 450° oven. Roast 15 minutes. Remove pork from pan and keep warm.

✶ Set pan over high heat and stir in broth and vinegar, scraping up browned bits. Bring to boil and cook until reduced by half. Whisk in butter, 1 tablespoon at a time. Stir in capers.

✶ Cut tenderloins into thick slices and serve with sauce.

Main Street Cowboys

BARBECUED PORK CHOPS

We liked this recipe using pork short ribs as well. The onions placed on top of the pork caramelize and are quite wonderful.

6 servings

1	cup ketchup	1	heaping tablespoon brown sugar
¼	cup vinegar	1½	cups water
1¾	teaspoons salt	1	medium onion, sliced
¼	teaspoon red (cayenne) pepper	6	pork chops
1½	teaspoons chili powder		Parsley

✱ Mix all ingredients except onion and pour over pork chops arranged in a 9x12-inch baking pan.

✱ Place sliced onions on top of pork chops.

✱ Bake uncovered in 300° oven for 3 hours. Turn once after 1½ hours.

✱ Garnish with sprigs of parsley, if desired.

SWEET & SOUR SHISH–KABOBS

Served on a bed of rice pilaf and garnished with parsley or cilantro, this makes a beautiful dish.

4 servings

½	cup pineapple juice	1½-2	pounds pork tenderloin, cut into 1-inch cubes
¼	cup soy sauce	2	cups assorted vegetables (onions, peppers, mushrooms, cherry tomatoes)
2	teaspoons brown sugar		
1	garlic clove, minced		
½	teaspoon Worcestershire sauce	½	cup pineapple chunks

✱ Mix marinade ingredients and add pork cubes. Marinate in refrigerator overnight. Thread meat onto skewers alternately with pineapple and your favorite vegetables. Grill until done.

Rodeo entertainer and bullfighter JJ Harrison at the Pendleton Round-Up Grounds

When planning a party that includes a casual meal, make sure there's plenty of seating. Most people really prefer to sit down while they're eating. It's never a problem for Round-up party givers. We just bring in bales of hay and scatter them around. Voila! Instant chairs!

PENDLETON WHISKY PORK KABOBS

The marinade gives this a very complex flavor ... intensely sweet and tangy.

4 servings

1   pound boneless pork loin, cut into ¾-inch cubes
4   tablespoons Dijon mustard
¼   cup packed brown sugar
2   tablespoons Pendleton Whisky

2   tablespoons soy sauce
1   green or red pepper (or combination), cut in 1-inch squares
1   onion, cut in 1-inch wedges

✳ In plastic re-sealable bag, combine pork, mustard, brown sugar, Pendleton Whisky, and soy sauce. Mix well. Refrigerate 6-24 hours.

✳ Remove pork from marinade and thread pork cubes onto skewers, alternating with the pepper and onion.

✳ Grill or broil kabobs 10-15 minutes until browned, brushing occasionally with reserved marinade.

If using wooden skewers, remember to soak them in water 30 minutes before using. Or they'll cook before your kabobs are done!

JAGERSCHNITZEL

This recipe came from Germany and it's always a hit at Round-Up time.

4 servings

1 chicken bouillon cube	1 medium onion, sliced
1½ cups hot water	1 4-ounce can sliced mushrooms, drained (fresh works too)
4 boneless lean pork loin steaks (fat removed)	
Salt and black pepper	1 tablespoon cornstarch
2 tablespoons butter or vegetable oil	½ cup sour cream
	Salt and black pepper

✱ Add bouillon cube to water and allow to soften.

✱ Pound pork steaks to ½-inch thick. Rub with salt and pepper. Brown both sides in melted butter or vegetable oil. Remove steaks from pan. Add onion to drippings and cook until onions begin to soften. Add mushrooms, bouillon/water, and steaks. Cover and simmer for 15-20 minutes. Remove steaks to platter.

✱ Mix cornstarch with sour cream and stir into sauce. Heat, but do not boil. Season with salt and pepper, and pour sauce over steaks.

Quince bushes and rose bushes were much treasured by women who lived on the ranches of Eastern Oregon and grown in the garden along with the standard vegetables. The roses were usually an old-fashioned and hardy variety with an abundance of sweetly scented petals to be put in a jam jar and made into a potpourri or jelly to serve with biscuits.

One woman, Bertha Kaepernick Blancett, 1911-1918 all around Cowgirl at the Pendleton Round Up, competed with the men and nearly always took home the prize money. She won the bucking contest many times. People say she was as skilled in the kitchen as she was as a trick rider and good at the relay racing contests too. Bertha eventually married a cowboy named Del and became almost as famous for her Quince Jelly, a staple in pioneer homesteads around Pendleton at the time. Bertha was inducted into the National Cowgirl Hall of Fame in 1999 for her riding abilities.

JACKLE GERMAN BRATWURSTS

Nobody loves brats (naughty children), but everyone loves brats (brots). These are a great addition to any Round-Up party, and you just let everyone "dress" their own.

12 servings

12 bratwursts	16 ounces sauerkraut
2 large onions, separated into rings	Mustard (brown is traditional, but any will work)
32 ounces dark beer (stout or heavy porter)	Prepared horseradish
1 teaspoon white pepper	Grated cheese
1 teaspoon garlic juice (or 1 tablespoon granulated garlic or 10 cloves garlic smashed and chopped)	Jalapeño rings
12 stadium rolls	Any other topping you'd like to add. Don't be confined by tradition on this.

✱ Place bratwursts in a pan appropriately sized to contain them. Pick a pan that allows enough sidewall to cover the sausages in liquid. Add the sliced onions to the pan with the sausages. Cover the sausages and onions in dark beer (the darker the better).

✱ Add the white pepper and garlic. Bring to a boil. Reduce heat and cook at a rolling boil with the lid off for 45 minutes. Readjust sausages occasionally to give the ones on top time on the bottom immersed in the liquid. The concoction is done when the beer has boiled the liquid down some and is starting to thicken (don't get in a hurry).

✱ When the brats are done, remove them from the liquid and set aside. Strain the onions from the liquid and keep warm in a bowl covered with foil.

✱ Place the brats on a barbecue grill at 375° and brown on both sides.

✱ At this time, it is optional to lightly toast the buns on the grill (do not overdo it) or the buns can be used un-toasted. Either will work. Place a brat on each bun and serve. Top the brats with any combination of your condiments. Serve the reserved onions as topping.

Other condiments might include ketchup, mayonnaise, chili, shredded lettuce, chopped tomatoes, sliced olives, grilled green or red peppers and/or mushrooms ... whatever! There are no wrong turns on this one.

1978 Round-Up Queen Kathie Schubert

SWEET AND SOUR SPARERIBS

Put these in the oven and they're ready by the time you've finished Crazy Aunt Sue's Margaritas!

4 servings

4 pounds pork spareribs, cut in serving size pieces	½ cup water
1 8-ounce can crushed pineapple, undrained	¼ cup finely chopped onion
⅔ cup dark brown sugar, firmly packed	2 tablespoons soy sauce
	2 tablespoons cornstarch
⅔ cup white vinegar	2 teaspoons dry mustard
½ cup ketchup	Salt and pepper

✱ Spread ribs, meaty side up, in a single layer in a large shallow pan. Brown in 375° oven for 45 minutes. Drain off fat.

✱ Combine pineapple, brown sugar, vinegar, ketchup, water, onion, soy sauce, cornstarch, and dry mustard in a saucepan and stir until smooth. Cook over medium heat until thick and glossy, stirring constantly.

✱ Sprinkle salt and pepper over browned ribs, spoon sweet-sour sauce over each piece using about half the sauce. Reduce oven heat to 300° and bake, covered, for 1 hour. Turn ribs, cover with remaining sauce and bake, uncovered, 45 minutes more.

In 1910, R.W. "Bob" Fletcher came up with the idea of forming a horseback band and made it happen. The band made its first official public appearance at the 1911 Round-Up. The band, known as the Pendleton Mounted Cowboy Band, led the Westward Ho! Parade that year. R.W managed the mounted band until the early 1920's when he organized the family Fletcher Round-Up Cowgirl Cowboy Band. Emery Worthington became the manager of the mounted band until 1938 when it disbanded. In 1985 the mounted band was reorganized for the 75th anniversary of the Round-Up and is still going strong today.

Cowgirls and Cowboys at an early Grand Entry, led by the Round-Up Mounted Band

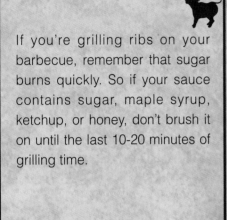

If you're grilling ribs on your barbecue, remember that sugar burns quickly. So if your sauce contains sugar, maple syrup, ketchup, or honey, don't brush it on until the last 10-20 minutes of grilling time.

Fred Westersund and Vic Gehling, Sr., masters of the grill

BULLISH ON SPARERIBS

Line your roaster with foil to save cleanup time later. These can be messy! But oh, they're good.

8–10 servings

5	pounds pork spareribs	1	16-ounce bottle ketchup
½	cup brown sugar	1	12-ounce bottle chili sauce
2	teaspoons salt	2	tablespoons Worcestershire sauce
2	teaspoons garlic salt		
¼	teaspoon pepper	1	tablespoon steak sauce

✱ Place spareribs in roaster and sprinkle the brown sugar, salt, garlic salt, and pepper over them generously.

✱ Mix together the ketchup, chili sauce, Worcestershire sauce, and steak sauce. Pour over the spareribs and bake uncovered 2-3 hours at 350°.

OVEN BARBECUED RIBS

Easy to do on the grill as well.

6 servings

6	pounds pork spareribs	½	cup lemon juice or vinegar
¼	cup butter or margarine	¼	cup Worcestershire sauce
2	large onions, chopped	½	cup packed brown sugar
2	cloves garlic, minced	1	teaspoon black pepper
1½	cups ketchup	½	teaspoon hot pepper sauce

✱ Place ribs in an 8-quart Dutch oven, cutting to fit if necessary. Add cold water to cover ribs. Over high heat, heat to boiling. Reduce heat to low. Cover. Simmer 1 hour or until fork-tender. Drain ribs.

✱ In 2-quart saucepan over medium heat, melt butter. Cook onions and garlic until tender. Stir in ketchup, lemon juice or vinegar, Worcestershire sauce, brown sugar, pepper, and hot pepper sauce. Heat to boiling. Reduce heat to low. Cover. Simmer 5 minutes.

✱ Place ribs in roasting pan. Spoon half of the sauce evenly over ribs. Bake at 400° for 45 minutes or until glazed, turning occasionally and basting with remaining sauce.

Basil Chicken

Marinate this recipe up to 2 days and pull it out of the refrigerator when you get home from the rodeo, pop them on the grill, eat dinner, and you won't be late for the Happy Canyon night pageant.

6 servings

6	skinless, boneless chicken breasts	2	tablespoons coarse-ground mustard
¾	cup buttermilk	2	tablespoons chopped fresh basil leaves (or 2 teaspoons dried basil)
⅓	cup plain yogurt		Dash black pepper
¼	cup honey		

✴ Combine buttermilk, yogurt, honey, mustard, basil, and pepper in plastic re-sealable bag. Add chicken and turn to coat well. Refrigerate several hours or up to 2 days. Turn chicken occasionally.

✴ To grill, remove chicken from marinade. Discard marinade. Grill 15-20 minutes or cook them in a 375° oven for 30-35 minutes.

Chicken Broccoli Casserole

Montie Montana was a fan of Chicken Divan, and his wife created this fast and easy version especially for him.

12 servings

1½-2	pounds broccoli crowns	½	cup sour cream
1	whole roasted chicken	½	cup mayonnaise
2	10½-ounce cans cream of chicken or cream of broccoli soup	2	cups grated Cheddar cheese

✴ Place broccoli on bottom of 9x12-inch greased casserole dish. Place chicken, cut into bite-sized pieces, on top of broccoli.

✴ In a large bowl, combine undiluted soup, sour cream, mayonnaise, and 1 cup cheese. Mix well. Spread over chicken and broccoli. Top with remaining 1 cup of cheese. Bake at 350° for 30 minutes or until hot.

Happy Canyon, the production, was formed following the Umatilla-Morrow County Fair held in Pendleton in 1912. Roy Raley, Lee Drake, and George Hartman are credited with believing that something was needed for evening entertainment for the Round-Up crowds. In 1914, Roy Raley wrote the script for a show involving stories of the "wild west" which was performed in the evenings following Round-Up. In 1916, the Indian portion was added and titled "The Pageant of the West — an outdoor dramatic production symbolizing the history and development of the great West." The name was eventually changed to Happy Canyon and thousands of rodeo-goers have enjoyed its story in the evenings following the Round-Up.

Montie Montana performing at Happy Canyon with cast members Nancy Bittner, Jan Terjeson, Karla Lewis, Susan Kelty, Susan Corey, and Candy Hawkins

Chipotle en Adobo Sauce [chee-POT-tleh] peppers are smoked jalapeño chili peppers and are also known as chili ahumado. These chiles are usually a dull tan to coffee color and measure approximately 2 to 4 inches in length and about an inch wide. As much as one fifth of the Mexican jalapeño crop is processed into chipotles. Normally packed in cans with a sauce made of spices, vinegar, tomato sauce and sometimes other chiles. You can use the chiles, the sauce, or both in recipes.

Root Digger

CHIPOTLE CHICKEN

The Chipotle chiles give this dish a slightly smoky flavor, but it's not too spicy-hot.

8 servings

8	skinless, boneless chicken breasts	2	tablespoons chopped fresh cilantro
¼	cup canned chipotle chiles in adobo sauce	1	tablespoon paprika
3	tablespoons olive oil	1	teaspoon ground cumin
2	cloves garlic, chopped	1	teaspoon chili powder
4	tablespoons chopped onion	1	teaspoon salt

✸ Combine chiles in adobo, olive oil, and garlic cloves in food processor and purée.

✸ Add onion, cilantro, paprika, cumin, chili powder, and salt, and process until onion is finely chopped. Transfer ¼ of this mixture to a bowl, cover, and refrigerate. Put chicken breasts in plastic re-sealable bag and pour marinade in. Seal and refrigerate overnight.

✸ To grill, remove chicken from marinade, discard marinade, and grill 25-30 minutes or cook them in a 375° oven for 30-35 minutes. Brush with reserved marinade (the ¼ of it you put in the fridge earlier) as it cooks.

CHICKEN MAGNIFICENT

This dish can be made on the spur of the moment, as long as you have the ingredients on hand. It's quick, easy, and wonderful! The sauce goes nicely on plain fettuccini, and a combination of plain and spinach fettuccini is beautiful.

4-6 servings

5	tablespoons butter	3	green onions, sliced
4	chicken breasts		Salt and black pepper to taste
6	tablespoons all-purpose flour	3	tablespoons dry sherry
1½	cups half-and-half		Parsley
2	cups sliced fresh mushrooms		

✱ Cut chicken breasts into 1-inch cubes. Sauté in 3 tablespoons butter until brown and tender, about 5-8 minutes. Remove to a holding platter.

✱ Stir flour into pan drippings until absorbed. Add half-and-half and stir until thickened.

✱ Cook mushrooms and green onions in 2 tablespoons butter. Add salt and pepper.

✱ Add mushrooms, onions, sherry, and chicken to cream sauce. Heat and serve. Garnish with parsley.

This is not the recipe for Kessler's famous chicken. We tried, and we tried again. No recipe, but Jim Kessler did share a couple of his finer points with us. He uses a curing salt (plus some other things) before the chicken quarters go on the grill. He never sticks a fork or anything else in the chicken to see if it's done, because all you do is let the juices run out. Instead, he wiggles a wing or drumstick and if it wiggles really good, it's done. And he cooks the chicken for an hour and a half, three feet from the flame. Here's what they look like on the grill. See what you can do.

SWEET-HOT MUSTARD STUFFED CHICKEN BREAST

A new addition to the Hamley Steakhouse menu.

4 servings

4	chicken breasts		Salt and black pepper
½	cup freshly grated Parmesan cheese	2	tablespoons white wine
1	Granny Smith apple, thinly sliced	3	tablespoons Stone Ground Sweet-Hot Mustard
2	ounces fresh spinach	2	tablespoons honey
	Oil for cooking	1½	cups heavy cream

✱ Place chicken breasts flat on a cutting board and with a filet knife "butterfly" the chicken breasts, slicing them lengthwise from the thicker side of the lobe towards the thinner side of the lobe, stopping about ¾ of the way through, allowing breast to be folded open. Lay all 4 chicken breasts out on your cutting board cut side up. Sprinkle the cheese over the chicken.

✱ Layer the apple over half of the chicken breast and place the spinach over the top. Gently fold the unused half of the chicken over and make a pocket with the chicken and all the stuffing inside.

✱ Season the outside of the chicken with salt and pepper then place in a sauté pan with cooking oil that has been pre-heated over high heat. Sear both sides to a golden brown before placing on a baking sheet or baking dish in a 375° oven to finish.

✱ Using the pan you seared the chicken with, pour out remaining oil, and return it to medium-high heat. Once hot, "deglaze" the pan with white wine, scraping the pan with a flat spatula to remove any residue from the pan. Reduce heat to medium as you add the honey and the mustard, whisking to combine. Gently pour in the heavy cream, whisking constantly. Add salt and pepper to taste.

✱ Remove chicken breasts from the oven when they are firm to the touch (about 15 minutes). Pour sauce from pan over chicken and serve.

CHICKEN NANCY

We always serve this to Round-Up guests because I can make it 2 or 3 days before and put it in the fridge. And everyone loves it ... Judy Rew

6 servings

1	cup sour cream		Salt and black pepper
2	tablespoons lemon juice	1	box chicken flavored stuffing mix
2	teaspoons Worcestershire sauce	3	pounds fryer breasts and thighs
1	teaspoon celery salt	½	cup butter, melted
1	teaspoon paprika		

✱ Mix sour cream, lemon juice, Worcestershire sauce, celery salt, paprika, salt, and pepper in a medium-size bowl.

✱ Dip chicken pieces and coat heavily. Crush dressing into crumbs. Roll chicken in dressing crumbs and place in 9x13-inch greased dish. Drizzle dish with melted butter.

✱ Bake, uncovered, at 350° for 1 hour.

If you want to use your chicken marinade for a baste, boil it first (ever notice how all those chicken marinade recipes say "discard marinade"). Just put it in a small saucepan over high heat and boil like crazy for one full minute.

Standing: Happy Canyon Princess Elizabeth Bill, Round-Up Princesses Bille Jensen, Robin Bothum, Hostess Colleen Burns, Round-Up Princesses Sara Mautz, Serena Baker, Happy Canyon Princess Bridget Kalama. Kneeling: Hostesses Carolyn Gerberding, Judy Rew, and Queen Lisa Ferguson.

We belonged to a group that met the Sunday before Round-Up to raise a teepee in one of our yards. We participated probably 30 years and it had been organized several years before we became involved. We took turns having the party in our yards and everyone brought something — a salad, a dessert or appetizer. We always had a considerable happy hour before dinner. Maybe that's why the guys had so much trouble with those teepee poles...*Helen Hawkins*

Hawkins' Hot Barbecued Chicken

*This recipe is easily doubled or tripled (or more!). You're only limited by the size of your pan as to how much you can make. I've made it for my family and when entertaining, and everyone loved it! It was enjoyed at several tepeee raising parties...*Helen Hawkins

6 servings

- 2 tablespoons brown sugar
- ¼ cup lemon juice
- 1 cup ketchup
- 1 cup water
- ½ cup chopped celery
- ½ tablespoon prepared mustard
- 3 tablespoons Worcestershire sauce
- 1 teaspoon salt
- ½ teaspoon red pepper flakes
- 2 tablespoons butter or vegetable oil
- 3-3½ pounds chicken pieces
- 1 medium onion, sliced

★ Simmer brown sugar, lemon juice, ketchup, water, celery, mustard, Worcestershire sauce, salt, and red pepper flakes for 30 minutes.

★ Brown chicken pieces in hot butter or oil. Add onions. Transfer to 9x12-inch roasting pan. Pour sauce over chicken. Bake uncovered at 325°-350° for 1 hour.

This sauce can be used for other meats as well.

Teepee Raising Party

SUE'S CHICKEN ENCHILADAS

One of the best!

12 servings

4   chicken breasts, boiled and cubed

2   10.5-ounce cans cream of chicken soup

2   cups sour cream

2   tablespoons seasoned salt

1   3.8-ounce can sliced black olives

1   4-ounce can diced green chiles

½   cup chicken broth

1   cup grated mozzarella cheese

1   10-ounce can green chile enchilada sauce

12   8-inch flour tortillas

1   cup grated mozzarella cheese

Paprika

✵   Place cubed chicken in a large mixing bowl. Add soup, sour cream, seasoned salt, olives, green chiles, chicken broth, and 1 cup of cheese.

✵   In 11x15-inch pan, cover bottom with half of the green chile enchilada sauce.

✵   Place 2 or 3 large spoonfuls of chicken mixture on each tortilla; roll-up and place seam side down in pan. When pan is full, cover with remaining green chile enchilada sauce and top with remaining cup of mozzarella cheese. Sprinkle with paprika.

✵   Cover with foil; bake at 350° for 75 minutes.

You can use 1½ pounds of frozen, diced chicken pieces, thawed and browned, and a 16-ounce package of shredded Mexican cheeses.

Sue Schultz attended Blue Mountain Community College from 1982-1986, and never missed a Round-Up. She loved to cook and was asked to prepare the prime rib dinner for the 1985 Queen's Court, and, as a thank you, was given a 75th Commemorative jacket of which she was very proud. Sue was killed in a car accident in 2004. This is her recipe.

✵   ✵   ✵

For many years Herb and I hosted a Friday night of Round-Up buffet supper. I often included enchiladas in my menu. Usually 35 or 40 guests were invited, and the list grew as a result of conversations at the Round-Up show that day. Several years, steer ropers were included. One year national roping champion Don McLaughlin joined us. We called him "Uncle" and added him to our family tree after that year...*Margaret McLaughlin*

Tracey Bray, Tasha Moody, Penny French, and Patty Matheny, four cowgirls on vacation.

COWGIRL COUNTRY CHICKEN ENCHILADAS

A cowboy country favorite!

6 servings

FILLING

2	tablespoons vegetable oil	½	teaspoon ground coriander
1	medium onion, chopped	¼	teaspoon ground cumin
1	clove garlic, minced	½	teaspoon salt
1	4-ounce can diced green chiles	¼	teaspoon black pepper
½	cup sliced green olives	2	10-ounce cans cooked chicken, drained
1	tablespoon Worcestershire sauce	3	cups grated Cheddar cheese
½	tablespoon chili powder	12	6½-inch (fajita size) flour tortillas

DIPPING SAUCE

½	cup water	2	tablespoons vegetable oil
¼	cup red taco sauce		

TOPPING SAUCE

¼	cup margarine	1	cup milk
2	tablespoons all-purpose flour	1	cup sour cream

★ Sauté onion and garlic in oil 5 minutes. Add green chiles, green olives, Worcestershire sauce, chili powder, coriander, cumin, salt, pepper, and chicken. Mix well.

★ In small frying pan, heat water, red taco sauce, and salad oil. With tongs, dip tortillas one at a time, long enough to soften (10-15 seconds).

★ Spray 9x12-inch pan with cooking spray. Fill tortilla with about 3 tablespoons chicken mixture and sprinkle with shredded Cheddar cheese. Roll. Set seam side down in pan.

★ Make white sauce: melt margarine, whisk in flour, and add milk. Stir until thick and bubbly. Remove from heat. Add sour cream, stir until smooth. Pour white sauce over enchiladas, sprinkle remaining cheese on top. Bake at 375° for 25 minutes.

★ Garnish with sliced green olives and black olives. Serve with salsa.

Pat's Chicken Enchiladas

This recipe takes only about 30 minutes to prepare, not nearly that long to make it disappear!

12 servings

5	boneless chicken breasts	¾	pound shredded Mexican 4-cheese blend
1	small onion, diced	12	7- to 8-inch flour tortillas
1	pint sour cream		Sour cream
2	cans cream of chicken soup		Salsa
½	cup milk		
1	4-ounce can diced green chiles		

✶ Boil chicken, shred meat.

✶ Mix onion, sour cream, soup, milk, and chiles. Spread 1 cup over bottom of 9x13-inch baking pan.

✶ One at a time, soften tortillas for 8-10 seconds in microwave. Place ¼ cup of the chicken and 2 tablespoons cheese on one side of tortilla and roll up. Place in 11x15-inch pan. Repeat with all tortillas. Sprinkle any leftover chicken over top of tortillas and spread remaining mixture over all, working it down in between the rolled tortillas with a spatula. Sprinkle on remaining cheese.

✶ Bake at 350° for 35-45 minutes or until bubbly. Serve with sour cream and salsa.

"When things do not go right with you, when the circumstances seem to be against you and Fate deals you a blow between the eyes, remember what the cowboys say in the great Northwest. 'Just grit your teeth, get another hold and let 'er buck!' ...the motto of the Pendleton Roundup 1911

SOUR CREAM CHICKEN ENCHILADAS

These enchiladas have been a tradition for the Levy Clan after the rodeo for many years. We double and triple it, add a salad, rice, and some fruit because we usually serve about 30...Linda Levy Carter, Round-Up Princess 1968

6–8 servings

2	whole chicken breasts	1	10-ounce can enchilada sauce
2	10½-ounce cans cream of chicken soup	12	7- to 8-inch flour tortillas
1	pint sour cream	¾	cup chopped onion
1	4-ounce can chopped green chiles (save some for garnishing)	3	cups grated Cheddar or Monterey Jack cheese (or a combination)
		1	2.25-ounce can black olives

✳   Boil chicken breasts 20-25 minutes. Remove meat from bone and chop.

✳   Mix chicken meat, soup, sour cream, and chiles together. Spread thin layer of creamed mixture over the bottom of a 9x12-inch pan.

✳   Spread equal amounts of creamed mixture down the middle of each tortilla (reserving some creamed mixture for top) and sprinkle with chopped onion and cheese (reserving some cheese for top).

✳   Roll up tortilla and place seam-side down in prepared pan.

✳   Pour remaining mixture over the top of rolled tortillas and sprinkle with remaining cheese.

✳   Bake 25-30 minutes at 350°.

✳   Garnish with black olives, additional chiles, and grated cheese.

Linda and Bob Levy in 1951, getting an early start.

SPICY CHICKEN BULGOGI

Bulgogi (pronounced [pulgogi] in Korean) is a Korean dish that usually consists of marinated barbecued beef, although chicken or pork may also be used. It is one of the most popular beef dishes in Korea.

6 servings

4	skinless boneless chicken breasts	2	tablespoons soy sauce
2	tablespoons granulated sugar	1	fresh garlic clove, minced
1	tablespoon red pepper	2	green onions, chopped
2	tablespoons white wine	1	tablespoon toasted sesame seeds

✳ Flatten chicken with meat pounder. Slice into thin strips.

✳ Combine sugar, red pepper, white wine, soy sauce, garlic, green onions, and sesame seeds in a medium bowl. Add chicken and mix well. Fry mixture in pan.

✳ Serve with white rice.

Toasting sesame seeds brings out the seeds full, nutty flavor. Heat the seeds in a dry pan over medium heat, or on a sheet in a 275° oven, until golden and fragrant, about 5 minutes.

"My favorite part of the Round-Up is the Cowboy Breakfast in Stillman Park. I like everything about it; the way the men pour a zillion pancakes on the griddle, the all-volunteer crew, the cowboy music. Everything always tastes better outdoors early in the morning. One year, long ago, before I was married to Mike, I thought I needed to leave to go back to work but when I heard the cowboy band playing "Stand By Your Man," I called in well…. *Pam Forrester*

Round-Up Director Ron Hudson

Ben and Lila Boone, long-time friends of my Mom and Dad, Cap and Ralph Hassell, would stay at our house during Round-Up. Ben was a judge, along with Bill Switzler, at the Round-Up. Cowboys invited for dinner were Slim Pickens, Sonny Hancock, Fritz Truan, Homer Pettigrew, Jerry Ambler, Bill McMacken, and Ross Dollarhide. This recipe was one of our favorites...*Mary Hassell Curl*

1941 Round-Up Princess Mary Hassell (second from left) with Princess Helen Proebstel, Queen Maxine McCurdy, Princesses Anne Thompson, and June Kirkpatrick.

Pendleton Round-Up Junior Queen and Court 1935, from the left: Princess Pauline Lieuallen, Adams; Carol Nelson, Pilot Rock; Queen Janet Thompson; Princesses Mary Hassell, Beverly Alexander, and Susan Sturgis, Pendleton. Princess Colleen Kilkenny, Heppner, was not present for this photo.

CUSTARD CHICKEN CASSEROLE

Don't call this "custard" in front of your cowboys, and they'll love it!

10–12 servings

1   whole chicken

DRESSING
1   16-ounce loaf bread, cubed
2   tablespoons minced onion
½   teaspoon celery salt

1   teaspoon sage
½   teaspoon black pepper
¼   cup chicken broth

CUSTARD
½   cup butter
¾   cup all-purpose flour

1   quart chicken broth
6   eggs

✱   Boil chicken. Remove meat from bones; reserve broth.

✱   Combine bread, onion, celery salt, sage, and pepper. Add ¼ cup chicken broth until moist. Spread dressing in 9x13-inch pan; cover with chicken meat.

✱   In saucepan, melt butter, stir in flour; add 1 quart chicken broth and cook until thickened. Remove from heat.

✱   In small bowl, add eggs, beat until frothy. Pour custard mixture into eggs. Stir gently. Pour mixture over chicken. Bake at 350° for 45-60 minutes or until custard is set.

Former Princess Mary Hassell returns to the Westward Ho! Parade for the Round-Up Royalty Reunion in 1981.

CHICKEN SPAGHETTI – 50's STYLE

This recipe spans generations. Blanch Holt passed it to Betty Graybeal, who gave it to Nancy Graybeal, and is now made by Corrin Graybeal. It's easily doubled or tripled.

8–10 servings

½	pound bacon, diced	1	8-ounce package frozen peas
1	Walla Walla Sweet onion, diced	1	28-ounce can crushed or petite diced tomatoes
1	pound spaghetti		Salt and black pepper to taste
1	whole roasted chicken, shredded		Grated cheese

✴ Cook bacon until crisp; add onions. Simmer until soft. Drain off fat.

✴ Meanwhile, cook spaghetti according to directions and drain.

✴ Mix in large bowl the chicken, frozen peas, tomatoes, bacon and spaghetti. Spray a 9x12-inch pan with non-stick cooking spray. Add mixture and top with grated cheese.

✴ Bake uncovered at 350° for 45 minutes.

One tester added a couple of tablespoons of Marsala wine while sautéing the bacon and onions, and liked the smoothness that resulted.

Like many Pendletonians, Jay & Betty Graybeal loved the Pendleton Round-Up — especially the parties! They didn't miss a one. They started the week before with a teepee raising party, hit all the parties during the week, and, of course, never missed the Buckle Club.

This picture is from a 1954 Round-Up party at 1209 NW King. As you can see, the North Hill was pretty bare back then. Six-year old Nancy Graybeal is talking with bartender Grandfather Walter A. Holt.

In 1965, Umatilla County Clerk Jessie M. Bell put an end to all the estimates about the Westward Ho! Parade. She and three others actually counted every participant. They came up with 2,145 people in the parade, including 512 Indians. Critters included 662 horses, 23 mules, 110 ponies, 12 burros, nine oxen, and three dogs. There were 16 bands and 19 rodeo and fair queens, two drum and bugle corps, 28 buggies, and two stagecoaches.

Don Hawkins and Donna Johns

ITALIAN PARMESAN CHICKEN

The taste is great! Very easy, very delicious.

6 servings

6	boneless, skinless chicken breast halves	1	teaspoon garlic salt
2	cups grated Parmesan cheese	½	teaspoon black pepper
1	cup dry bread crumbs	1-2	tablespoons fresh or dried chopped parsley
1	tablespoon Italian Seasoning	½	cup butter, melted

✱ Melt butter in medium bowl.

✱ In separate bowl, mix Parmesan cheese, bread crumbs, Italian Seasoning, garlic salt, pepper, and parsley.

✱ Line large cookie sheet with foil, and dab with small amount of butter under where each piece of chicken will be.

✱ Dip chicken pieces first in melted butter and then roll in Parmesan mixture. Place coated pieces on baking sheet. Drizzle any excess butter or dry mixture over pieces. Bake at 425° for 35-40 minutes, or until juices run clear.

QUICK & EASY CHICKEN POT PIE

Just about the easiest thing to do with leftover chicken, more cost effective and more nutritious than you can buy at the store, and so much better!

6–8 servings

2	10.75-ounce cans cream of potato soup	½	cup milk
1	16-ounce can mixed vegetables	½	teaspoon thyme
2	cups cooked chicken breast, cubed	½	teaspoon black pepper
		2	9-inch pie crusts

✱ Arrange one pie crust in bottom of 9-inch pie plate.

✱ Combine soup, vegetables, chicken, milk, thyme, and pepper. Spoon into pie plate. Cover with top crust. Crimp edges to seal. Put slits in crust. Bake at 375° for about 40 minutes.

CHICKEN AND RICE CASSEROLE

Handy to have on hand, or great to have the following Sunday.

10–12 servings

4	chicken breasts	1	10.5-ounce can cream of mushroom soup
4	envelopes dry chicken noodle soup mix	1	2.5-ounce can sliced mushrooms
5	cups chicken broth	1	cup mayonnaise
1	cup raw white rice	1	cup butter cracker crumbs
5	stalks celery, chopped		
1	onion, chopped		

✶ Cook chicken in salted water until tender. Remove chicken and cool. When cool, cut into chunks.

✶ In medium saucepan, mix 4 envelopes chicken noodle soup, rice, and chicken broth.

✶ In pan, sauté celery and onion in butter. When soft, add cream of mushroom soup, and mayonnaise. After stirring together, add this sauce mixture to soup/rice mixture; add chicken chunks. Place in 9x13-inch baking dish; cover with butter cracker crumbs. Bake at 350° for 1 hour.

This is a great casserole to make ahead and freeze a week or two before Round-Up. If I don't need it during the week, it's nice to have the Sunday after Round-Up when everyone is getting ready to leave, doing laundry and everything else that is put off until Round-Up is over...*Jan Levy*

Marge Jones, Creagh Hawes,
Karin Power

TURKEY TAMALE POT PIE

You can use ground beef as well, but this is a fun thing to do with ground turkey.

10–12 servings

FILLING

1	cup chopped onion
¾	cup chopped red bell pepper
4	garlic cloves, minced
1	pound ground turkey breast
1	tablespoon chili powder
1	teaspoon dried oregano
½	teaspoon salt
1	14.5-ounce can diced tomatoes, undrained

1	15-ounce can kidney beans, drained and rinsed
1	15.5-ounce can black beans, drained and rinsed
1	large bunch turnip greens (about 8 to 10 ounces), center stem cut away, leaves cut into 1-inch pieces (mustard or collard greens can be substituted if turnip greens are unavailable)

TOPPING

1	cup all-purpose flour
¾	cup yellow cornmeal
1	teaspoon baking powder
½	teaspoon salt

¼	teaspoon baking soda
1	cup low-fat buttermilk
1	large egg, lightly beaten
1	teaspoon honey

✳ Prepare filling: heat a large skillet over medium-high heat. Coat pan with cooking spray. Add onion, bell pepper, garlic, and turkey. Cook 5 minutes or until turkey loses its pink color. Add chili powder, oregano, salt, tomatoes, beans, and turnip greens. Cook 3 minutes or until greens are wilted. Spoon turkey mixture into a 9x12-inch pan coated with non-stick cooking spray.

✳ Prepare topping: combine flour, cornmeal, baking powder, salt, and baking soda in a bowl. Combine buttermilk, egg, and honey and add to dry ingredients, stirring just until moist. Spread cornmeal mixture evenly over turkey mixture. Bake at 425° for 20-25 minutes or until topping is golden.

BUTTERFLIED LEG OF LAMB

This is moist and tender, very tasty.

6–8 servings

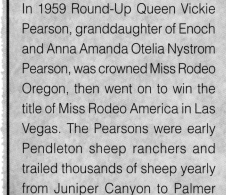

3	pound leg of lamb, boned and butterflied	2	teaspoons curry powder
	Juice of 2 large lemons	1	teaspoon ground coriander
3	tablespoons olive oil	1	teaspoon ground ginger
2	tablespoons grated or finely diced onion	1	clove garlic, mashed or minced
1-2	tablespoons chili pepper		Sea salt and lemon pepper to taste

✶ Trim fat from leg of lamb. Lightly score meat.

✶ Mix lemon juice, olive oil, onion, chili pepper, curry powder, coriander, ginger, and garlic. Pour mixture over leg of lamb. Marinate in plastic bag or non-metallic pan with cover for 1-3 days, turning 3-4 times a day.

✶ Let meat come to room temperature before cooking, approximately 30 minutes. Prepare charcoal grill or bring gas grill to medium heat.

✶ Drain marinade from leg of lamb.

✶ Cook over indirect heat for 1 hour and 30 minutes or until internal temperature reads 140°-145° for rare, 150° for medium-rare, or 160° for medium well.

✶ Let the meat rest for about 10 minutes before carving.

For a leg of lamb weighing more than 6 pounds, double the mixture part of the recipe.

In 1959 Round-Up Queen Vickie Pearson, granddaughter of Enoch and Anna Amanda Otelia Nystrom Pearson, was crowned Miss Rodeo Oregon, then went on to win the title of Miss Rodeo America in Las Vegas. The Pearsons were early Pendleton sheep ranchers and trailed thousands of sheep yearly from Juniper Canyon to Palmer Junction, a distance of almost 100 miles. Enoch and Anna were both from Sweden, and homesteaded on the Columbia River. He died in 1935 from complications of a sliver in his hand, before the days of penicillin.

1959 Round-Up Queen Vickie Pearson

The fine wool herds of Umatilla County are famous throughout the west and their wool demands a premium on the market. The county boasts the largest purebred Rambouillet herd in the world, as well as other herds of sheep bred for a superior quality of wool. Two hundred thousand head of sheep are grazed in the county each year. The wheat stubble lands and the irrigated alfalfa tracts adjoining winter range give exceptionally good opportunities for wintering. Pendleton is well known for its lamb industry, and the wool from the local Rambouillet sheep goes to make blankets and shirts for the Pendleton Woolen Mills.

Verne Pearson on sheep with his mother and sister on the Pearson Sheep Ranch, 1912.

ROBUST AND HEARTY LEG OF LAMB

Any size leg of lamb will work with this tasty recipe. According to the French, the lamb is done when it's so tender you can eat it with a spoon.

8-12 servings

6   medium onions, quartered

6   carrots, quartered

1   head of garlic, cloves peeled and halved

6   bay leaves

1   large sprig of fresh thyme or 1 teaspoon dried thyme

1   4-6 pound leg of lamb, trimmed of visible fat

1   teaspoon salt

¼   teaspoon fresh ground black pepper

2   bottles (750 ml each) dry white wine

4½   pounds large boiling potatoes, peeled, and cut into 1½-inch chunks

5   large tomatoes, peeled, seeded, and chopped or one 28-ounce can crushed Italian tomatoes

✱   Layer the onions, carrots, garlic, bay leaves, and thyme in a large roasting pan. Place lamb on top of vegetables and herbs. Roast lamb for 30 minutes in a 425° oven.

✱   Remove the pan from the oven and season with salt and pepper. Return lamb to the oven and roast for 30 minutes longer.

✱   Remove the pan from the oven and set it over two burners turned on high heat. Reduce the oven temperature to 350°. Slowly pour the wine over the lamb and bring to a boil. Cover the lamb with aluminum foil and return it to the oven. Roast for about 3-4 hours longer, until the meat is moist and falling off the bone. (Timing will vary depending on the size of the lamb and the type of roasting pan used. Check the lamb periodically, reducing the oven temperature to 325° if the lamb begins to burn or the liquid begins to evaporate too quickly. Add more wine or broth if necessary).

✱   About 1 hour and 30 minutes before the lamb is done, add the potatoes and the tomatoes with their liquid and submerge them in the liquid in the roasting pan.

✱   Transfer the lamb and vegetables to a carving board. Pour the pan juices (the carrots and onions will have been cooked almost to a liquid) into a small saucepan and boil over high heat for a few minutes to intensify the flavors (or blend in food processor).

✱   Carve the lamb into thick slices. Place slices on a serving dish and surround with potatoes. Serve pan juices separately.

Rosemary and Garlic Lamb Chops

Lamb flavored with a big hit of garlic and an overlay of rosemary is a classic combination.

4 servings

8	lamb chops, 1½-inches thick (about 5 ounces each)	6	tablespoons extra virgin olive oil
2	tablespoons minced garlic (about 6 cloves)	1	teaspoon kosher or sea salt
3	tablespoons minced fresh rosemary	1	teaspoon freshly ground black pepper
			Fresh rosemary sprigs

✱ Place room-temperature lamb chops on a flat baking sheet.

✱ In a small bowl, combine the garlic, rosemary, olive oil, salt, and pepper and mix thoroughly. Rub the lamb chops on both sides with the garlic mixture.

✱ Over a hot fire, grill the chops on one side for 3 minutes for rare, or 4 minutes for medium-rare. Turn and cook for 3 minutes more, or until an instant-read thermometer registers 120° for rare and 130°-135° for medium-rare.

✱ Remove the chops from the grill and let rest 5 minutes. Arrange 2 chops on each dinner plate, pour accumulated juices over, and garnish with fresh rosemary.

Lamb Chops with Pepper Herb Crust

A little spicy

4 servings

1	tablespoon coarsely ground black pepper	¾	teaspoon salt
1	teaspoon dried thyme	½	teaspoon dried mint
1	teaspoon paprika	⅛	teaspoon cayenne pepper
		4	large or 8 small lamb chops

✱ In a small dish, combine black pepper, thyme, paprika, salt, mint, and cayenne. Rub mixture over lamb chops. Arrange chops in a shallow glass baking dish, cover, and refrigerate 1 hour or more.

✱ On a medium-hot grill, grill the lamb chops, turning once, until they are cooked as desired. Rare should take 8-10 minutes. Serve hot.

Mario Zubiria of Mario's Basque Barbecue is a chef extraordinaire and his lamb and beef kabobs are high on everyone's list at Round-Up time. His is a family run catering business that has introduced so many of us to the delights of Basque cooking.

Our teepee raising group, which had 20-25 couples as members was started in about 1972 and continued for almost 30 years. We met the Sunday before Round-Up to put up the teepee in a different couple's yard each year. It was decorated with Indian designs and was signed by all the members.

After a considerable amount of firewater, the fellows would put up the poles and erect the teepee with the wives offering suggestions and giving advice. Dinner was potluck, although one year members enjoyed a Pitchfork Barbecue.

One year we had no ladder, so Joan Corey, the smallest person there, was lifted to the top of the teepee to start closing the front with the pegs. No injuries were reported...*Helen Hawkins*

SEAFOOD LASAGNA

Very rich, very good!

12 servings

8	lasagna noodles, uncooked	2	10.75-ounce cans cream of mushroom soup
1	large onion, chopped	⅓	cup milk
2	tablespoons butter	⅓	cup dry white wine
1	8-ounce package cream cheese, softened	1-2	pounds fresh or frozen shelled shrimp, cooked and halved
1½	cups cream-style cottage cheese	1	7.5-ounce can crabmeat, drained, flaked
1	egg, beaten	¼	cup grated Parmesan cheese
2	teaspoons crushed dried basil	½	cup shredded sharp Cheddar cheese
½	teaspoon salt		
⅛	teaspoon black pepper		

✶ Arrange four lasagna noodles on the bottom of a greased 15x11x2-inch baking dish. Do not overlap.

✶ Cook onions in the butter until tender but not brown. Blend in cream cheese. Stir in cottage cheese, egg, basil, salt, and pepper. Spread half of this mixture on top of the noodles.

✶ Combine soup, milk, and wine. Stir in the shrimp and crabmeat. Spread half of the shrimp/crab mixture over the cottage cheese layer. Repeat layer of noodles, cottage cheese mixture and shrimp/crab mixture. Sprinkle top with Parmesan cheese and bake uncovered at 350° for 45 minutes.

✶ Top with Cheddar cheese and bake until the cheese melts, 2 or 3 minutes more.

✶ Let the lasagna sit for 15 minutes before serving.

The teepee has been raised — let's eat!

Ruth's Round-Up Escalloped Oysters

Ruth Duff often made this dish to accompany her pre- or post- parade party or for the Teepee raising party.

2 servings

1	pint medium oysters	⅛	teaspoon black pepper
½	cup butter, melted	1½	cups fresh cracker crumbs
½	teaspoon salt	¾	cup heavy cream
½	teaspoon cumin powder	1	teaspoon Worcestershire sauce

✶ Drain oysters, saving liqueur. Cut oysters in bite-sized pieces.

✶ Combine butter, salt, cumin and pepper. Pour over cracker crumbs and mix thoroughly. Spread one-third of the crumbs in bottom of a 2-quart casserole dish. Cover crumbs with one-half of the oysters. Spread another one-third of the crumbs over the oysters. Cover crackers with remaining oysters.

✶ Combine reserved oyster liqueur, cream, and Worcestershire sauce. Pour liquid mixture over the oysters. Top oysters with remaining crumbs.

✶ Bake at 350° for 40 minutes.

From the *East Oregonian*, August 13, 1910:

"Round-Up" headquarters have been established in the offices of James Gwinn in the basement of the American National Bank building. The headquarters will be maintained until after the big frontier celebration is pulled off in Pendleton. Sheriff Til Taylor has been named chairman of the committee to obtain horses, bulls, and steers for the show.

Round-Up Party

Unless you can catch a fish directly out of the Umatilla River, which flows right through Pendleton (do we have a great River Parkway or what?), really fresh fish in Pendleton is not always available. But if the label says "fresh-frozen," it's probably fresher than the "fresh" fish we can buy in our local grocery stores.

FISH ROYALE

This works with any kind of fish you have.

4 servings

MARINADE

2	tablespoons cold water	¼	teaspoon salt
4	tablespoons lemon or lime juice	¼	teaspoon paprika

FISH

4	fish fillets	1	medium onion, chopped
½	cup butter	2	cloves of garlic, chopped
1	bell pepper, sliced		

✖ In a bowl, combine water, lemon juice, salt, and paprika.

✖ Place fish fillets in a shallow pan. Pour marinade over the fish fillets. Refrigerate fish for 30 minutes. Turn the fish and continue marinating for an additional 30 minutes. Remove the fish from the marinade and discard marinade.

✖ Place the fish in a shallow, greased, baking dish. Bake at 400° for 10 minutes.

✖ Melt butter in a skillet over medium heat. Add bell pepper and onion. Cook vegetables until the onions are tender and translucent. Add garlic and cook for an additional minute.

✖ Remove fish from baking dish and top with vegetables.

CRAB DUMPLINGS

Great addition to vegetable or fish chowders.

18 dumplings

¼ cup butter or margarine, room temperature

¼ cup all-purpose flour

1 teaspoon dry sherry or dry white wine

1 egg yolk

⅓ cup shredded cooked crabmeat

Pinch white pepper

★ Combine butter or margarine and flour in a small bowl. Cream with the back of a spoon until smooth. Stir in sherry and egg yolk. Add crabmeat and white pepper; stir until blended.

★ Dust your hands with flour. Shape rounded teaspoonfuls of dumpling mixture into small balls. To cook, drop dumplings in simmering soup 15 minutes before soup is done. Cover and simmer until dumplings are firm, about 15 minutes.

Substitute diced cooked shrimp, shredded cooked lobster or tuna for crabmeat.

CRAB QUICHE

This recipe is very easy to make, and it's a good thing, because you'll be wanting seconds.

6 servings

1 9-inch pie shell, unbaked

1 egg white, unbeaten

3 eggs

1¼ cups heavy cream

1½ cups grated Swiss cheese

½ teaspoon salt

Dash of cayenne pepper

¼ teaspoon thyme

¼ pound crabmeat, roughly chopped

1 6½-ounce jar artichoke hearts, marinated or not, depending upon preference

★ Brush pic shell with egg white and let dry.

★ Beat eggs and heavy cream just to blend. Add cheese, salt, pepper, thyme, and crabmeat. Pour crab mixture into pie shell. Arrange artichokes on top of egg mixture.

★ Bake at 375° for 1 hour or until an inserted knife comes out clean.

From the *East Oregonian*, September 6, 1910

The Commercial Association has agreed to look for accommodations for the hundreds of visitors expected to attend the Round-Up. Mark Moorhouse urges hotels and restaurants "not to practice extortion methods" on visitors. "Nothing could kill off an annual celebration more quickly." said Moorhouse.

Old Time Pendleton

Several of the Pendleton Round-Up queens and princesses have been crowned Miss Rodeo Oregon over the years:

1958 - Judy Lazinka Currin,

1959 - Vickie Pearson Bafus,

1960 - Jan Beamer Bothum,

1963 - Marilyn Foster Corfield,

1977 - Julie Rugg Williams,

1981 - Janice Healy Davis,

1989-90 - Robin Bothum Nansel.

Pictured below is Marilyn Foster with Round-Up President Fred Hill.

1962 Round-Up Queen and 1963 Miss Rodeo Oregon Marilyn Foster with Round-Up President Fred Hill

SAUTÉED SCALLOPS WITH LEMON MUSTARD SAUCE

These are nice served on mashed potatoes, mashed cauliflower, or on toasted garlic bread.

4 servings

1	pound large sea scallops	2	tablespoons butter
	Salt and black pepper	2	tablespoons fresh lemon juice
2	tablespoons all-purpose flour	2	tablespoons water
1	tablespoon olive oil	1	teaspoon Dijon mustard

✶ Sprinkle scallops with salt and pepper and dust with flour.

✶ Heat oil in large skillet over high heat. Add scallops and sauté until brown and just cooked through, about 3 minutes per side. Remove from heat and put scallops on platter.

✶ Mix the butter, lemon juice, water, and mustard in a small bowl and add them to the skillet, scraping up any browned bits. Place skillet on medium-low heat. Whisk until sauce simmers and thickens, about 2 minutes. Spoon sauce over scallops.

ROUND-UP CRAB CASSEROLE

Easy to throw this together, easy to wow your guests

8–10 servings

2	6-ounce cans crabmeat	2	3-ounce cans chow mein noodles
2	cups chopped celery		
4	tablespoons chopped onions		Salt and black pepper to taste
2	10.5-ounce cans creamed soup, your choice		

✶ In a bowl, combine crabmeat, celery, onions, soup and noodles.

✶ Pour crab mixture into a buttered casserole dish. Bake at 325° for 1 hour or until bubbly.

PENDLETON UNDERGROUND ASIAN SKEWERS

These work as appetizers or as a main dish, and they're as beautiful to serve as they are to eat!

18 kabobs

MARINADE

½	cup soy sauce	½	teaspoon ground ginger
¾	cup brown sugar	½	teaspoon garlic powder
1	teaspoon rice vinegar	⅛	teaspoon red pepper flakes
½	tablespoon sesame oil	½	teaspoon cornstarch

KABOBS

1	8-ounce can pineapple chunks	6	slices bacon, cut into thirds
1	8-ounce can whole water chestnuts	2	tablespoons sesame seeds
18	large shrimp, peeled, deveined, tails intact	2	limes, cut into wedges
			Wooden or bamboo skewers

✴ Soak the skewers in cold water for at least 30 minutes before cooking.

✴ Drain and reserve juice from canned pineapple. Set aside.

✴ In a bowl, whisk together soy sauce, brown sugar, rice vinegar, sesame oil, ginger, garlic powder, red pepper flakes, pineapple juice, and cornstarch. Add shrimp, water chestnuts and bacon to marinade. Refrigerate mixture for at least 1 hour.

✴ Wrap each water chestnut in a piece of bacon, set aside.

✴ Push wooden skewers through 1 shrimp, 1 bacon-wrapped water chestnut, and 1 pineapple chunk. Repeat until all pieces of shrimp have been skewered.

✴ Set oven rack to the second highest level from the broiler and set the oven to broil. Arrange the skewers on a greased broiling pan and place under broiler for about 6 minutes. Turn skewers over and broil for another 5 minutes or until golden brown.

✴ Arrange skewers on a serving platter and sprinkle with sesame seeds. Serve with lime wedges.

You can easily grill these on the barbecue.

Pendleton's underground tunnels, dug by the Chinese between 1870 and 1930, cover over 70 miles underneath Pendleton's historic district. In 1989, some of the tunnels were restored and exhibits and mannequins used to recreate the businesses that used to be located there. These businesses included ice plants, butcher shops, and Chinese laundries, as well as illegal saloons, bordellos and opium dens.

SHRIMP KABOBS

RAPHAEL'S INDIAN SALMON

We were so excited to get this recipe! It's been one of our favorites for many, many years.

1 serving

SALMON

1   8-ounce salmon fillet, skin removed
1   shallot, finely diced
1   tablespoon butter
3   thin tomato slices

1½ ounces fresh spinach leaves
2   cups dry vermouth
1   tablespoon huckleberry purée

★ Sprinkle diced shallot over salmon. Melt butter in sauté pan or skillet, add salmon. Top with tomato slices and cover with spinach leaves. Place over medium heat and add vermouth. Cover and simmer for approximately 10 minutes (depending on the thickness of the fillet).

★ Remove spinach covered salmon fillet from pan. Place on plate and top with huckleberry purée.

HUCKLEBERRY PURÉE

1   cup huckleberries (blackberries, marionberries, raspberries can be substituted, but it's just not quite the same)

¼   cup water
2   tablespoons granulated sugar
1   teaspoon arrowroot

★ In a blender, purée huckleberries and water. Transfer to small saucepan and bring to a boil.

★ Mix arrowroot and sugar in a small bowl and add to the boiling purée. Mix well and cool to room temperature.

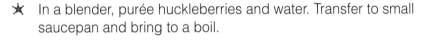

Michelle Kordatsky

JAY-MAN'S BAKED SALMON

I hope that you enjoy this, as many a cowboy has come through camp and turned up their noses to fish. Once they have tried it, they always come back for more ...Jim Harrison

8 servings

1	3-pound salmon fillet	2	tablespoons Cajun Blackening seasoning (depending on how spicy you like your fish)
1	tablespoon garlic salt		
1	clove garlic, sliced	1	large lemon
		½	cup Parmesan cheese

✱ Rinse salmon in cold water and let dry (try really hard to get fresh salmon). Place fillet on aluminum foil large enough to fold over fish. Sprinkle garlic salt onto fillet and spread garlic over. Sprinkle with blackening seasoning. Slice the lemon and spread over fillet. Top with Parmesan cheese.

✱ Fold the foil to form an envelope to completely seal fish. Place on grill or oven at 350° for about 30 minutes.

One way to make sure the fish has cooked throughout is the foil will puff up when the fish is done.

Jim Harrison (Jay-Man)

Jay-Man (whose real name is Jim Harrison), lives in the Pendleton area and while he looks like he's native Indian, he is really half Korean. Every year since 1991 he has cooked at the Round-Up grounds for the pickup men and the stock crew. He brings down a couple of big barbecue grills, several large coolers, and cooks two and sometimes three meals a day for the pickup men and their families and the stock crew, contractors, and bullfighters for the entire Round-Up...for just about an entire week's worth!

The rodeo season is starting to wind down by the time of the Pendleton Round-Up, and after a long summer on the rodeo road, it's almost like being at home having Jay-Man do the cooking for us. Having him there at "camp" it's like there's always someone there, to keep an eye on things and to chat with. Not only that, but Jay-Man's an excellent cook and we always have a salmon dinner one night...*Jody Rempel*

MAPLE-CHILE GLAZED SALMON

This is called Madame Stella's Salmon at Hamley's Steakhouse.

6 servings

SALMON

6	6-ounce salmon fillets	Kosher or sea salt and freshly ground black pepper
2	tablespoons vegetable oil	

GLAZE

1½	cups pure maple syrup	¾	cup fresh lime juice
2	ounces chile-garlic sauce (do not confuse with Sambal or Shiracha)	2	tablespoons honey
		1	tablespoon butter (added later)

✳ Mix syrup, chile-garlic sauce, lime juice, and honey. Set aside.

✳ Salt and pepper the salmon fillets enough to taste. Heat thin layer of vegetable oil, just enough to coat the pan, in a large (not non-stick) frying pan until it is very hot.

✳ Place salmon fillets in frying pan, sear on high heat until salmon is cooked about one-third of the way through. Turn to sear the other side until it's cooked one-third of the way through.

✳ Remove fillets to baking dish and place in 375° oven until firm to the touch, about 10 minutes.

✳ Keep frying pan at high temperature, and add pre-mixed glaze ingredients. When glaze starts to bubble, scrape the remnants of salmon from the pan to mix with the glaze. One it is bubbling nicely, add butter and continue to mix. Reduce heat until it barely simmers.

✳ Remove salmon from oven and place on serving plate. Pour glaze from pan over salmon and serve with coconut rice. (See recipe on Page 129.)

In the early years, there was a huge tree down at the Indian Village. It's been gone for probably 50 years now, but it was used to dry salmon. The Native people would clean the fish and lay the fillets out in the branches to dry in the sun.

COLD POACHED SALMON
WITH HORSERADISH AND HERB SAUCE

Cold poached salmon at your buffet table makes a beautiful centerpiece.

12 servings

HORSERADISH AND HERB SAUCE

1 cup mayonnaise

⅔ cup chopped fresh basil, plus whole leaves for garnish

½ cup fresh chopped chives

¼ cup fresh chopped tarragon

2 tablespoons white wine vinegar

2 tablespoons creamy horseradish

SALMON

2 18½x10½-inch foil pans

3 cups dry white wine

3 cups water

1 tablespoon peppercorns

3 bay leaves

1 lemon, sliced

1 2½- to 3-pound salmon fillet, skin on

Kosher salt

Olive oil

✱ In food processor, blend mayonnaise, basil, chives, tarragon, vinegar, and horseradish. Place mixture in a bowl, cover, and refrigerate.

✱ Place wine, water, peppercorns, bay leaves, and lemon slices in a large saucepan. Bring to a boil, turn down heat and simmer for 10 minutes. Remove from heat and allow to cool to room temperature.

✱ Place salmon fillet skin side down in one foil pan. Pour cooled liquid over the top. Cover pan tightly with aluminum foil and bake at 350° for 20 minutes. After 10 minutes remove the foil and baste salmon with poaching liquid, then reseal foil and finish baking. After 20 minutes, remove pan from oven and remove foil. Allow salmon to cool. When cool enough to handle, place foil pan over the sink, and with a sharp knife, puncture several holes into the bottom of the foil pan to allow the poaching liquid to drain. Place the pan into the second foil pan. Brush olive oil onto the surface of the salmon, cover with foil and refrigerate until thoroughly chilled. This can be done a day ahead.

✱ To serve, cut the end off of the foil pans. With the help of a spatula, slide the salmon out of the pans onto a serving platter. Top with the Horseradish and Herb Sauce. Use whole basil leaves to garnish platter.

For nearly 70 years, salmon were not present in the Umatilla River. Irrigation diversions and habitat damage extinguished them in the early 1900s. Today, salmon are once again living in the Umatilla River and making a remarkable comeback, thanks to a cooperative effort led by the Confederated Tribes of the Umatilla Indian Reservation.

Jenny VanPelt

213

Indian leader Poker Jim, father of Clarence Burke, issued a special written invitation to publisher George Palmer Putnam and a group of "rough writers."

"The Indians of Pendleton are pleasured to see some of the cowboys from New York. You are welcome to our tepees. When I sign my name to a paper, I nearly always lost something, but I will do it for you. Allow 'er to buck. *Poker Jim."...1922*

The tenderloin of venison is the choicest cut. Soaking venison in buttermilk reduces the wild or gamey taste.

ELK MEDALLIONS

A specialty of Chef Rob at Raphael's Restaurant.

1 serving

1	tablespoon olive oil	½	teaspoon extra fine diced Anaheim pepper
6	ounces elk loin, sliced into three 2-ounce medallions, ⅜-inch by ½-inch thick	1	Morel mushroom, sliced
		1	teaspoon huckleberries
1	teaspoon extra fine diced red onion	2	ounces water
		2	ounces demi-glaze or other brown sauce

✶ Heat olive oil in sauté pan until oil is hot (it will start to smoke). Carefully add elk medallions and sear about 1 minute on each side. Add onion, pepper, mushroom, and huckleberries.

✶ Pull medallions from pan and place on plate. Add demi-glaze to sauté pan and mix well. Add 2 ounces water to demi-glaze; cook until it's a light gravy consistency, then pour sauce over pan-seared elk medallions and serve.

TASTY GAME BURGERS

A pretty basic recipe for good old hamburgers, but with a bit of a wild twist.

6-8 servings

1	pound ground beef	1	tablespoon barbecue sauce
1	pound ground game	¼	cup cold water

✶ Mix beef, game, barbecue sauce, and water.

✶ Shape into patties.

✶ Grill until no longer pink in the center.

PHEASANT FLORENTINE

If you're not a bird hunter, talk someone out of a couple of their pheasants, or substitute chicken.

4 servings

PHEASANT

2   10-ounce packages frozen spinach, thawed, chopped

2   teaspoons lemon juice

½   teaspoon salt

¼   teaspoon black pepper

2-3 cups cooked and diced pheasant

¼   cup grated Parmesan cheese

Paprika

CREAM SAUCE

2   tablespoons butter

2   tablespoons all-purpose flour

1   cup half-and-half or heavy cream

✱   Spread spinach in bottom of casserole dish. Sprinkle lemon juice, salt and pepper on top. Spread pheasant on spinach mixture.

✱   Melt butter in small saucepan. Add flour and stir until well blended. Add half-and-half or cream gradually, stirring constantly, until thickened. Pour hot cream sauce over mixture. Sprinkle cheese and paprika on top. Bake at 350° for 20-25 minutes.

Looks like we're either going to have Pheasant Florentine or Squirrel Stew.

215

Roy and his wife Eva gave a very large garden party every Round-Up. There was always a variety of dignitaries, Round-Up participants, and local people in attendance. Their home was where Raphael's Restaurant now operates. His Mountain Stew was a basic "after the hunt" meal at the family cabin, Tamarack Temple, in the Blue Mountains. This was most likely a "man's meal."... *Sally Raley Brady*

Roy Raley, father of both Happy Canyon and the Pendleton Round-Up, was a true Pendleton pioneer. He was a lawyer, legislator, cattleman, banker, surveyor, engineer, sportsman, businessman, and creator of community celebrations. He was the first President of the Pendleton Round-Up, a position he held for two years. His vision for a show highlighting his Indian friends gave birth to Happy Canyon, the evening show performed during the Round-Up, which portrays Indian village life before the coming of the white man. He wrote the script, planned the scenery, and directed the first show in 1913. He also was the organizer of the Indian beauty contest, still held annually before the Westward Ho! Parade. Roy Raley was one of the first inductees into the Pendleton Round-Up and Happy Canyon Hall of Fame.

ROY RALEY'S MOUNTAIN STEW

This recipe is adaptable to other vegetables and spices, and freezes well.

6–8 servings

1	tablespoon olive oil	5	peppercorns
1½	pounds venison, cut up (or stew meat)	5	cloves
2-3	14-ounce cans beef broth	1	cup red wine
1	tablespoon celery salt	½	cup chopped onions
1	tablespoon parsley flakes	4	carrots, sliced
½	tablespoon red pepper flakes	2	turnips, chopped
1	bay leaf	2	medium potatoes, chopped

✶ Add olive oil to a stew pot and heat. Add meat to pot and brown.

✶ Add beef broth and bring to a boil, scraping the bottom to pick up brown bits. Reduce heat and simmer 30 minutes.

✶ Add seasonings and wine and simmer for 1 hour.

✶ Add vegetables and cook until tender, 30-40 minutes.

Eva and Roy Raley, founder and first president of the Pendleton Round-Up

THAI CURRIED PHEASANT/CHUKAR/QUAIL

Any bird will work in this exotic recipe.

4 servings

8	ounces rice noodles, cooked	2	teaspoons curry powder
2	tablespoons vegetable oil	1	tablespoon fish sauce
2	garlic cloves, finely chopped	1	teaspoon lemon juice
2	teaspoons red curry paste	1	teaspoon granulated sugar
1	cup coconut cream	1	scallion, coarsely chopped
2-3	cups wild fowl, chopped bite-size	2	shallots, finely diced
12	shiitake mushrooms, cleaned, halved	¼	cup chopped fresh cilantro
		1	lemon or lime, cut into wedges
2	cups chicken stock	1	tablespoon pickled cabbage

✳ In a frying pan, heat the oil and sauté garlic until golden, about 1 minute. Stir in curry paste and cook for a few seconds. Pour in coconut cream and cook until reduced and thickened. Do not boil.

✳ Add wildfowl, stir, then add mushrooms and stir fry for a minute. Add chicken stock, curry powder, fish sauce, lemon juice, and sugar, stirring constantly.

✳ Place cooked rice noodles in the bottom of a soup bowl. Pour wildfowl mixture over noodles. Garnish with scallions, shallots, cilantro, and pickled cabbage for each serving. Serve with lemon or lime wedges on the side.

1936 Round-Up princess Beverly Simpson Raley Gantz

Steve Corey, Round-Up President, lost his coveted "director name badge" when making his final lap around the rodeo arena on Saturday. That wouldn't seem like much of a loss to most people, but the misplacement of a director badge carries with it a lot of baggage: will the finder of the badge present the badge as his own at the gate and gain free admission to the rodeo forever thereafter? And, of course, the more serious loss is one of "good face" among friends — will Steve be known thereafter as the director who lost his name badge? The good news came the following September, when Judge Ron Pahl, also a Round-Up director, was walking in the arena track as it was being worked up for the next rodeo, and stumbled upon Steve's badge. Being a good and judicious person, Judge Pahl promptly returned it to Steve, but not without a few cautionary remarks.

STEVE'S FAVORITE PHEASANT

Ahhhhh…Just lovely. Substitute chicken if you're short on pheasant.

4 servings

4	pheasant breasts	½	cup brown sugar
1	cup all-purpose flour	2	tablespoons Worcestershire sauce
¼-½	cup olive oil or butter	¼	teaspoon garlic powder
1	medium onion, chopped	1	cup sherry
½	cup seedless raisins	1	16-ounce can dark, pitted, sweet cherries, drained
1	cup chili sauce		
½	cup water		

✶ Dust the pheasant breasts with flour. Heat butter or oil in a heavy skillet. Brown pheasant. Place pheasant in a deep casserole dish.

✶ In the same skillet, combine onions, raisins, chili sauce, water, brown sugar, Worcestershire sauce, and garlic powder. Boil briefly, scraping the brown bits from the bottom of the skillet. Pour mixture over the pheasant.

✶ Bake covered at 325° for 1 hour 30 minutes. Remove the cover. Add sherry and cherries. Bake for an additional 10-20 minutes. Serve over rice.

2003 Round-Up President Steve Corey

WHEN THE DUST SETTLES PASTA

The sauce can keep in the refrigerator for up to a week and is great with seafood or chicken.

6–8 servings

SAUCE

1	32-ounce can crushed tomatoes	⅓	cup chopped green or sweet onions
1	cup fresh basil	1	tablespoon minced garlic
2-3	tablespoons olive oil	1	teaspoon salt
¼	cup white wine	½	teaspoon black pepper
2	tablespoons balsamic vinegar	1	10-ounce can artichoke hearts, chopped

PASTA

4	quarts water	1	cup freshly grated Parmesan cheese
1	teaspoon salt (optional)		
12-16	ounces linguini		

✳ In large pan, add tomatoes, basil, olive oil, wine, vinegar, onions, garlic, salt, pepper, and artichoke hearts. Bring to light boil.

✳ Reduce heat, simmer until mixture reduces by half, approximately 30 minutes.

✳ In a large saucepan, bring water to a boil, season with salt if desired. Add linguini and cook until al dente, or with a bite, approximately 8-10 minutes.

✳ Plate the pasta, add the sauce, and generously sprinkle with Parmesan cheese.

Bill Duff and Royal Raymond

For the last twenty five years, some of my family (Joe, Ann and her husband Mike) have been coming down to Pendleton for the Round-Up. At night we used to go over to Bill Severe's saddle shop (known as Hotel de Cow Punch, a popular "bunkhouse" for rodeo contestants), meet some of his cowboy friends and listen to some of them play guitar late into the evening.

Bill always had a pot of coffee on the wood stove and we noticed that he was constantly making coffee so we all pitched in and bought him a big campfire pot. It was blue with white specks and Bill really enjoyed having that pot. His recipe for campfire coffee was to fill the pot with water, add a cup of ground coffee, a pinch of salt, and half cup of cold water to settle the grounds, then bring it to a full boil. He never emptied out the old grounds — he just kept adding coffee. Whew, you had to have an iron stomach. Bill had a pot of beans on the wood stove for the cowboys and he told us his secret recipe: you count out only 239 beans, one more would make it 2-farty! He had the best sense of humor...*Raphael Hoffman*

BUCKLE BUNNY SPAGHETTI

This is a recipe you can add or subtract ingredients and quantities depending on your family's likes and dislikes.

10-12 servings

When cooking pasta for pasta salads do not rinse the pasta. The sauce will cling much better to pasta that hasn't been rinsed.

½ cup butter
2 tablespoons olive oil
1 medium onion, chopped
2 tablespoons minced garlic
6 large mushrooms, sliced
1 teaspoon dried oregano
2 pounds Italian sausage
1 pound lean ground beef

2 6.5-ounce jars marinated artichokes, drained, chopped
1-2 6-ounce cans black olives, drained, sliced
1-2 cups white wine or water
4 quarts water
1 teaspoon salt
16 ounces fettuccini

✶ Melt the butter in a skillet over medium heat. Add the olive oil. Sauté onion until softened. Add garlic and cook for additional minute. Add mushrooms and cook for 3 minutes. Add the oregano and cook for additional 2 minutes.

✶ In another skillet, brown the sausage and ground beef. Drain the fat. Add the garlic and onion mixture to the meat. Add artichokes and olives. Add wine or water and simmer until thickened.

✶ In another pot, bring water to a boil and season with salt. Cook pasta according to directions.

✶ Plate the pasta and pour meat mixture over noodles and serve.

PENDLETON ROUND-UP
HAPPY CANYON

The Pickup Chicks: Marlo Ward, Jody Rempel, Linda Russell, Deb Northcott, wives of the pickup men.

BROCCOLI SPAGHETTI

A nice side dish for meat, poultry, or seafood.

6 servings

1 bunch fresh broccoli or two
10-ounce packages frozen
broccoli spears

16 ounces spaghetti

2 garlic cloves, sliced

½ cup (or more) shredded
Parmesan cheese

½ cup butter

Salt and black pepper

✷ Heat to boiling in large saucepan 4 quarts water, add spaghetti
and cook for 2 minutes. Cut broccoli into 1-inch pieces and add to
spaghetti. Cook for 8 minutes and drain into a colander.

✷ Brown garlic in melted butter, then remove garlic. Pour over broccoli
spaghetti and sprinkle generously with grated Parmesan cheese to
your taste. Serve immediately.

RAPHAEL'S GREEK PASTA

*Chef Rob Hoffman has been making this pasta for over 20 years and it never fails
to please.*

2 servings

¼ cup butter

2 boneless, skinless chicken
breast halves, cut into strips

1½ cups sliced mushrooms

½ cup red bell pepper, cut into
strips

½ cup red onion, cut into strips

2 packed cups fresh spinach, cut
into strips

1 medium tomato, finely diced

8 ounces fettuccine, cooked

2 teaspoons seasoning salt

1 cup freshly grated
Parmesan cheese

✷ In large skillet, melt butter over medium-high heat. Continue to
cook and stir butter until it turns golden brown. Add chicken,
mushrooms, bell pepper, and onion. Sauté until the chicken is
almost cooked through, about 3 minutes. Add spinach and tomato.
Cover until spinach has wilted. Reduce heat to low and add
fettuccine. Toss while slowly adding seasoning salt and cheese.

✷ When the cheese has melted, remove from heat. Serve immediately.

I remember my Cousin Mickey always talking about the Pendleton Round-Up and how he was going to go back and ride the bulls and win at the stick games late in the evening and early in the morning. Cousin Mickey was going to do a lot of things. I went to my first Round-Up when I was living in Lapwai with my cousins. It was so exciting to see all of the animals, everyone dressed up to look like a cowboy or a cowgirl AND the Native people on the levy selling jewelry. The levy was dangerously narrow and very dusty, but today it's in Roy Raley Park, on the flat with shade and very comfortable. Most of the jewelry makers were from the Plateau area, a few from Montana, and more from the Southwest. There was so much to choose from and it was so fun listening to their stories about how they learned from the grandmothers who had taught them the technique (and the patience it required!). I purchased a silver buffalo pin that I still have to this day...*Raphael Hoffman.*

CHEF MIGUEL'S
"DEATH BY CANNELLONI" CANNELLONI

*It's a lot of cream and butter, but you only live once...*Mike Brown

8 servings

FILLING

1	tablespoon olive oil
1	medium onion, finely diced
1	clove garlic, minced
¾	pound ground chicken
½	pound ground ham
¾	pound ground veal (optional)

1	15-ounce can spinach, drained very well
1	teaspoon ground ginger
⅓	cup dry sherry
1-2	cups freshly grated Parmesan cheese

PASTA

4	quarts water
1	teaspoon salt (optional)

1	16-ounce box cannelloni or manicotti shells

SAUCE

¼	cup butter
2	tablespoons all-purpose flour
4-5	cloves garlic

3	cups heavy whipping cream or half-and-half
1-2	cups fresh Parmesan cheese, grated
	Pinch fresh or dried basil

✴ Heat the olive oil in a large frying pan. Sauté onions until soft. Add garlic and cook for additional minute. Brown the ground chicken, ham and veal. As the meat mixture browns, add the spinach. Add ginger and wine. Continue simmering until the sherry has reduced by half. Let mixture cool. Once cooled, mix in Parmesan cheese.

✴ Bring water to a boil and season with salt if desired. Cook pasta 1 minute less than specified, until al dente. Drain shells and let cool.

✴ Grease lasagna or casserole dish. Fill cooled shells with meat mixture. Arrange shells in dish.

CHEF MIGUEL'S "DEATH BY CANNELLONI" - CONTINUED

✷ In a large saucepan, melt butter and sauté garlic for 1 minute. Add flour to pan and stir for 1 minute, stirring constantly, so flour turns a light golden color. Slowly add 1 cup of cream whisking constantly. Add more cream and continue whisking until reaching desired thickness. Add Parmesan cheese and continue stirring. Pour sauce over stuffed shells. Sprinkle with basil.

✷ Bake in a 400° oven for 30-40 minutes until lightly golden and bubbly.

Connie Reeves was the oldest inductee into the Cowboy Hall of Fame when she died at 101 after being thrown from her horse Dr. Pepper. She is credited as telling all the other cowgirls to "Always saddle your own horse."

MEAN MANICOTTI

Use your own spaghetti red sauce or your favorite ready-made.

8 servings

1	pound Italian sausage	1½	cups dry bread crumbs
4	tablespoons olive oil	¾	cup cottage cheese
2	teaspoons minced parsley	¾	cup Parmesan cheese
2	cloves garlic, minced	5	eggs
2	10-ounce packages frozen chopped spinach (or 2 bunches fresh spinach, cooked, drained, and finely chopped)	1	8-ounce package manicotti, cooked until barely tender
		1½	cups mozzarella cheese

✷ Lightly brown the sausage in oil. Drain. Add parsley and garlic and simmer about 3 minutes more.

✷ In large bowl, combine meat, spinach, bread crumbs, and cheeses. Let stand for 10 minutes. Vigorously beat in eggs, one at a time.

✷ With a spoon (or however it works for you), pipe mixture into manicotti tubes. Pour a little sauce into a 9x13-inch pan. Arrange stuffed manicotti in a single layer, spoon sauce over the top, and top with grated or sliced mozzarella cheese.

✷ Bake in a 325° oven until hot, about 45 minutes. Let rest 10 minutes.

*1967 Round-Up Queen
Susan Olsen Corey*

The cowgirl most responsible for bringing back to life the cowgirls of the past is Polly Helm, originally from Pendleton. She discovered a photo of Kitty Canutt and started collecting other images and information about "lady buckaroos." In 1986 she put it all together in the form of the Pendleton Cowgirl Company, which produces calendars, note cards, magnets, T-shirts, and more that featured old prints on the front and its story on the back. Polly says, "The cowgirl spirit is a state of mind and heart. The mystique is built around the idea of women doing what they love to do, despite the risks involved. It's about being true to oneself."

CHEESY NOODLES

This is a great side dish for barbecued meats.

8–10 servings

1	8-ounce package wide noodles	½	cup milk
1	8-ounce carton cottage cheese	¼	teaspoon garlic salt
1	8-ounce carton sour cream	½	cup sharp Cheddar cheese
1	10-ounce can cream of chicken soup	¼	cup diced green onions
			Chives or parsley

✶ Cook noodles according to package directions, drain.

✶ Mix the cottage cheese, sour cream, soup, milk, and garlic salt and combine with the noodles. Place in buttered casserole dish. Sprinkle with grated sharp cheese, onion tops, chives, or parsley.

✶ Bake covered at 300° for 30 minutes.

PARMESAN AND BRIE POLENTA

Homemade polenta will change your mind about polenta.

10 servings

5½	cups water	5	ounces Brie, rind removed and cut into ½-inch pieces
1	cup powdered milk	1½	cups freshly grated Parmesan cheese
1	teaspoon salt		Cayenne pepper
1	garlic clove, minced		Ground white pepper
1½	cups polenta (coarse ground cornmeal)		Ground nutmeg

✶ Bring water, powdered milk, salt, and garlic to a boil in a heavy saucepan. Gradually add polenta, whisking until smooth. Reduce heat to medium and simmer until thick and creamy, whisking constantly, 8-10 minutes. Mixture will get thick.

✶ Stir in Brie and half of Parmesan cheese. Season to taste with peppers and nutmeg. Transfer to large bowl and sprinkle with remaining Parmesan cheese.

SESAME NOODLES

This is without a doubt the most popular recipe ever used in our house and we have been doing it for 30 years. It is usually served as a cold dish and is particularly good in the summer with barbecue. Some of these ingredients may be new to you - but not to worry. You will make this recipe again and again...Celia Currin

4 servings

1	pound thin noodles (Vermicelli or Capellini), cooked and drained	1	tablespoon granulated sugar
½	cup soy sauce (black is best)	2	tablespoons Tahini (can substitute creamy peanut butter)
¼	cup sesame oil	2	bunches of scallions, sliced
¼	cup hot sesame oil (brands vary in heat)	2	cloves of garlic, diced
¼	cup peanut oil	1	cup sesame seeds, toasted

✷ Mix soy sauce, sesame oils, peanut oil, sugar, Tahini, scallions, and garlic and pour over noodles.

✷ Sprinkle with sesame seeds.

This can be served at room temperature or chilled.

Cubed cooked chicken breasts and a little broccoli make this a full meal.

War Paint or Chemulwick (his Klamath Indian name meaning painted horse) was one of the greatest saddle broncs of all time. During his lifetime of almost 20 years in the rodeo arena, War Paint bucked off about 90% of his riders. He was awarded the silver mounted halter three times for Bucking Horse of the Year. After his death in 1975, War Paint was mounted and became a permanent exhibit in the Round-Up Hall of Fame, which houses cowboy and Native American displays dating back to the first Round-Up in 1910.

Score another for War Paint, bucking off Glen Evans

225

Buford and Ruth Kinnison
"what did he just say?"

Buford Kinnison was a musician, a chute boss for Round-Up Hall of Famer Harley Tucker of Enterprise, and was the head painter of the Main Street Cowboy benches. Most people remember him for his generous heart and singing along with him as he and his cohorts played every morning at the Cowboy Breakfast during Round-Up.

BEER SHRIMP SAUCE

Can be served as a delicious appetizer or over pasta as a main dish.

4 servings

2	pounds raw shrimp, shelled and deveined	2	tablespoons all-purpose flour
3	tablespoons minced onion	1	cup beer
4	tablespoons butter	3	tablespoons lemon juice
1½	teaspoons salt	1	bay leaf
¼	teaspoon hot sauce	½	teaspoon thyme
			Pasta

★ Wash and dry shrimp thoroughly. Sauté shrimp and onion in butter for 1 minute on each side. Add salt, hot sauce, flour, beer, and lemon juice. Bring to a boil stirring constantly. Add bay leaf and thyme. Cook over low heat for 5 minutes. Remove bay leaf. Serve over your choice of pasta, or garnish with parsley and serve as an appetizer with canapé toothpicks.

PESTO SAUCE

Stir some of this over hot pasta and top with 2 tablespoons grated Parmesan cheese for a quick and hearty meal.

2 cups

6	cups fresh basil leaves	½	cup freshly grated Parmesan cheese
1	cup fresh cilantro leaves		
8-10	cloves garlic	⅔	cup olive oil
8	tablespoons pine nuts		Salt and black pepper

★ Blend basil, cilantro, garlic, and pine nuts in a blender until it becomes a paste. It will be stiff. Don't grind your wooden spoon!

★ Add Parmesan cheese and continue blending. While blending, drizzle the olive oil, and add the salt and pepper.

You can substitute walnuts for the pine nuts.

CHUTE

Desserts

BLACK BOTTOM CUPCAKES

This recipe was submitted by several past court members. It was a favorite that dates back to the 60's, when the Families Purchase, Thompson, Rice, and Davis traveled to Junior Rodeos. These cupcakes were always taken along for snacks. And they're not as hard as the recipe makes them look.

2 dozen cupcakes

1	8-ounce package cream cheese	1	teaspoon baking soda
1	egg	1	cup water
⅛	teaspoon salt	1	tablespoon vinegar
⅓	cup granulated sugar	1½	cups sifted all-purpose flour
1	6-ounce package chocolate chips	½	cup cocoa
1	cup granulated sugar	½	teaspoon salt
		⅓	cup vegetable oil
		1	teaspoon vanilla

✳ Thoroughly beat together cream cheese, egg, ⅛ teaspoon salt, and ⅓ cup granulated sugar. Stir in chocolate chips. Set aside.

✳ Combine 1 cup granulated sugar, baking soda, water, vinegar, flour, cocoa, salt, oil, and vanilla. Beat until blended.

✳ Fill paper-lined cupcake tins ⅓ full. Top each with heaping teaspoon of cream cheese mixture. Bake at 350° for 30-35 minutes.

If you don't have enough batter to fill all the cupcake tins, pour 1 tablespoon of water into the unfilled spots. This helps preserve the life of your pans.

From the *East Oregonian*, September 12, 1910

C.S. Spain of Joseph has announced that the Spain Brothers of Union County will be here for the Round-Up with a string of relay and bucking horses. John A. Spain won the bronc-b at Walla Walla last fall. Spain is a trick rider and spinner.

Grand Marshall Paul Rice, Sr., carrying the American Flag to start the 1994 Westward Ho! Parade

If you have some ice cream on hand and a few liqueurs around, you can always serve dessert with a flair. Just put scoops of the ice cream in pretty individual serving bowls, then put out an assortment of liqueurs so your guests can drizzle a favorite on their ice cream. Another great topping is Pendleton Whisky mixed with your favorite caramel sauce and then poured over vanilla ice cream. This is also really good over apple pie served with or without vanilla ice cream. Or just eat it with a spoon.

YUMMY RUMMY CAKE

This cake will make you feel like you've just hit the Rainbow Tavern and the church potluck all at once.

16 servings

CAKE

1 cup finely chopped pecans or walnuts	4 eggs
1 package yellow cake mix	½ cup vegetable oil
1 3.4-ounce package instant vanilla pudding mix (4 serving size)	½ cup cold water
	½ cup dark rum

GLAZE

½ cup butter	1 cup granulated sugar
¼ cup water	½ cup dark rum

✶ Sprinkle nuts in bottom of non-stick sprayed Bundt pan.

✶ Mix together cake mix, pudding mix, eggs, oil, and water. Add rum and stir. Pour batter over nuts in pan. Bake at 325° for 1 hour. Cool on rack. When cool, invert cake onto a serving platter. Mix glaze while cooling.

✶ Melt butter, add water, and sugar. Boil for 5 minutes, stirring constantly. Remove from heat, cool slightly, and then stir in rum. Poke holes in cake and drizzle glaze over it until soaked in.

Jennifer and Tim Hawkins and Jo and Jerry Simpson

CHAMPION'S CHOCOLATE BROWNIE CAKE

As smooth as Jim Shoulders made a bareback ride look.

10-12 servings

This cake is a favorite of Jim Shoulders, Pendleton Round-Up's 1958 and 1959 Bareback Champion, 1959 Bull Riding Champion, 1958 Oregon Journal Trophy winner, and a 1999 inductee to the Pendleton Round-Up and Happy Canyon Hall of Fame. Winning 16 world titles, a major factor in amassing such a record of championships was his exceptional ability to withstand pain and compete when injured. Following retirement from competition, Jim became a Pro Rodeo stock contractor.

CAKE

2	cups all-purpose flour	1	teaspoon soda
2	cups granulated sugar	½	cup buttermilk
½	cup shortening	2	eggs
½	cup margarine	1	teaspoon cinnamon
4	tablespoons cocoa	½	teaspoon salt
1	cup water	1	teaspoon vanilla

ICING

½	cup margarine	1	1-pound box powdered sugar
4	tablespoons cocoa	1	teaspoon vanilla
6	tablespoons milk	1	cup chopped pecans

✳ Sift flour and sugar in a large bowl.

✳ In a saucepan, bring shortening, margarine, cocoa, and water to a boil. Slowly add liquid mixture to flour mixture.

✳ Dissolve baking soda in buttermilk. Add soda-buttermilk mixture, eggs, cinnamon, salt, and vanilla to batter and mix well. Pour into greased and floured 15½x10½x1-inch pan. Bake at 400° for 20-25 minutes.

✳ While cake is baking, combine margarine, cocoa, and milk in saucepan. Bring to a boil. Add powdered sugar. Remove from heat and add vanilla and pecans. Spread carefully on hot cake.

Jim Shoulders

Instead of the traditional flour, dust cake pans with sifted cocoa powder for chocolate cakes, finely ground nuts for carrot cakes, or superfine sugar for white cakes.

✶ ✶ ✶

Bring eggs to room temperature to get more volume when beating.

MRS. WARNER'S CHOCOLATE NUT CAKE

This cake recipe is over 100 years old. Mrs. Warner cooked for a sheep rancher on Butter Creek and she mixed a lot of her cooking in the top of a flour sack. Her cooking was wonderful. She didn't make a mess and never used too much flour... Bev Dick.

12 servings

½	cup cocoa powder	2	teaspoons cream of tartar
1	teaspoon baking soda	½	teaspoon salt
1	cup boiling water	2	eggs
2	cups granulated sugar	1	teaspoon vanilla
½	cup butter	¾	cup milk
3	cups all-purpose flour	¾	cup chopped nuts

✶ Combine cocoa powder, baking soda, and water. Boil until thickened a bit; keep hot (not boiling) until ready to add to rest of cake mixture.

✶ Cream together sugar and butter. Add flour, cream of tartar, and salt and mix well.

✶ Beat eggs until light; add vanilla, milk and nuts. Add to flour mixture.

✶ Bring chocolate mixture to a boil quickly and add to cake the last thing. Pour into 9x13-inch pan. Bake at 375° for 28-30 minutes. Test with toothpick until it comes out clean.

This cake is even great without frosting, and it's even better the second day.

GERRY'S CHOCOLATE CAKE

The expert spoke and we listened!

10–12 servings

CAKE

2½	cups all-purpose flour	1¾	cups granulated sugar
1½	teaspoons baking soda	2	large eggs
1	teaspoon baking powder	½	cup water
½	cup cocoa powder	1	teaspoon vanilla
½	teaspoon salt	1	cup buttermilk
⅔	cup butter		

FROSTING

1	6-ounce package semisweet chocolate chips	1	cup butter
½	cup whipping cream	2½	cups powdered sugar
			(Have a bowl of ice ready)

✱ Butter and flour two 9-inch cake pans. Line the bottom of each with parchment paper, then butter and flour this paper as well.

✱ Sift together the flour, baking soda, baking powder, cocoa, and salt. Set aside.

✱ Cream the butter in a bowl with an electric mixer. Gradually add the sugar, and beat at medium speed for 1 minute. Add the eggs, one at a time, beating for 1 minute after each egg. Gradually add the water and vanilla, and beat for 1 minute more. Do not overbeat. With the mixer on low speed, add one-quarter of the flour mixture, then one-third of the buttermilk, then another quarter of the flour mixture, then another third of the buttermilk, until both are completely added. Each time you add the flour mixture, continue blending only until the flour no longer shows, then add the next portion of buttermilk. Do not overbeat. Pour the batter into the prepared pans, and tap each once to settle. Bake for 30 minutes at 350°, or until a toothpick inserted in the center comes out clean. Cool the cakes for 10 minutes, then remove from pans by inverting on wire racks. Cool completely before frosting.

✱ For the frosting, combine the chocolate chips, whipping cream, and butter in a double boiler over medium heat, stirring constantly until the mixture is smooth. Remove from heat. Whisk in the powdered sugar. Beat icing in a bowl set over ice until the frosting holds its shape, about 10 minutes.

Gerry Frank, a descendant of the well-known Frank family associated with the Meier & Frank department store, long-time politico, and oft-Round-Up attendee, is also a known chocoholic. Gerry is co-owner of Gerry Frank's Konditorei in Salem, a gourmet cake shop and restaurant, and has been sole judge of the *Gerry Frank Chocolate Layer Cake Contest* for the Oregon State Fair since the contest inception in 1959. He writes the *Frankly Speaking* column for the travel section of *The Oregonian*, often keying on places to experience, eat, and stay throughout the state. As prescribed by Gerry Frank, if a cowboy or cowgirl experiences any bumps and bruises, chocolate will help take away the pain!

Gerry Frank and George Corey

CHOCOLATE ANGEL FOOD CAKE

A "must have" in the refrigerator during Round-Up. The family is in and out between the rodeo and Happy Canyon, and everyone hits the kitchen for a piece of this yummy cake...Jan Levy.

10–12 servings

CAKE

1¾	cups egg whites	1	tablespoon lemon juice
2	teaspoons cream of tartar	¾	cup all-purpose flour
1½	cups granulated sugar	¾	teaspoon salt
¼	teaspoon almond extract	¼	cup cocoa
1	teaspoon vanilla		

FILLING/FROSTING

1½-2	pints heavy whipping cream	1	teaspoon vanilla
½-¾	cup granulated sugar		Cocoa to taste, sifted

✳ Beat egg whites with mixer until frothy. Add cream of tartar and beat until stiff. Slowly add 1 cup of sugar, almond extract, vanilla, and lemon juice.

✳ Sift remaining ½ cup sugar with flour, salt, and cocoa. Combine (by hand — not with mixer) with egg white mixture. Spoon into angel food cake pan. Bake on lowest rack at 375° for 35-40 minutes. Cool; split into 3 layers.

✳ Whip cream, fold in ½-¾ cup sugar, vanilla, and cocoa to taste. Fill between layers and frost cake.

Try a nondairy whipped topping mixed with hot chocolate mix for the filling.

To split a cake into layers, loop a length of waxed dental floss around the outside of the cake at the point you want the cut, then cross the ends and pull gently but firmly. The floss will cut right through the cake.

BLACK RUSSIAN CAKE

Don't wait for the Russians to come to serve this cake.

10–12 servings

CAKE

1	yellow cake mix	1	cup vegetable oil
½	cup granulated sugar	4	eggs
1	5.9-ounce package chocolate instant pudding mix (6 serving size)	¼	cup coffee flavored liqueur
		¼	cup vodka
		¾	cup water

GLAZE

½	cup powdered sugar	¼	cup coffee flavored liqueur

✱ Combine cake mix, sugar, and pudding into bowl. Add oil, eggs, coffee flavored liqueur, vodka, and water to dry mixture. Beat for 4 minutes. Pour mixture into Bundt pan that has been sprayed with non-stick spray. Bake at 350° for 45-50 minutes. Cool 10 minutes, then invert pan.

✱ While cake is cooling, mix together powdered sugar and coffee flavored liqueur. Let glaze stand while cake is cooling. Poke holes in top of cake with meat fork to allow glaze to soak into cake. Pour over cake. Dust with powdered sugar.

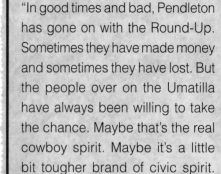

"In good times and bad, Pendleton has gone on with the Round-Up. Sometimes they have made money and sometimes they have lost. But the people over on the Umatilla have always been willing to take the chance. Maybe that's the real cowboy spirit. Maybe it's a little bit tougher brand of civic spirit. Anyhow, in Pendleton, the show goes on, regardless of hazards, and the whole state benefits."…
1933 Eugene Register Guard, after the Pendleton Round-Up had weathered the Depression.

Ferguson Wheat Field

When making torten (tortes), never grease the pan sides. Tortes are good just as baked, but hey, who are we to say you shouldn't add some whipped cream or fruit sauce?

★ ★ ★

A delicacy of the early Oregon Pioneers was fern pie. It was made from fiddleheads, the tender stalks of young ferns.

MOCHA CHOCOLATE SIN CAKE

Don't we just love chocolate flourless cakes? We do! We do!

16–24 very rich servings

12	ounces semisweet chocolate, coarsely chopped	1	cup French or Italian roast coffee, brewed to triple strength
4	ounces unsweetened chocolate, coarsely chopped	1	cup brown sugar
1	pound butter, chopped	8	large eggs, lightly beaten

✶ Line bottom of 9-inch cake pan with 2-inch sides with parchment paper. Place chopped chocolate in a large bowl.

✶ Bring butter, coffee, and sugar to a boil in a medium saucepan, stirring to dissolve sugar. When sugar is dissolved, pour over chocolate and stir until smooth. Slowly add about ¼ of the chocolate mixture to eggs, stirring as chocolate is added. Whisk egg and chocolate mixture back into large chocolate bowl, mixing thoroughly. Pour batter into prepared pan. Place cake pan in a roasting pan. Pour enough hot water into roasting pan to come halfway up the sides of the cake pan.

✶ Bake at 350° for about 1 hour or until a toothpick inserted into center of cake comes out with just a few moist crumbs.

✶ Chill cake for at least 3 hours. Cut around the sides of the cake to loosen and invert cake pan over a serving platter. Use a blow dryer turned on high to warm the bottom of the cake pan. Lift off cake pan and peel off parchment paper. Keep chilled until ready to serve.

✶ Serve with huckleberry sauce or raspberry sauce (recipes following).

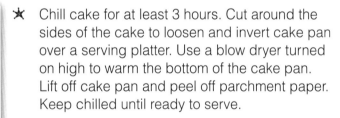

HUCKLEBERRY SAUCE

Blueberries may be substituted for huckleberries. This sauce also is a great pancake syrup. This can be made 2 days ahead. Keep covered and refrigerated.

2 cups

1   pound huckleberries
     (fresh or frozen)
½   cup granulated sugar

1½   teaspoons grated orange peel
1   tablespoon Cointreau or other
     orange liqueur

✳ Combine huckleberries and sugar in a medium saucepan. Bring to a simmer over medium heat, stirring until sugar dissolves. Simmer until the mixture is reduced by half (about 15 minutes). Add orange peel and liqueur.

RASPBERRY SAUCE

This can be made 2 days ahead and stored covered in the refrigerator. If you are not bothered by the raspberry seeds you can skip the straining part, but the strained sauce is much nicer.

2 cups

1   12-ounce package frozen
     raspberries, thawed
½   cup granulated sugar

1½   teaspoons grated orange peel
1   tablespoon Cointreau or other
     orange liqueur

✳ Purée raspberries and sugar in food processor until smooth.

✳ Place raspberries in a strainer set over a bowl. Press berries with the back of a large spoon to extract as much liquid as possible. Discard the solids left in the strainer. Stir grated orange peel and Cointreau into the berries.

For several years, Jim and Rose Donnelly have hosted a Round-Up huckleberry pancake breakfast. On the Saturday of Round-Up, friends and family gather in the yard of the Donnellys to enjoy the Round-Up tradition. Friends and family step up to help feed the crowd. The huckleberries are gathered from Mt. Adams in late August by Jim and Rose and friends. The syrup consists of huckleberries and sugar, the less sugar the better, then cooked down to syrup consistency.

The Pendleton Round-Up is in my blood and in my heart! As a 10 year old usher wiping down the grandstand seats and showing Round-Up attendees where their seats were; riding in the arena as part of the Mustangers drill team on horseback at 15; riding in the Westward Ho! Parade as a flag bearer; to my dream come true — September 1959 — when I jumped the rail as a member of the Round-Up Court and we raced around the track to the cheers of the crowd! Each and every year, my heart beats a little faster and tears form in my eyes as the current year's court enters the gates. Yes, I have many memories of that second week of September. Let 'er Buck! ...*Lynda Ferris Maselli*

Mom's Easy German Chocolate Cake

Absolutely a blue ribbon winner with your guests. Every year at Round-Up, we gather with friends for our version of the tailgate party in the EconoLodge parking lot, and everyone makes me promise to bring this cake...Lynda Ferris Maselli

8-10 servings

CAKE

1	white cake mix	1	5.9-ounce instant chocolate pudding mix (6 serving size)
3	egg whites (save yolks)	3	cups milk

ICING

1	cup evaporated milk	1	teaspoon vanilla
1	cup granulated sugar	2	cups chopped pecans or walnuts (optional)
3	egg yolks		
½	cup butter		

✶ Combine cake mix, egg whites, pudding mix, and milk. Mix with electric mixer on medium to high setting for 5 minutes. Pour into greased and floured 9x12-inch cake pan. Bake at 350° for 30 minutes or until cake springs back when pressed in center.

✶ While cake is cooling, combine milk, sugar, yolks, butter, and vanilla in saucepan. Cook, stirring constantly to blend, until thick — about 12-15 minutes. Pour over cooled cake.

In place of nuts, another option is 1½ cups shredded coconut and 1 cup nuts.

Linda Ferris

CHOCOLATE POTATO CAKE

This brownie-like cake is a must-have for any chocolate lover's recipe book!

10–15 servings

¾	cup butter or margarine	1	teaspoon nutmeg
2	cups granulated sugar	½	cup milk
4	eggs, beaten	1	cup mashed potatoes
2	cups all-purpose flour	1	cup cocoa powder
2	teaspoons baking powder	1	teaspoon vanilla
1	teaspoon cinnamon	1	cup chopped walnuts

★ Cream butter/margarine and sugar. Add beaten eggs. Mix well.

★ Mix flour, baking powder, cinnamon, and nutmeg together. Add to butter mixture. Stir in milk and mashed potatoes. Add powdered chocolate, vanilla, and nuts. Mix well.

★ Pour into two 9-inch round cake pans or 13x9x2-inch pan. Bake at 350° for 30 minutes or until toothpick comes out clean.

★ After cake is cool, frost with chocolate frosting.

Use a 9x13-inch cake pan and serve it with vanilla ice cream and chocolate or raspberry topping.

This recipe belonged to my grandmother, Blanch Rothrock. It was my dad's favorite cake (Bob Rothrock). My mother would make this cake on his birthday and for special dinners during the year. We always had it at Round-Up...
Karen Rothrock McAnally

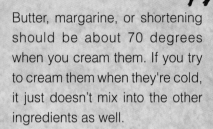

Butter, margarine, or shortening should be about 70 degrees when you cream them. If you try to cream them when they're cold, it just doesn't mix into the other ingredients as well.

OATMEAL CAKE

This is a cake that gets better the second day if it lasts that long.

12 servings

CAKE

1½	cups oatmeal	3	eggs
1½	cups butter	1½	teaspoons vanilla
1¼	cups boiling water	1¼	cups all-purpose flour
1½	cups brown sugar	1½	teaspoons baking soda
1¼	cups granulated sugar		

FROSTING

½	cup melted butter	1	teaspoon vanilla
2-3	beaten eggs	2	cups coconut
½	cup granulated sugar	1	cup coarsely chopped walnuts

✱ Pour boiling water over oatmeal and 1½ cups butter. Let stand until soft. Add brown sugar, 1¼ cups granulated sugar, 3 eggs, and 1 teaspoon vanilla to oatmeal mixture and mix well.

✱ Slft together flour and baking soda and add to oatmeal mixture and mix well. Pour into greased 9x12-inch pan. Bake at 350° for 35 minutes.

✱ Put ½ cup butter, eggs, ½ cup granulated sugar, and 1 teaspoon vanilla in saucepan and cook on low, stirring constantly until melted and it starts to turn brown. Stir in coconut and nuts. Frost cake.

Duveen and Jerry Schubert,
1984 Round-Up President

CARROT CAKE

This carrot cake has it all.

24 servings

CAKE

1½	cups vegetable oil	1	teaspoon salt
2	cups granulated sugar	1	teaspoon vanilla
4	eggs	3	cups grated carrots
2	cups all-purpose flour	1	cup chopped walnuts
2	teaspoons cinnamon	1	15-ounce can crushed and drained pineapple — set aside ⅓ cup
2	teaspoons baking soda		
2	teaspoons baking powder		

CREAM CHEESE FROSTING

1	8-ounce package cream cheese, softened	½	cup margarine or butter
1	1-pound package powdered sugar	¼	teaspoon vanilla
		⅓	cup pineapple
		¼	cup chopped nuts

✵ Mix vegetable oil, granulated sugar, and eggs in large bowl. Add flour, cinnamon, baking soda, baking powder, and salt. Mix well. Add 1 teaspoon vanilla, carrots, nuts, and pineapple, reserving ⅓ cup pineapple for frosting. Pour into a 9x12-inch greased and sugared cake pan and bake at 375° for 55-60 minutes.

✵ Mix together until smooth cream cheese, powdered sugar, margarine or butter, and ¼ teaspoon vanilla. Add reserved ⅓ cup pineapple and ¼ cup nuts. Frost cooled cake and serve.

Queen for a Day

I have always been so moved by the grand entry by the Queen and Court, which opens the rodeo every day, and while I never considered trying out for the court, I always wanted to make that entry. Only in my dreams. On my 40th birthday, my husband surprised me with just that. He rented the Round-Up grounds, had a friend bring a horse, invited 250 people for a birthday bash, drove me there, and said, "have at it." I did it. I made the Grand Entry, and made the front page of the sports section of the East Oregonian, jumping nicely over the first fence. The second fence was a different story, because as I raced across the infield, my friends in the south grandstand stood up and roared their approval, at which point the horse stopped and went straight up in the air. I got off (I think I kind of slipped off the rear), got the horse under control, got back on, and with some cajoling, got the horse over the second fence, and cantered around the track. Yes! It was thrilling. And then we all gathered in the Let 'er Buck Room for dinner and birthday cake. This is the recipe for the cake that my friends made for me. I hope you enjoy it too!...*Mary Alice Ridgway*

His real name was Howard Choteau Webster, and he dominated steer roping from 1949 to 1955, winning four world championships and twice finishing runner-up. At the Round-Up, Shoat Webster was bulldogging champ in 1949, steer roping champ in 1949 and 1951, calf roping champ in 1950, and all-around champion in 1949, 1950, 1951, and 1952. He retired the Sam Jackson all-around cowboy trophy at the Pendleton Round-Up by winning it three times in a row, and was inducted into the Round-Up Hall of Fame in 1975. Don't ever let it be said that a real champion doesn't know his fruit cake!

To keep loaf cakes fresher longer, cut slices from the middle rather than from the end. When you're finished slicing, firmly push the two leftover sections together to reform a loaf. This way, you eliminate leaving an exposed, quick-to-dry-out "end" slice.

Shoat Webster

SHOAT WEBSTER'S FRUIT CAKE

Place a small pan of water in the oven baking to make it moister.

12 servings

1 pound dates, cut up	1 pound shredded, flaked coconut
1 small jar red cherries, chopped, with juice	1 14-ounce can low-fat sweetened condensed milk
1 small jar green cherries, chopped, drained	
1 pound pecans, cut up	

✸ Mix together dates, red cherries (with juice), green cherries (drained), pecans, and coconut. Add sweetened condensed milk; mix well.

✸ Line loaf pan with wax paper. Pour in mixture. Bake at 300° for 2 hours.

PINEAPPLE CAKE

This is a very moist cake and will keep in the refrigerator easily for a week.

12–16 servings

CAKE

2 cups all-purpose flour	1 cup vegetable oil
2 cups granulated sugar	3 beaten eggs
2 teaspoons baking soda	1 teaspoon vanilla
1 teaspoon salt	2 cups crushed pineapple with juice
2 teaspoons cinnamon	

CREAM CHEESE FROSTING

½ cup butter	1 8-ounce package cream cheese
4 cups powdered sugar	2 teaspoons vanilla

✸ Mix together flour, granulated sugar, baking soda, salt, and cinnamon. Add oil, eggs, and 1 teaspoon vanilla. Mix well. Fold in pineapple. Pour into two 9-inch round cake pans, greased and floured, or one 9x12-inch greased and floured cake pan. Bake at 350° for about 45 minutes or when a knife inserted in middle comes out clean.

✸ With mixer, cream together butter, powdered sugar, cream cheese, and 2 teaspoons vanilla until smooth. Frost cooled cake.

FRESH APPLE CAKE

A thin cream cheese frosting, whipped cream, or ice cream is suggested to top this off, but it's good without any icing at all. The Rum Sauce is just another option.

12–15 servings

CAKE

4	cups peeled and diced apples	2	teaspoons vanilla
2	cups granulated sugar	2	cups all-purpose flour
½	cup vegetable oil	2	teaspoons baking soda
2	eggs, well beaten	2	teaspoons cinnamon
1	cup chopped nuts	1	teaspoon salt

RUM SAUCE

½	cup butter or margarine	½	cup cream or half-and-half
1	cup granulated sugar	1	teaspoon rum flavoring

✱ Mix apples and sugar in a large bowl. Add oil, eggs, nuts, and vanilla

✱ Mix flour, soda, cinnamon and salt together. Add to the oil and egg mixture and mix well. Pour into a greased 9x13-inch glass baking pan and bake at 350° for 1 hour.

✱ For rum sauce, combine butter or margarine, sugar, cream or half-and-half, and rum flavoring. Heat thoroughly in double boiler until sugar is dissolved. Pour over cake.

Pick-up men Bobby Marriott and Gary Rempel

This Fresh Apple Cake recipe is from Rita Kirkpatrick, who was born May 3, 1905, the last of seven children. "I grew up with the Round-Up, and in 1928 I began my career in the Happy Canyon show, first as an immigrant, then a dance hall girl in the street scene. I was in the show for 18 years, and after the show I sold bucks in the gambling hall upstairs in the dance hall. This is where I met Chester Kirkpatrick, my future husband.

My older sister, Margaret Pigg, was Clerk of the Course for many years until the "Turtles" took over. We had tickets in the grandstand for family and friends. In 1950 she bought box seats, and when she died in 1980 I took over the box. I have gone every day to the rodeo for over 62 years and hope to go again this year."...*Rita Kirkpatrick*

Rodeo cowboys had formed a union called the Cowboys Turtle Association and in 1937 the Round-Up refused to meet a Turtle demand that the judges of the show also be Turtles. A rival group, the Northwest Cowboys Association, organized at Pendleton with differing policies. Turtles were not allowed in the 1937 and 1938 Round-Ups, but differences were resolved early in 1939, and a four-day rodeo was planned. This also was the time new bucking chutes were introduced at the Round-Up, a new method to replace snubbing.

SOUR CREAM LEMON CAKE

A glazed lemon cake, made with fresh lemon and sour cream.

12 servings

CAKE

2	cups all-purpose flour		2	cups granulated sugar
2	teaspoons baking powder		3	eggs
1	teaspoon salt			Grated zest of 1 large lemon
1	cup butter, room temperature		1	cup sour cream

LEMON GLAZE

¼	cup melted butter		2	cups sifted powdered sugar
2	tablespoons fresh lemon juice			

✻ Generously butter and flour a 10-inch Bundt pan.

✻ In a bowl, sift together the flour, baking powder, and salt. Set aside.

✻ In a mixing bowl with hand-held electric mixer, cream 1 cup butter and granulated sugar; beat at high speed until mixture is very light and fluffy, about 5 minutes. Beat in eggs, one at a time, beating well after each addition and scraping down side of bowl frequently. Blend in lemon zest. Add flour mixture to the creamed mixture alternately with sour cream, adding each in 3 additions. Scrape sides of bowl frequently.

✻ Pour batter into prepared cake pan; bake at 325° for 65 minutes. Do not open oven door, do not test for doneness. Just trust it. Cool in pan 10 minutes.

✻ Meanwhile, combine lemon glaze ingredients in a bowl, blending until smooth. Carefully turn cake out onto a platter; drizzle evenly with glaze.

The first teepee raising party I was able to attend in Pendleton was at Betty Jane and Jay Graybeal's home in September of 1994. For a long time I had been hearing about this annual event, which occurred on the Sunday before Round-Up week.

The guidelines were pretty straightforward. The three or four host couples got together and decided on the location and the main entrée, which they would be responsible for furnishing. The men got the goods to supply the bar, delivered it to the chosen location and on the day of the raising, set up and tended the bar. Meanwhile the women got together and decided what foods they wanted, and who they should ask to make it. I remember Helen Levy saying, "Oh let's ask Teddie

(continued on next page)

Pumpkin Cake Rolls

One 29-ounce can of pumpkin makes four pumpkin rolls, and this recipe is easy to quadruple. This recipe is for one pumpkin roll. But you'll want more than one, for sure!

8–12 servings

CAKE

3	eggs	1	teaspoon ginger
1	cup granulated sugar	½	teaspoon nutmeg
⅔	cup pumpkin	½	teaspoon salt
¾	cup all-purpose flour	1	cup walnuts or pecans (optional)
1	teaspoon baking powder		
2	teaspoons cinnamon		

FILLING

1	8-ounce package cream cheese, softened	1	cup powdered sugar
4	tablespoons butter	½	teaspoon vanilla

✱ Grease a 15-inch jelly-roll pan. Line with waxed paper. Grease and flour the waxed paper.

✱ Beat eggs on high for 5 minutes. Beat in 1 cup of sugar. Fold in pumpkin (do not use mixer). Fold in the flour, baking powder, and spices. Spread mixture evenly over the waxed paper. If using nuts, sprinkle on top. Bake at 375° for 15 minutes.

✱ After baking, sprinkle a thin, cotton towel with powdered sugar and turn cake upside down on towel. Gently peel off waxed paper while warm. Roll towel and cake together while warm and let cool.

✱ Beat cream cheese and butter until light and fluffy. Beat in sugar and vanilla.

✱ Unroll the cake and towel, spread filling over cake, and re-roll without the towel. Chill in freezer. Cut into slices.

Can be frozen up to 3 months, and it is best kept in the freezer until ready to use.

(continued)

(Pearson) to make her lemon cake. I love that!"

The day arrived. The men made and served the drinks. Helen and Don Hawkins brought in the teepee that Steve and Gwen Thompson had given the group when they moved to Charbonneau and had been in one of their barns since the previous Round-up. Several fellows got the poles and carefully laid them out so the decision could be made about which ones to use first, which were to be used last, and finally the all-important decision: where exactly on the lawn the teepee should be placed. Level ground and vantage point seemed to be uppermost in their minds. Before you knew it, the teepee was up, standing solid and tall, and Joan Corey was climbing up a huge ladder to put the peg and the feather in the flap of the entrance — just so!...
Shirlee McGreer

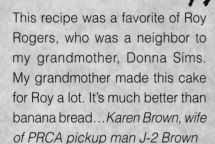

This recipe was a favorite of Roy Rogers, who was a neighbor to my grandmother, Donna Sims. My grandmother made this cake for Roy a lot. It's much better than banana bread...*Karen Brown, wife of PRCA pickup man J-2 Brown*

ROY ROGER'S FAVORITE BANANA CAKE

This cake is great as is but can also be topped with a vanilla frosting of your choice.

10-12 servings

½	cup shortening	1 teaspoon baking powder
½	cup buttermilk	1 teaspoon baking soda
1	cup bananas, very ripe	¾ teaspoon salt
2	eggs	1⅞ cups cake flour
1¼	cups granulated sugar	Walnuts, optional

✶ Blend shortening, buttermilk, bananas, and eggs. Stir in sugar, baking powder, baking soda, salt, flour, and nuts. Mix well. Pour into greased 9x13-inch pan.

✶ Bake at 350° for 25-30 minutes.

Make sure your bananas are really ripe, super black.

J-2 Brown

CHERRY BERRIES ON A CLOUD

Former Court Chaperone Helen Cook would serve this at her Round-Up parties for the courts. And yes, there were etiquette lessons given! This recipe was a favorite of all the girls...Ann Lorenzen Hulden

MERINGUE BASE

3	egg whites	8	ounces semisweet chocolate, melted
¼	teaspoon cream of tartar		
¾	cup granulated sugar		

CAKE

1	8-ounce package cream cheese, softened	2	cups miniature marshmallows
1	cup granulated sugar	2	20-ounce cans cherry pie filling
1	teaspoon vanilla		Few drops of red food coloring, if desired
2	cups chilled whipping cream	2	teaspoons lemon juice

✳ Cover bottom of 9x13-inch pan with heavy brown grocery sack.

✳ Beat egg whites with cream of tartar until foamy. Beat in ⅔ cup sugar, 1 tablespoon at a time, until stiff and glossy. Cover bottom of pan evenly. Bake at 275° for 1 hour. Turn off oven. Leave meringue in oven with door closed for 2 hours or overnight.

✳ Melt chocolate and cover meringue with it. Let cool in refrigerator a few minutes.

✳ Blend cream cheese, 1 cup sugar, and vanilla.

✳ In a chilled bowl, beat whipping cream until stiff. Gently fold in whipped cream and marshmallows into cream cheese mixture. Spread mixture into chocolate meringue pie shell. Cover with cherry pie filling mixed with lemon juice.

From the *East Oregonian*, August 19, 1910

Major Lee Moorhouse has received a letter from Poker Jim, prominent Walla Walla Indian, in which the brave promises his support for the "Round-Up." He said if suitable prizes are posted he will bring his race horses down and will persuade Indian friends to attend and bring their race horses.

I was a princess of the Pendleton Round-Up in 1950. I lived in Heppner, Oregon, and Kathryn "Kite" Lazinka was the queen at that time. In later years, my young brother, Paul Hisler, married Queen Kite's daughter Susie.

Since then I lived in Portland for fifty years and have just recently moved to Rockaway Beach, Oregon.

There are certain songs I hear that will remind me of certain times and places. When I hear "Good Night, Irene" I remember the Round-Up court staying at the old Temple Hotel in Pendleton. We had a hard time sleeping because the people in the streets were ending the night singing "Good Night Irene." This was in the year 1950…
Francine Bristow-Hisler

★   ★   ★

Store your cake with half an apple in the container, and the cake will retain its freshness longer.

If you're afraid your baking powder may be "dead," test it by putting 1 teaspoon into a cup of hot water. If it fizzes actively, it's okay. If not, buy a new box.

SINFULLY SCRUMPTIOUS DESSERT

Incredibly rich, incredibly tasty, submitted by 1950 Princess Francine Bristow-Hisler. A similar recipe, called The Next Best Thing to Robert Redford (and we think this is!), was submitted by Bev Dick.

24 servings

1 cup all-purpose flour	1 4-ounce package vanilla instant pudding mix (4 serving size)
½ cup butter	
¾ cup chopped pecans	1½ cups cold milk
1 8-ounce package cream cheese, softened	1 4-ounce package chocolate instant pudding mix (4 serving size)
1 cup powdered sugar	1½ cups cold milk
1 32-ounce tub frozen whipped topping	1 square semisweet chocolate, shaved or semisweet mini chocolate chips

✻ Combine flour, butter, and pecans and press into a 9x13x2-inch baking pan. Bake at 350° for 25 minutes. Cool in pan on rack.

✻ Combine cream cheese and powdered sugar; spread over pecan mixture. Spread one-half of whipped topping over cream cheese layer.

✻ Mix package of vanilla pudding with 1½ cups milk. Spoon over whipped topping; spread until layer is even. Mix package of chocolate pudding using remaining 1½ cups milk. Spoon on top of vanilla pudding; spread evenly. Spread remaining whipped topping on top and sprinkle with shaved semisweet chocolate or mini chocolate chips. Refrigerate until ready to serve.

REFRESHING STRAWBERRY FREEZE

Easy, fast, and good - a wonderful summer dessert.

20 servings

BOTTOM LAYER AND TOP LAYER

½	cup margarine	1	cup all-purpose flour
¼	cup brown sugar		

FILLING

2	10-ounce packages frozen strawberries, thawed	1	tablespoon lemon juice
2	egg whites	1	teaspoon vanilla
1	cup granulated sugar	1	cup whipped cream

✱ In an ovenproof pan or bowl, mix together margarine, brown sugar, and flour. Put pan/bowl in 400° oven for 15 minutes, stirring every few minutes. Spread half onto a sheet cake pan. Set aside remaining half.

✱ Beat strawberries, egg whites, sugar, lemon juice, and vanilla for 20 minutes until peaks form. Fold in whipped cream. Spread strawberry mixture over bottom crust in sheet cake pan. Sprinkle remaining half of crumbs onto strawberry mixture.

✱ Freeze until ready to eat.

The first Dress-Up Parade in 1927 was designed to inspire local folks to get ready for the Round-Up, adopt a western mood if it wasn't there already, and get their cowboy duds on. Prizes were given for all sorts of fancy dress, and there was a time when anyone looking like a dude, a very serious offense, was thrown into the paddy wagon. For years, the Dress-Up Parade was held the Saturday evening before Round-Up, and today it's a Saturday morning parade with floats, marching bands, fancy trucks, car clubs, riding groups, politicians, celebrities, and just about anyone who wants to enter.

Dress-Up Parade Float

With a goal the same as it is today, getting the citizens of Pendleton into the Round-Up mood and dress, the first Dress-Up Parade was held in 1927.

A boy rode a high-wheeled bicycle to herald the approach of the parade of 800 men and boys through downtown Pendleton. President Henry Collins, on horseback and bearing the American flag, led the parade. In earlier years, Pendleton had observed "Dress-Up Day" anywhere up to a month before the show opened.

The Dress-Up Parade grew to include floats and marching units and now is staged on the Saturday before Round-Up week.

SCRUMPTIOUS STRAWBERRY SURPRISE

Easy to assemble, inexpensive to make, and scrumptious on the palate!

10 servings

2	cups crushed pretzels	1	pint whipping cream, whipped
½	cup butter or margarine, melted	1	6-ounce package strawberry-flavored gelatin
4	tablespoons granulated sugar	1¾	cups boiling water
1	8-ounce package cream cheese	1	10-ounce package frozen strawberries, thawed
1	cup granulated sugar		

✶ Mix crushed pretzels, butter/margarine, and 4 tablespoons sugar and pat into 9x13-inch pan. Bake at 400° for 8 minutes. Cool.

✶ Cream together cream cheese and 1 cup sugar; fold into whipped cream. Spread over cooled pretzel mixture.

✶ Prepare gelatin using boiling water. Stir gelatin mixture into frozen strawberries. Pour on top of cream layer and refrigerate until firm.

Happy Canyon Directors in Dress-Up Parade

HUCKLEBERRY CRÈME BRÛLÉE

Be aware of the burning desire to eat two of these desserts!

4 servings

2	cups heavy cream	2½	teaspoons vanilla
¼	cup whole milk	4	teaspoons huckleberries (or more)
4	large egg yolks	¼-⅓	cup super fine granulated sugar
½	cup granulated sugar		

✳ Combine cream and milk in double boiler. Heat mixture until the milk just begins to steam. Remove from heat.

✳ In a small bowl, whisk egg yolks and sugar. Whisk a small amount of cream mixture into egg mixture. Now whisk the egg mixture into the cream mixture. Strain through a fine-meshed sieve into a bowl. Set the bowl into a larger bowl of ice for approximately 30 minutes to cool, stirring occasionally. Stir in vanilla extract.

✳ Place approximately 1 teaspoonful (or more) huckleberries in bottom of 4 to 6-ounce flameproof ramekins. Pour cream mixture over berries. Place the filled ramekins in an 11x13-inch baking pan that has been filled with boiling water to reach halfway up the sides of the ramekins. Place in cold oven and bake at 325° for 35-50 minutes, or until the custards quake just a bit in the middle and are not quite set. Remove ramekins from the pan and let cool completely. Refrigerate for at least 4 hours and up to 12 hours.

✳ Sprinkle each custard with 2-3 teaspoons of superfine sugar. Use a small butane torch to caramelize the sugar. Let cool a few minutes before serving.

You may also use your broiler to caramelize the sugar. Just be careful not to burn it.

The cream mixture can be made a day in advance and stored in the refrigerator.

Unique to mountainous areas of the Pacific Northwest, across eastern Washington, Oregon, northern Idaho, and into western Montana, juicy huckleberries embody the spirit of the region. Though worthwhile if you have time, finding and picking huckleberries is a tedious task; they are very small and you can pick for hours and only have enough for a small pie.

Ah, but they are so worth it! Our resident huckleberry expert, Raphael Hoffman of Raphael's Restaurant, reports there are 58 different varieties and each one, we like to say, is worth its weight in gold. Huckleberries have come to personify the Northwest wilderness, and we've heard of fights breaking out over arguments about secret huckleberry patches. As for why people would fight over huckleberries, well, you just have to taste some.

Each year on Friday of Round-Up, the 1984 court gets together after the rodeo at McKay Creek Park for a picnic. Most all the parents of the '84 court come, plus the court with their husbands and families. Queen Lisa's grandmothers even attend. Many times we have brothers or sisters with their families attend too! Court members were Lisa Martin Lundin, Nancy Miller Weinke, Katy Sorey Holdman, Candi Turner Willis, and Cindy Insko Secor. This group has met every year for over 20 years. It's always great to see everyone and get caught up with what everyone is doing. I made this cherry cheesecake one year for the picnic, and Lisa's grandmother said that "I must have wings"…guess that she liked it!...
Darlene Turner

Nancy Miller (Weinke), Lisa Martin, Katie Sorey (Holdman), and Candi Turner (Willis) reuniting in 2000.

CHERRY ANGEL CHEESECAKE

A rather unusual recipe, but very good. The longer it sits, the better it gets.

8 servings

1	11-ounce size angel food cake	½	pint whipping cream, unwhipped
1	8-ounce package cream cheese, softened	1	21-ounce can cherry pie filling
1½	cups powdered sugar		

✻ Break cake into pieces and place in 8x11-inch glass baking dish.

✻ Mix softened cream cheese and powdered sugar. Add whipping cream and mix until smooth. Pour over cake.

✻ Spread pie filling over top and refrigerate 6 hours or overnight.

FRUIT FLUFF

This cheesecake-like dessert has a very light flavor with great taste.

6–8 servings

1	graham cracker pie crust or chocolate crust	2	teaspoons vanilla
1	8-ounce package cream cheese, softened	1	8-ounce tub non-dairy whipped topping, thawed
½	cup granulated sugar	1	20-ounce can of pie filling (your flavor choice but cherry is delicious) OR about 2 cups of the fruit of your choice.
1	cup sour cream		

✻ Mix cream cheese, sugar, sour cream, whipped topping, and vanilla together with electric mixer. Pour into pie shell. Chill at least 4 hours.

✻ Top with pie filling or fruit choice.

This makes a very full pie. Be sure that the cream cheese and cool whip are both soft — if not, they will leave lumps.

Easy Peach Cobbler

This is an old family recipe, and can be served hot or cold with ice cream, if desired...Grace Lund

8 servings

PEACHES

2 cups peeled and sliced peaches	1 cup granulated sugar

BATTER

1 cup granulated sugar	¾ cup milk
¾ cup all-purpose flour	¼ teaspoon salt
2 teaspoons baking powder	½ cup butter or margarine

✳ Put peaches in 8½x10-inch pan. Sprinkle with a cup sugar. Set aside.

✳ Mix sugar, flour, baking powder, milk, and salt in medium size bowl. Pour over peaches, but do not stir. Melt butter and pour on top of batter. Do not stir. Bake at 350° for 1 hour.

A-1 Cobbler

Apricots and Apples, easier than a pie, and one of the best cobbler recipes we've seen.

12 servings

1½ quarts halved apricots or sliced apples	1 cup all-purpose flour
½ cup granulated sugar	½ cup granulated sugar
½ cup water	Butter
1 teaspoon vanilla OR nutmeg	½ cup chopped walnuts or pecans

✳ Mix together fruit with ½ cup sugar and water. For apricot cobbler, add vanilla; for apple cobbler, add nutmeg. Place fruit mixture into 10x10-inch pan. Mix together remaining ½ cup sugar, butter, and flour until crumbly. Dot with butter.

✳ Press crumbs on top of fruit. Top with nuts. Bake 350° for 35 minutes.

In the mid-80's I was in a golf competition soon after Round-Up. I was not a particularly good golfer. On the Monday following Round-Up, I went out to practice. A young fellow walked up and asked if he could golf with me. I told him that I wasn't very good. He said that was OK, that he needed help watching his ball. He introduced himself as Mel Coleman, and I said, "Oh yes, you ride Saddle Bronc and you're from Canada." We golfed and he helped me with my game. He was an excellent golfer, driving the golf ball 200 or 300 yards. And I won my golf match, thanks to all his help. I wished I had a piece of my peach cobbler to give to him... *Grace Lund*

Fruits that contain acids should be thickened with tapioca, cornstarch, or arrowroot starch, because the acidity of fruit may not thicken just using flour.

The Marionberry is a bright, glossy blackberry with medium to large fruit, somewhat longer than wide. It is a native Oregonian, and a cross between a Chehalem blackberry and an Olallieberry. Named after Marion County, it is known as the "Cabernet of Blackberries" for its complex and rich, earthy flavor.

Gifts of Marionberry jams and syrups have been offered to lure potential football players to the University of Oregon. Hmmmm.... wonder if a cowboy or cowgirl has ever been offered that .....

MARIONBERRY COBBLER

Specialty of the house at Rooster's Restaurant

24 servings

COBBLER

3	gallons marionberries	3	cups all-purpose flour
7½	cups granulated sugar	3	tablespoons cinnamon

TOPPING

12	cups flour	¼	cup cinnamon
9	cups oatmeal	2	pounds melted butter
4½	cups granulated sugar		

✶ For topping, mix the flour, oatmeal, sugar, and cinnamon. Stir in the melted butter.

✶ For cobbler, combine sugar, flour, and cinnamon and mix with marionberries. Place 8-ounce portions in bowl and top with ½-¾ cup topping.

✶ Bake at 350° until topping is golden brown and filling begins to bubble, about 30 minutes.

BLACKBERRY DUTCH OVEN DELIGHT

For those who like cooking their cobbler in the ground!

12 servings

2	cups blackberries	2	cups all-purpose flour
2	cups granulated sugar, divided	2	teaspoons baking powder
1	cup butter	½	cup milk

✶ Coat blackberries with 1 cup sugar.

✶ Melt butter in Dutch oven over coals. Mix flour, 1 cup sugar, baking powder, and milk. Pour over melted butter. Pour sugared fruit over batter. Put lid on.

✶ Bake 30-45 minutes with 12 briquettes underneath and 8 briquettes on top of the Dutch oven. Check for browning because the time differs with the briquettes.

✶ Serve with whipped cream or ice cream.

You can use peaches (add a little cinnamon), rhubarb, strawberries, apples — the choice is yours.

KARINA'S COLORADO APPLE CRISP

Very easy and delicious with a dash of cinnamon or nutmeg sprinkled on top and served with vanilla ice cream or cream.

6–8 servings

5	cups peeled and sliced apples	½	cup butter, melted
1	cup oatmeal	⅓	cup all-purpose flour
½	cup brown sugar		

✶ Place apples in an 8-inch square pan.

✶ Combine oatmeal, brown sugar, butter, and flour, mixing until crumble. Sprinkle on top of apples. Bake in a 375° oven for 30-45 minutes, until apples are tender.

With the recipe came a note stating that she never measured her apples - "just keep peeling and slicing apples until it looks right, and sprinkle with cinnamon"... Beth Mills

Henry Knoche was a Grand Marshal for the Westward Ho! Parade in 1995. He brought his teams and Studebaker freight wagon for years to give rides on the streets of Pendleton. Loving pies was a hobby of his, and there were only two kinds of pie that he liked — hot or cold. Blackberry Dutch Oven Delight was always on the top of his "gotta have" list.

Dave Peterson and Henry Knoche

CHOCOLATE SUNDAY PUDDING

This is like a pudding cake, and can be eaten cold or right out of the oven. The directions seem wild, but it works!

6 servings

PUDDING

1 cup all-purpose flour	½ cup milk
⅔ cup granulated sugar	2 tablespoons butter, melted
2 teaspoons baking powder	1 teaspoon vanilla
1 teaspoon salt	½ cup chopped walnuts
3 tablespoons cocoa powder	

TOPPING

3 tablespoons cocoa powder	1 cup boiling water
¾ cup granulated sugar	1 teaspoon vanilla
Pinch of salt	

✱ Sift together flour, ⅔ cup sugar, baking powder, salt, and chocolate powder. Set aside.

✱ Mix together milk, melted butter, 1 teaspoon vanilla, and walnuts; then add to flour mixture. When well mixed, pour into large oiled bread pan.

✱ For topping, mix together cocoa powder, ¾ cup sugar, and pinch of salt. Sprinkle over batter in bread pan.

✱ Mix together boiling water and 1 teaspoon vanilla and pour over all. Bake at 350° for 50 minutes.

✱ Serve with whipped cream or ice cream. Or not. It's good all by itself.

The early Pearson family

256

Miss Patti's Ole-Fashioned Bread Pudding with Let 'er Buck Whisky Sauce

Just like your grandma used to make, with one big exception.

16 servings

BREAD PUDDING

1	loaf white bread or leftover biscuits	2½	cups granulated sugar
1	cup raisins soaked in brandy for 20-30 minutes until plump	6	cups half-and-half
1	tablespoon cinnamon	3	tablespoons vanilla
10	eggs	3	tablespoons butter, cut into 10-12 pieces

LET 'ER BUCK WHISKY SAUCE

½	cup butter	4	tablespoons water
1	cup granulated sugar	⅓	cup Pendleton Whisky
2	egg yolks, beaten		

✱ Cut or pinch the bread into small pieces. Add raisins and half the cinnamon. Place in 9x12-inch pan.

✱ Beat eggs, sugar, half-and-half, and vanilla in large saucepan. Heat until very warm, but not boiling. Add remaining cinnamon. Pour all over bread and raisins. Top with sliced butter. Let sit 30 minutes for bread to soak up cream mixture.

✱ Bake at 350° for 45 minutes or until knife inserted in the middle comes out clean. Let rest at least 30 minutes before cutting.

✱ For sauce, in small saucepan, melt butter. Stir in sugar and cook until sugar dissolves. Add egg yolks and water. Cook until mixture boils. Remove from heat and stir in whisky. Serve over warm bread pudding.

Miss Patti (Fairbank) fixes dinner for special guests of Round-Up and Happy Canyon each Monday and Tuesday of Round-Up week before PBR (Professional Bull Riding). We don't think she's ever run out of it, but people in the know head for the bread pudding first ... and then they go get the main course.

In early times, the colonists sliced off pumpkin tops, removed the seeds, and filled the insides with milk, spices, and honey. It was then baked in hot ashes and is the origin of pumpkin pie.

The largest pumpkin pie ever made was over five feet in diameter and weighed over 350 pounds. It used 80 pounds of cooked pumpkin, 36 pounds of sugar, 12 dozen eggs and took six hours to bake.

Pumpkins were once recommended for removing freckles and curing snake bites.

The largest pumpkin ever grown weighed 1,140 pounds.

FLAKY PIE CRUST

This recipe can be kept in the refrigerator for 3-4 days before rolling out.

Two 9-inch pie crusts / Three 8-inch pie crusts

3	cups sifted all-purpose flour	1	egg
1	teaspoon salt	1	tablespoon vinegar
1¼	cups shortening	5	tablespoons water

✻ Combine flour and salt. Cut in shortening until size of small peas.

✻ Mix egg, vinegar and water and add to dry mixture. Take ⅓ or ½ of the dough and roll out until it fits a 9-inch pie pan.

PUMPKIN PIE FROM SCRATCH

You will have enough pumpkin to make at least 2 pies, maybe more. You can refrigerate the cooked pumpkin for 2-3 days if you like. This would be fun to make with grandchildren after Halloween so they can see where pumpkin pies come from.

6 servings

PUMPKIN PREP

1 small to medium-sized pumpkin

✻ Cut the pumpkin into about 4 pieces, cleaning the insides; if using the kids' Jack-O-Lantern, be sure to scrape out the charred part first.

✻ Place pumpkin pieces on a cookie sheet lined with foil. Bake at 350° about 45 minutes to 1 hour. Scrape out the meat with a large spoon. Measure out 1 cup of cooked pumpkin. Set aside.

PIE FILLING

2	eggs	2-3	teaspoons pumpkin pie spice (more is better)
1	tablespoon butter or margarine, melted	½	teaspoon salt
1	cup evaporated milk	1	cup cooked pumpkin
1	cup granulated sugar		

✻ Combine eggs, butter or margarine, milk, sugar, spice and pumpkin in blender. Blend about 20 seconds. Pour into unbaked 9-inch pie shell. Bake at 450° for 15 minutes, then lower oven to 350° and bake an additional 40 minutes.

FROSTY PUMPKIN PIE

It's easy to make two while you're at it ... the gingersnap box makes 3 cups of crumbs, and a 28-ounce of canned pumpkin has about 3 cups in it.

6-8 servings

1½	cups fine gingersnap crumbs	½	teaspoon ginger
¼	cup powdered sugar	½	teaspoon cinnamon
¼	cup margarine, melted	½	teaspoon nutmeg
1	cup canned pumpkin	1	quart vanilla ice cream, softened
½	cup packed brown sugar		
½	teaspoon salt		

✱ Mix crumbs with powdered sugar and margarine. Press into 9-inch pie pan. Refrigerate.

✱ Combine pumpkin, brown sugar, salt, ginger, cinnamon, and nutmeg. Mix well. Stir in ice cream, beating just until blended. Pour into unbaked pie shell. Freeze until firm. Cut into wedges. Garnish with whipped cream.

FROZEN PEANUT BUTTER PIE

This recipe can be assembled in less than 10 minutes, and can be frozen for several weeks.

8 servings

1	8-ounce package cream cheese, softened	½	cup milk
¾	cup peanut butter, creamy or chunky	1	8-ounce tub extra creamy whipped topping, thawed
1	cup powdered sugar	1	9-inch graham cracker crust

✱ In medium bowl with electric mixer, beat cream cheese on low until fluffy. Mix in peanut butter and sugar. Slowly add milk, beating until blended. Fold in whipped topping. Spoon into pie crust, mounding the top. Freeze until firm. When solid, cover with foil.

✱ Remove from freezer 15-30 minutes before serving.

We have been attending the Round-Up for the past 14 years, since our daughter moved to Pendleton, and look forward to coming each year to see family and friends. I have been a chaperone for several of my granddaughter's school functions and we enjoy watching our granddaughter Crystal perform at numerous horse shows and riding in the parades as one of the pennant bearers for the Round-Up Court. This frosty pumpkin pie has been a favorite in our family for years. It's the gingersnap crust that makes it so good...*Mary Ann Mitchell*

BERYL GRILLEY'S APPLE PIE

The secret to this recipe is letting the apples stand in the spices all night. All the juices come out of the apples and when you fill your pie shell the next day, the apples have already been reduced.

6–8 servings

Beryl had a cabin up in the Blue Mountains, just off the Deadman's Pass Exit and she loved having people come up with their horses and ride. And after a good ride through her cherished mountains, the riders would gather in her little living room, she'd bring out the soda pops and ask everyone to write about their day in her journal. She'd usually have some sort of extra treat and one day she served pieces of this huge apple pie. I mean it was huge. She shared the recipe and although it takes 2 days, it is worth it...*Sue Nelson*

9 cups apples (5-6 pounds)	¼ teaspoon salt
½ cup granulated sugar	2 tablespoons lemon juice
½ cup brown sugar	3 tablespoons all-purpose flour
1½ teaspoons cinnamon	1 tablespoon butter or margarine
¼ teaspoon nutmeg	1 double pie crust, unbaked
1 teaspoon vanilla	

✶ Peel, core and slice apples into large bowl. Mix the apples with the granulated sugar, brown sugar, cinnamon, nutmeg, vanilla, salt, and lemon juice. Cover and let stand overnight. No need to refrigerate.

✶ The next day, with a slotted spoon, pile the apples into your unbaked pie shell (high, high and higher), mounding them up with your (well washed) hands. Whisk the flour into the liquid remaining in the bottom of your apple bowl. Pour this mixture over the apples in the pie shell, dot with butter and cover with the top crust.

✶ Bake at 425° for 40-50 minutes.

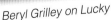

Beryl Grilley on Lucky

WESTWARD HO! APPLE PECAN PIE

This is Jack Shaw's favorite pie. Scratch that. It's his favorite food.

6–8 servings

PASTRY

½	cup butter, softened
⅓	cup brown sugar, firmly packed
1½	cups all-purpose flour
½	cup chopped pecans

FILLING

6	Granny Smith apples or Red Delicious apples (if using Red Delicious, add 1 tablespoon lemon juice
⅔	cup granulated sugar
½	cup water
2	tablespoons cornstarch
¼	cup water
1	tablespoon butter
½	teaspoon cinnamon
	Pinch of nutmeg

TOPPING

½	cup all-purpose flour
½	cup chopped pecans
¼	cup brown sugar, firmly packed
½	teaspoon cinnamon
¼	teaspoon ginger
⅛	teaspoon mace
¼	cup butter

★ Work butter, ⅓ cup brown sugar, 1½ cups flour, and ½ cup pecans to fine granules and press into pie pan. Refrigerate for 10 minutes.

★ Peel and thinly slice apples into saucepan. Add ⅔ cup granulated sugar and ½ cup water. Bring to simmer, cover and cook 5 minutes.

★ Dissolve cornstarch in remaining ¼ cup water. Stir into apple mixture. Cook for 2 minutes, stirring occasionally. Remove from heat. Stir in butter, cinnamon, and nutmeg. Cool and put in pastry.

★ For topping, combine flour, ½ cup pecans, brown sugar, cinnamon, ginger, mace, and butter. Work into crumbs and sprinkle on top of apples. Bake at 425° for 10 minutes. Reduce heat to 375° and bake 30 minutes. Cover loosely with foil to keep from becoming too brown.

A review of pecan and other nut research, published in the *American Journal of Clinical Nutrition* suggests that nuts like pecans may aid in weight loss and maintenance. Hey, that's good enough for us! I'll have another piece of this pie, thank you very much.

My mother Mary Wallan, a returning D-Day veteran, rode on a float honoring veterans in one of the first Dress-Up Parades after World War II. Her nurse's cap was used in the Happy Canyon doctor scene for years. My dad William Wallan was a Happy Canyon Director in charge of Buildings and Grounds in the early fifties. His mother, Dora Wallan, of Adams, taught me how to make pies. This one has received numerous first places and Best of Shows at my local district fair in Redding, California...*Mary Wallan Trevor*

*2006 Round-Up Princess
Celeste Hillock*

BLUE RIBBON LEMON PIE

We've never met a lemon pie we didn't love, and this one is exceptional.

6 servings

CRUST

1	cup all-purpose flour	⅓	cup plus 1 tablespoon shortening
½	teaspoon salt	2	tablespoons ice water

FILLING

4	eggs yolks, room temperature	1	cup boiling water
	Grated rind from 1 lemon	3	tablespoons cornstarch
3	tablespoons fresh lemon juice		Salt
1	cup granulated sugar		

MERINGUE

4	egg whites, room temperature	½	teaspoon vanilla
¼	teaspoon cream of tartar	⅓	cup granulated sugar

✻ Mix flour and salt together. Cut in shortening until mixture is like peas in size, then add water. Form into a ball and roll out on a floured surface. Place in pie pan and flute edges. Bake for 10 minutes at 400°, until slightly golden.

✻ Mix sugar, salt, and cornstarch together in a medium saucepan. Add boiling water and stir over medium heat.

✻ Mix egg yolks and lemon juice together, stirring well. Add to water-sugar mix and continue cooking over medium heat. Add butter. Mixture will begin to thicken. Remove from burner when consistency is that of pudding. Place filling in baked pie shell.

✻ Beat egg whites, cream of tartar, and vanilla in bowl until mixture forms soft peaks. Slowly beat in sugar until egg whites are stiff. Place meringue over pie filling, taking care to completely seal pie crust edges. Bake at 350° for 15 minutes. Pie should be golden brown. Remove and cool at room temperature before serving.

When lemons are on sale, buy several or a bag of them, and put them in the freezer. When you need fresh lemon juice, pop one in the microwave for 60 seconds and you have fresh lemon juice.

Never Fail Meringue

So many things can go wrong with meringue, but follow these directions, and your pie meringue should work just fine.

Enough for 1 pie

1	tablespoon cornstarch	3	egg whites
7	tablespoons granulated sugar		Few grains of salt
½	cup water		

✳ In saucepan, mix cornstarch, sugar, water, and salt. Cook until thick and clear. Cool slightly.

✳ In separate bowl, beat egg whites until frothy. Continue beating while slowly pouring cooked mixture into egg whites. Continue beating for 5 minutes. Spoon meringue over cooked filling of your choice in pie shell, sealing edges to crust.

✳ Bake at 450° for 5-6 minutes or until golden brown.

1966 Round-Up Queen Paulette Rice

Hints for a perfect meringue:

✳ To prevent it from weeping, add ¼ teaspoon cornstarch to each tablespoon of sugar before adding to egg whites.

✳ To prevent it from shrinking, make sure it touches the crust all around, and bake it in a moderate oven. Turn off the oven and open the door a crack when the meringue has finished browning and let the pie cool slowly in the oven. This will keep the meringue from cracking and "weeping."

✳ For the highest meringue, add a pinch of baking powder to room-temperature egg whites before beating.

Grandfather Mervin Meiners, Main Street Cowboy, had a lifetime membership to Round-Up. My Grandma, Stella Meiners, was a Side Saddler past president, and donated many hours pouring coffee and giving donuts to the cowboys during the Pendleton Round-Up over the years. They both were in parades and whatever was needed to help to make Round-Up the best rodeo to this day. Family member Bill Steagall, an EMT, helps with the medical crew every year at Round-Up. Even though we no longer have the family wheat ranch, we still enjoy coming to Round-Up and bringing new generations and friends to one of our favorite events of the year! Let 'er Buck! This recipe for mincemeat goes back several generations...*Cindy Carter*

MINCEMEAT (THE REAL THING)

For those of you who don't want to use bottled mincemeat, here is a recipe for homemade mincemeat that is over 100 years old.

12–16 quart canning jars

4	pounds venison (deer or elk)		1	gallon apple cider
8	pounds apples (firm and tart cooking apples)		1	pound currants
	Fruit fresh or lemon		1	pound raisins
1	pound suet (beef ground fat — available at meat departments)		3	teaspoons cloves
			6	teaspoons salt
			10	teaspoons cinnamon
5	pounds granulated sugar		1	jigger of brandy per jar (optional)

✱ Prepare meat in crockpot the night before — cook 6-8 hours.

✱ Peel and core apples — either cube or cut into chunks. Sprinkle with fruit fresh or lemon to keep from browning. Set aside.

✱ In extra large stock pot, at least 6 gallon, start adding meat, suet, sugar, and enough apple cider to make juicy. (You may only need three-fourths of the gallon.) Bring to slow boil to dissolve sugar and melt down suet. Stir often to keep bottom of pot from burning.

✱ Add apples, currants, raisins, cloves, salt and cinnamon, stirring frequently on a slow boil until apples soften.

✱ Place jars on lowest temperature in the oven. Remove one jar at a time from oven and fill with hot mincemeat mixture, leaving 2 inches at the top. Add jigger of brandy, if desired. Place lids that have been covered with boiling water on each jar and seal. (Make sure all ingredients and jars are hot.)

✱ For pie, make two crust pie recipe; pour 1 quart jar of mincemeat into bottom pie shell. Cover with top crust. Bake at 375° for 1 hour or until crust is golden brown.

CHOCOLATE CHIP OATMEAL COOKIES

Oatmeal and wheat germ make these cookies almost healthy! We think they're really good for us! These cookies freeze well and can be prepared several days in advance.

5 dozen

1½ cups all-purpose flour	1 tablespoon hot water
1 teaspoon baking soda	½ cup chopped walnuts or pecans
½ teaspoon salt	1 12-ounce package chocolate chips
1 cup butter or margarine	1 teaspoon vanilla
¾ cup brown sugar	1 cup quick-cooking oatmeal
¾ cup granulated sugar	1 cup wheat germ
2 eggs	

✳ Mix together flour, soda, and salt. Set aside.

✳ Cream butter. Beat in brown sugar and granulated sugar. Add eggs, one at a time, beating after each. Mix flour mixture into sugar mixture. Add hot water, walnuts, chocolate chips, vanilla, oatmeal, and wheat germ.

✳ Drop by teaspoonfuls on ungreased cookie sheets. Bake at 375° for 10 minutes.

Events of the Pendleton Round-Up include a special Children's Rodeo for exceptional youngsters on Wednesday, and "Tough Enough to Wear Pink" on Thursday, supporting cancer research. The tougher the hombre, the pinker the shirt.

Longtime Round-Up volunteer and PRCA cowboy Tom Sorey bonds with Children's Rodeo participant Austan Turk. This was Austan's last Round-Up. He died on December 20, 2007, at the age of 8.

RANGE COOKIES

Take these on your wild horse round-ups or your wild goose chases.

6 dozen cookies

1	cup margarine	1	teaspoon baking soda
1	cup granulated sugar	2	cups oatmeal
1	cup brown sugar	2	cups cornflakes
¼	teaspoon salt	2	cups coconut
2	eggs	2	cups chocolate chips
1	teaspoon vanilla	1-2	cups chopped nuts
2	cups all-purpose flour		

✳ In a large bowl, cream margarine, granulated sugar, brown sugar, and salt together. Add eggs and vanilla, mix well.

✳ Combine flour, soda, oatmeal, cornflakes, coconut, chocolate chips, and nuts. Add to creamed mixture. Drop by teaspoonfuls onto baking sheet for 1 inch cookies.

✳ Bake at 350° for 8-10 minutes.

To get cookie dough to drop without sticking, dip the spoon in milk first.

COWBOY COOKIES

As rich and sweet as my memories of the Pendleton Round-Up, these cookies are good!...Claudine Willis

4 dozen cookies

1	cup golden raisins	2	teaspoons baking powder
1	cup boiling water	1	teaspoon baking soda
¾	cup shortening	¼	teaspoon salt
1½	cups granulated sugar	1	teaspoon cinnamon
2	eggs	½	teaspoon cloves
1	teaspoon vanilla	2	cups oatmeal (not instant)
2½	cups all-purpose flour	1	cup coarsely chopped walnuts

✸ Put raisins in boiling water and simmer until plump, about 20 minutes. Drain raisin liquid off into measuring cup — add water to make ½ cup. Cool.

✸ Mix shortening, sugar, eggs, and vanilla together, blending well. Stir in liquid from raisins.

✸ Sift flour, baking powder, baking soda, salt, cinnamon, cloves, and oatmeal together and add to egg mixture. Fold in walnuts and raisins.

✸ Drop rounded teaspoonfuls of dough 2 inches apart on an ungreased cookie sheet.

✸ Bake in 400° oven for 8-10 minutes until golden brown.

✸ Remove from cookie sheet to cooling rack.

It was Round-Up time and I was at the Pendleton Club with my date. The music swirled around us; the dance floor was crowded with pretty girls in summer dresses and good looking cowboys in Western shirts. A tall, dark, and handsome lad walked over to our table and asked me to dance. I declined his invitation because I was with my boyfriend, Lary. A cowboy sitting at the next table leaned over to me, and said, "Do you know who that is, lady? That's Bill Linderman, King of the Cowboys." Well. I had passed up a once-in-a-lifetime chance to dance with the King...
Claudine Willis

Bill Linderman regularly competed in saddle bronc riding, bareback riding, bulldogging, and calf roping while earning the crown as All-Around World Champion three times (1945, 1950, and 1953) along with numerous individual titles. Bill was the epitome of what a cowboy should look like and perform - tall, handsome, and strong. Many claim that he was the greatest rodeo cowboy that ever lived, earning him the moniker "The King" by his fellow competitors. Bill lived for rodeo and died for rodeo, perishing in a plane crash on his way to Northwest Washington Fair at Puyallup when his United Airlines flight crashed at the Salt Lake City airport in 1965.

The Schweizer family's favorite pastime for over 38 years has been the Pendleton Round-Up. It was always Mother's rule that you must be 21 years old to attend. In the beginning we stayed in Pendleton at the Temple Hotel, where there was always fun to be had by all. Now we stay in Hermiston and it's a treat to get together every year. We enjoy Margie Gribble's sugar cookies every year as we sit around the beds in the hotel room, catching up on all the year's happenings. Mother and Daddy have since passed away, but the tradition lives on through their nine daughters and their grandchildren. Here's to another 100 years in Pendleton! Let 'er Buck!

SUGAR COOKIES

Not all sugar cookie recipes are created equal. This one is a keeper.

10–11 dozen cookies

1 cup margarine or butter (room temperature)	1 cup powdered sugar
1 cup vegetable oil	1 teaspoon cream of tartar
1 cup granulated sugar	4½ cups all-purpose flour
1 tablespoon vanilla	1 teaspoon baking soda
2 eggs	1 teaspoon salt
	Extra sugar for dipping

✱ Cream butter, oil, and sugar. Add vanilla and unbeaten eggs. Add powdered sugar, cream of tartar, flour, soda, and salt. Chill dough until it will roll into walnut-sized balls.

✱ Place balls on ungreased cookie sheet. 2-3 inches apart, depending on size of ball. Flatten balls to ¼-inch thick with flat-bottomed glass which has been dipped in granulated sugar (colored, white - any grind). Sprinkle more sugar on cookies before baking, if desired.

✱ Bake 10-12 minutes in 350° oven. Cookies should be barely browned on edges, so watch the first batch to see how long to bake.

Cookies will expand a bit so be sure to allow space in between flattened cookies.

To start the flattening process, it helps to lightly moisten the bottom of the glass in water before dipping it in sugar.

GRANDMA'S GINGERSNAPS

When cooled, these cookies get crisp.

2-3 dozen cookies

1	cup granulated sugar	1	teaspoon cinnamon
¾	cup shortening	2	teaspoons baking soda
1	egg	1	tablespoon ginger
⅓	cup molasses	½	teaspoon salt
2	cups all-purpose flour		Granulated sugar for dipping

✱ Cream sugar and shortening. Add egg and molasses. Beat well.

✱ Sift flour, cinnamon, soda, ginger, and salt together and mix thoroughly with sugar mixture. Roll into balls and dip in granulated sugar. Bake at 350° for 12-15 minutes.

CHOCOLATE COCONUT BARS

The end result is worth all the crushing of the graham crackers; it looks good and tastes great.

15-20 bars

¾	cup butter	1	14-ounce can sweetened condensed milk
2	packages (36 squares) crushed graham crackers	1	12-ounce package chocolate chips
1	14-ounce package coconut	½	cup peanut butter

✱ Melt butter in 9x13-inch pan. Stir in cracker crumbs and spread evenly in pan. Top with coconut. Pour sweetened condensed milk over coconut. Bake in 350° oven for 25 minutes. Remove from oven and set aside.

✱ Melt chocolate chips, add peanut butter. Mix well. Pour over coconut spread. Cool for 30 minutes. Refrigerate for 2 hours. Cut into small squares.

For many years the Purchase Family met at Grandma P's (Kathreen Purchase) every day before Round-Up. The family all brought salads and potluck dishes. Grandma would cook a ham and she always had ice cream for dessert with a cookie tin of her homemade Gingersnaps... *Kathi Purchase McElroy*

Just the aroma of ginger cookies baking brings back the memories of these delicious cookies permeating every room of my grandmother's (Clara Hamley) large house up on Despain Street. The aroma always reminds me of home...*Polly Helm*

1946 Round-Up Queen Jackie Hales Purchase, 1946 Princess Pauline Lieuallen Thompson, 1944 Princess Marilyn Glenn Lieuallen, 1944 Queen Janet Thompson DeWaal

To feed 500 people home cooked food at a Round-Up supper is a gigantic task, but the hosts at the Dr. D.V. Glenn ranch went blithely at it and gave a marvelous party Friday night.

Hosts included the D.V. Glenns, the Dick Glenns, the Sheldon Lieuallens, the Lester Hursts, the Alan Samuelsons, the Hill Hughes and daughter Jean Casentini, the Bob Brogoittis, the George Alkios, the Bill Purchases Jr., the George Coreys, and the Lou Levys.

Everyone had a job to do and the whole thing showed the result of careful preparation. The Hursts made huge gobs of old-fashioned coleslaw, and Lester also cooked the wieners in a great iron caldron over a blazing fire, serving them piping hot. The Levys were the chefs for those delectable beans. Hill and Frances Hughes got out their paring knives at 7 am Friday, and cut 200 tomatoes into quarter size pieces. The Bill Purchases were on the coffee detail. The Lieuallens peeled all those onions. Wonderful cakes were baked and kept in the deep freeze by various hostesses. The little red and white aprons, and the matching ties, worn by hostesses and hosts, were the work of Betty Purchase.

The great outdoors was a fine setting for the affair, with bales of hay to sit on. The entertainment was terrific. Mrs. C.M. Bentley played, with her usual skill, that darling old-time accordion. Dr. Glenn, Dick Glenn, and Dr. Earle P. Cochran were members of a quartet joined at other times by various fourths. Finally everybody was singing. Special solo numbers were by Governor McKay, Sen. William Knowland, Jess Gard, and Sid Unander, office holders or office seekers, all told to "sing for their suppers" which they did right well....
Elsie Dickson of the East Oregonian

FROSTED BANANA BARS

These bars are always a hit, moist and delicious, and the icing melts in your mouth.

24 bars

BARS

½	cup margarine, softened	1	teaspoon vanilla
2	cups granulated sugar	2	cups all-purpose flour
3	eggs	1	teaspoon baking soda
1½	cups mashed bananas (3 medium)		Pinch of salt

FROSTING

½	cup margarine, softened	4	cups powdered sugar
1	8-ounce package cream cheese, softened	2	teaspoons vanilla

✶ For bars, in mixing bowl, cream margarine and sugar. Beat in eggs, bananas, and vanilla.

✶ Combine flour, baking soda, and salt. Add to creamed mixture and mix well. Pour into greased 10x15x1-inch jelly-roll pan. Bake at 350° for 25 minutes or until bars test done. Cool.

✶ For frosting, cream margarine and cream cheese in mixing bowl. Gradually add powdered sugar and vanilla and beat well. Spread over cooled bars.

These bars should be stored in a refrigerator because of the cream cheese frosting.

Front: Marilyn Lieuallen, Pauline Thompson, Donna Johns, Bece Carter, Betty Duff, Betty Purchase, Creagh Hawes; Back: Elnor Alkio, Dorothy Perry, Jean McGough, Mary Koch, Virginia Tubbs, Vida Bittner, Wilma Raymond

CHOCOLATE CARAMEL BROWNIES

A couple of these brownies and you'll be good for all afternoon at the rodeo! But just to be sure, stick a couple in your pocket.

15–20 bars

BROWNIES

⅓ cup evaporated milk

1 package German Chocolate Cake Mix

¾ cup melted butter or margarine

1 cup finely chopped walnuts

CARAMEL TOPPING

⅓ cup evaporated milk

1 14-ounce package caramels

1 6-ounce package chocolate chips

✱ Mix together milk, cake mix, butter or margarine, and walnuts. Pat one-half of this mixture into a 9x12-inch pan. Set aside other one-half for later. Bake at 350° for 10 minutes. Cool.

✱ Melt the milk and caramels in microwave. Pour caramel mixture over cooled cake. Sprinkle 6-ounce package chocolate chips over cake and spread. Crumble the remaining one-half of the cake mixture over the entire cake.

✱ Bake at 350° for 18 minutes.

In 1974, the Pendleton Chamber of Commerce took over the job of registering and finding space for trailers and campers at Round-Up. The local schools offered their playgrounds after Tuesday afternoon, and now we have School Trailer Parks during Round-Up week.

Rodeo Clown Lloyd Ketchum

One of the most original parties ever given in the history of the Pendleton Round-Up was that for which a group of the younger set were hosts at Glenn's Gulch near Pendleton, on the Oregon Trail.

Hosts were Mr. and Mrs. Robert Brogoitti, Mrs. Jean Casentini, Mr. and Mrs. George Alkio, Mrs. Ellen Samuelson, and Mr. and Mrs. Richard Glenn.

The spot should not be called a "gulch;" the name does not describe the charm of the place with its white fence, picturesque stables and tack room, and the beauty of the setting — the tawny rolling hills, and by special order, a glorious big moon in the blue of the August sky.

The hostesses themselves cooked the food for the hundreds in the hungry horde, and 1100 sandwiches with a variety of delicious insides were served on a merry-go-round off shining tin buckets.

A program of western entertainment was enjoyed — solos, quartets, ukulele numbers — and Mr. Slim Pickens, Round-Up clown extraordinaire, obliged with an inimitable number, chuckful of pathos and drammer. Other performers, though in the amateur class, did right well too...*Elsie Dickson of the East Oregonian*

BROWNIES FOR A CROWD

This recipe must be good! It was submitted by three different people. We believe it's from an old Farm Journal cookbook.

48 brownies

BROWNIES

½	cup margarine	1	cup + 1 tablespoon sifted flour
1	cup granulated sugar	½	teaspoon baking powder
4	eggs	¼	teaspoon salt
1	teaspoon vanilla	½	cup chopped walnuts (optional)
1	16-ounce can chocolate syrup		

ICING

6	tablespoons margarine	½	cup semisweet chocolate chips
6	tablespoons milk		
1	cup granulated sugar	1	teaspoon vanilla

✳ Beat margarine and sugar until light and fluffy. Beat in eggs, two at a time. Add vanilla. Stir in chocolate syrup.

✳ Sift together flour, baking powder and salt. Add to chocolate mixture. Pour into well greased 15x2x10½-inch jelly-roll pan and spread evenly. Bake at 350° for 20-25 minutes. Cool.

✳ For icing, combine margarine, milk, and sugar in 2-quart saucepan. Bring to a boil, stirring constantly, and continue boiling and stirring for at least 30-45 seconds. Remove from heat and add chocolate chips, stirring until mixture thickens slightly, cools, and begins to set up. This frosting loses its gloss and begins to crackle on top when it is beginning to cool and set up. Stir in vanilla and spread over cooled brownies.

It's important to stir icing long enough to thicken and cool before spreading on brownies. Icing will set up and is delicious.

Front: Jim Perry, Harold Thompson, Bill Duff, Bob Hawes, Rich Koch, Sheldon Lieuallen; Back: Bill Purchase, Frank Tubbs, Stan McGough, Maurice Johns, Royal Raymond, Jules Bittner, Sprague Carter, George Alkio

THE BUTTER QUEEN'S BROWNIES

This recipe originated with 1957 Round-Up Queen Ann Terry Hill's mother, whom they called "The Butter Queen."

20–24 brownies

BROWNIES

½ cup butter, softened	1 16-ounce can chocolate syrup
1 cup granulated sugar	1 cup all-purpose flour
4 eggs, beaten	1 cup chopped walnuts

ICING

2 tablespoons unsweetened cocoa	2 tablespoons black coffee
2 tablespoons butter	1 teaspoon vanilla
	1 cup powdered sugar

✱ In mixing bowl, cream butter and sugar. Add beaten eggs. Add chocolate syrup and flour. Mix well. Add nuts. Spread into greased 9x13-inch pan. Bake at 350° for 30-35 minutes

✱ Combine cocoa, butter, coffee, vanilla, and powdered sugar. Mix well and spread on cooled brownies.

Linda and Anna Mautz with Ann Terry Hill

Long considered the unofficial kick-off to the Pendleton Round-Up, the Twilight Breakfast is held Thursday evening, the week before Round-Up. Sponsored by the Sidesaddlers, the VFW, and the Main Street Cowboys, the event is held at Stillman Park in downtown Pendleton, and attracts many townspeople and early Round-Up arrivals each year.

The first Twilight Breakfast was held in 1959. The Sidesaddlers were originally the wives of the Main Street Cowboys, but today the membership is open to all women. The first breakfast was held in the back room of Stewart's Market, but so many people turned out that evening, that the next year they moved it to the parking lot of Stewart's. They soon outgrew that location, moved it to Stillman Park where it remains today.

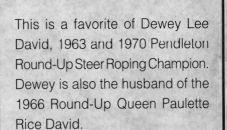

SAND ART BROWNIES

This recipe is a great idea for gift giving — for that busy person before Round-Up who would like some homemade goodies for her company to enjoy.

1 quart jar

You'll need a 1 quart canning jar with lid and ring (wide mouth is best).

✳ Layer in the jar in the order given, leveling the ingredients as you layer.

¾	teaspoon salt	⅔ cup granulated sugar
½	cup + ⅛ cup all-purpose flour	½ cup chocolate chips
⅓	cup cocoa	½ cup vanilla chips
½	cup all-purpose flour	½ cup chopped walnuts
⅔	cup brown sugar	

✳ Make sure the jar is full to the top.

✳ Screw on lid and ring and cover with a 7½-inch circle of fabric tied with a ribbon or raffia.

✳ Print and attach a tag that lists the liquid ingredients and baking instructions as follows:

3 eggs, well beaten   1 teaspoon vanilla

⅔ cup vegetable oil

✳ In a large mixing bowl, combine the contents of the quart jar with eggs, vegetable oil and vanilla. Stir well to combine all ingredients.

✳ Pour batter into a well-greased 9x13-inch cake pan. Bake in 350° oven for 30-35 minutes. Cool, cut and enjoy.

This is a favorite of Dewey Lee David, 1963 and 1970 Pendleton Round-Up Steer Roping Champion. Dewey is also the husband of the 1966 Round-Up Queen Paulette Rice David.

1970 Steer Roping Champion
Dewey Lee David

PENDLETON WHISKY ICE CREAM

Developed by Hamley's Steakhouse just for fun, this is serious ice cream!

6–8 servings

2	cups whole milk	8	egg yolks
2	cups heavy cream	1	cup + 2 tablespoons granulated sugar
½	cup Pendleton Whisky		

✷ Combine milk, cream, and whisky in a medium saucepan and heat over medium heat until 170°, stirring constantly to prevent scalding.

✷ Combine egg yolks and sugar in a medium mixing bowl and whisk to combine completely. Temper the egg mixture by adding a bit of the cream mixture, a spoonful at a time. Place back on medium heat. Stir constantly until temperature reaches between 175° and 180°.

✷ Pour into a clean container and chill completely, overnight, if possible. Place into an ice cream mixer and follow manufacturer's instructions.

VERY RASPBERRY ICE CREAM

This is very easy to make and has a great flavor. You'll need an ice cream freezer.

2 quarts

1	3-ounce raspberry-flavored gelatin	1	cup whipping cream
½	cup boiling water	1	3.4-ounce package instant vanilla pudding mix (4 serving size)
1	10-ounce package frozen raspberries, thawed and sieved	¾	cup granulated sugar
2	eggs	2	teaspoons vanilla
		1	quart milk

✷ In mixing bowl dissolve raspberry-flavored gelatin in boiling water. Stir in sieved raspberries.

✷ In separate bowl, beat eggs; add whipping cream, dry pudding mix, granulated sugar, and vanilla. Stir into raspberry mixture. Pour into 1 gallon ice cream freezer container; add milk and stir until blended. Freeze, according to freezer manufacturer's directions.

At the request of the Hamley Steakhouse manager, Rory Rittenbach started developing a recipe for ice cream using Pendleton Whisky. After many tries (this wasn't easy!), he came up with this recipe, and introduced it at one of tasting parties. There wasn't near enough to go around.

DENA'S SHERBET

An easy and delicious light dessert

4–6 servings

1	cup whipping cream	½	cup granulated sugar
2	eggs, separated	1	cup fruit juice
¼	cup milk		Juice of 1 lemon

✳ Beat whipping cream and egg whites until stiff. Add egg yolks, milk, and ¼ cup of the sugar. Beat and pour into an ice cube tray with the dividers removed. Freeze slightly, until mushy.

✳ Add the remaining ¼ cup sugar, fruit juice, and lemon juice. Mix well. Freeze until firm.

Dena Loiland was a Round-Up princess in 1929 and 66 years later, her granddaughter Corey Loiland followed in her footsteps, representing Pendleton on the 1995 court.

1995 Pendleton Round-Up Court Corey Loiland, Marty Perkins, Queen Kimberly Hoeft, Jodi Severe, and Molly McEwen

Agri-Times
Mary Esther Brock Alford
Sally Allen
Doris Amort
Claire Anderson
Caryn Appler
Athena Doubletree
    Restaurant
Cindy Bailey
MaKenzie Bailey
Marijo Baird
Dave & Susie Balcom
Dell Rose Banks
Jean Lazinka Barbouletos
Jan Barhyte
Suzie Barhyte
Darin Bathrick
David Bellefeuille-Rice
Michele Evans Bergstrom
Tyler Biddle
Becky Bishop
Sharon Bishop
Vida Bittner
Delores Bjerke
Jan Thompson Bliss-Beach
Heidi Bonbright
Angela Boston
Sandy Bowen
Fred Boyles
Judy Bracher
Sally Raley Brady
Sarah S. Brady
Betty Branstetter
Daphna Branstetter
Francine Bristow-Hisler
Peggy Morris Bronson
Cindy Brower
Karen Brown
Mike Brown
Tammy Burnett
Jolene Burnette
Minalou Byler
Kay Byrd
Cathy Cambier
Gladys Carmichael
Cindy Carter
Linda Levy Carter
Brenna Cave

Cyd Cimmiyotti
Gregory Cimmiyotti
Judy Purchase Clark
Patti Clark
Sylvia Clawson
Peggy Clough
Kamae Coffman
Jessica Collins
Shannon Cimmiyotti Collins
Doris Collis
Natalie Anderson
    Constantine
Dianne Ransier Conway
Helen Cook
Mary Wynn Cook
Sonja Cooley
Valarie Cooley
Pam Cooper
Cydney Corey
Heather Hales Corey
Joan Hoke Corey
Susan Olsen Corey
Robin L. Corey
Marilyn Foster Corfield
Charlotte Cresswell
Cindy Criswell
Deb Weathers Croswell
Carl R. Culham
Mary Hassell Curl
Celia Currin
Marlene Currin
Jeanne Daly
Sara Mautz Danzelaud
Paulette Rice David
Dewey Lee David
Jennifer Raymond Davis
Laura Davis
Patricia Dawson
Patty Alford DeGrofft
Tiah DeGrofft
Bev Dick
Shirley Warner Dickerson
Judy Dickey
Katy Thorne Doba
Mabel Dobbs
Rose Donnelly
Cheryl Doyle
Eloise M. Duarte

Karen Dubuque
Betty Duff
Glenda Duff
Sally Duff
Shelley Swanson Dunlap
Jean Eckles
Lynne Erickson
Josilyn Evans
Lynn Evans
Rebecca Raymond Evans
Wendie Every
Deanna Ferguson
Mike Fiore
Annette Fitterer
Mary Lou Fletcher
Pamela Forrester
Gerry Frank
Carolyn Frasier
Amy F`reeman
Mary Lieuallen Freeman
Jayne Frink
Julie Garrett
Pamela Garza
Dr. Vic & Mary Gehling
Carolyn Gerberding
Richard Gerttula
Rachel Getman
Bruce Gianotti
Dicy Strom Graham
Connie Graybeal
Corrin Graybeal
Nancy Graybeal
Margaret I. Green
Margie Gribble
Pam Griffith
Beryl Grilley
Mildred Grilley
Alice Grondahl
Dorys Grover
Dwan Guenther
Lauradele Guthrie
Rhonda Hack
Hamley's Steakhouse
Mary Ann Hamley
Bill & Ginny Hardie
Margaret Harned
Jim Harrison
Leslie Hartwig

Hallie Harvey
Creagh Hawes
Helen Hawkins
Melanie Heald
Polly Helm
Carolyn Hendricks
Michele Allen Henson
Ann Terry Hill
Susan Healy Hisler
Mrs. Bill Hodgen
Jan Terjeson Hoffman
Raphael Hoffman
Rob Hoffman
Betty Lou Holeman
Betty Jean Holmes
Diane Holt
Pat Hopper
Lois Horton
Kathy Houk
R. Jack Howland
Katy Hudson
Nancy Hudson
Feather Huesties
Ann Lorenzen Hulden
Will B. Hulden
Colleen Hunt
Evelyn Huston
Shar Hutchison
Nita Hyatt
Harriet Isom
Jamie Jenson
Lori Anderson Johnson
Polly Johnson
Dianne Byrne Johnston
Susan Jones
Cristy Katsol
Colleen S. Keller
Susan Kelley
Jennifer Kennedy
Sarah Kent
Jerry Keown
Kateari Kerwin
Janet Kilby
Betty Kilkenny
Kaye Killgore
Susan Fitterer Kingham
Dan and Bev Kinsley
Rita Kirkpatrick

Sharon Kline
Mary Koch
Ann Kottkamp
Julie Kromer
Marlene Krout
Peggy Krueger
Jessica Larson
Roberta Lavadour
Jordan Lebsock
Cadie Ledbetter
Ruby Levandowski
Jan Levy
Karla Lewis
Marilyn Lieuallen
Darlene Linnebur
Rilla and Sharon Livingston
Billy Lorenzen
Ida Lorenzen
Ila Lorenzen
Judy Lovitt
Katie Low
Mary Ann Low
Grace Lund
Jan Lysek
Vi Main
Judy Malcolm
Lynda Ferris Maselli
Willie Mason
Linda Pearson Mautz
Karen Rothrock McAnally
Janie McArtor
Birdine McBee
Carolyn McBee
Carole McCarty
Pat McClintock
Kathi Purchase McElroy
Brenda McGirr
Shirlee McGreer
Patrick McLarney
Margaret McLaughlin
Ronda Meagher
Cheryl Meloy
Kylee Milby
Beth Mills
Toni Minthorn
Miss Patti's Country Cuisine
Dr. Christine Mitchell
Crystal Mitchell

Mary Ann Mitchell
June Mohrland
Marilee Montana
Betty Montoya
Mike & Barbara Morehead
Bob Mumm
Nettie Murphy
Berle Nash
Jimmy Naughton
Suzanne Dick Nekrasawicz
George Nelson
Laurie Nelson
Sue Nelson
Linda Neuman
Betty Nichols
H.T. (Joe) Nichols
Nita Nichols
Kathie Schubert Nooy
Oregon Wheat Growers
    League
Dorothy O'Rourke
Mary Lou Lazinka O'Rourke
Connie Palmer
Danise Parrish
The Plateau Restaurant
Anita Palmer-Pranger
Sandy Patchin
Vonnie Perkins
Debra Jean Peterson
MaryBeth Phelan-Coho
Melissa Price
Jill Quesenberry
Mary Thompson Rabb
Kathryn Furnish Ramey
Michael Ramm
Gladys Raymond
R. Royal Raymond
Raphael "Ruff" Raymond
Wilma Jean Raymond
Raymond Reeder
Julie Reese
Jody Rempel
Judy Rew
Norma Rickman
Jack Rider
Bob Ridgway
Mary Alice Ridgway
Rory Rittenbach

Charline R. Rooper
Rooster's Restaurant
Joan Isaac Rose
Teri Roselle
Beth Roth
Marla Royal
Diane Levy Salmon
Roberta Sankey
Jean L. Schiewe
Judy Thompson Schneider
Duveen Schubert
Janice Schulze
Sue Schulze
Cindy Insko Secor
Jack Shaw
Sharon Shoulders
Janet Simons
Kayella Simons
Marina Simrell
Linda Sink-Fleming
Marilyn Smiley
L. Darlene Smith
Shannon Mahoney Smith
Tia Smith
Lois Speaks
Mary Jane Guderian
    Stangier
Stetson's House of Prime
Teresa Sweek Stone
Darla Stoneman
Lucille Straughan
Lucille Stroble
Shauna Stroble
Maxine Conley Stuart
Blake & Kristin Swaggart
Gloria Kelty Swanson
Helen Swanson
Gene Sweek
Susan Talbot
Lori Teal
Laurie Terjeson
Marilyn & James Terjeson
Pat Terjeson
Matthew Ternes
Carolyn Thompson
Katie Thompson
Jill Thorne
Kay Thorne

Laure Thorne
Andrea Timmermann
Rona Toman-Keown
Mary Wallan Trevor
Margaret Troedson
Virginia Tubbs
Darlene Tucker Turner
Gail Turner
Betty Udy
Christina vanderKamp
Karen Vander Plaat
Shannon VanDorn
Sandy VanEpps
Vivian Vaughan
Brian von Eggers
Marjorie Waheneka
Lynn Whitacre Walker
Diane Weatherspoon
Shoat Webster
Ellyn Weeks
Katie Weinke
Carole Cassens Wells
Adam West
June Whitten
Leslee Temple Williams
Candi Turner Willis
Claudine Willis
Virginia Wilson
BJ Winburn
Julie Wunderlich
Kristen Yunker
Gere Zacharias
Mario Zubiria

SPECIAL THANKS TO:

Barhyte Specialty Foods
Raphael's Restaurant
Hamley's Steakhouse
Let 'er Buck, a History of
    the Pendleton Round-
    Up, by Virgil Rupp
The East Oregonian
The Pendleton Round-Up
    Staff
Round-Up and Happy
    Canyon Hall of Fame
Don Erickson Photograph
    Collections

INDEX

INDEX

INDEX

THE BULL

A 100 Year celebration of kickin' it up with good food and great parties
at the

PENDLETON ROUND-UP

PO Box 609
Pendleton, OR 97801
(541) 276-2553
(800) 457-6336
www.pendletonroundup.com

Name _____

Address _____

City _____ State _____ Zip _____

Telephone _____

Please send _____ copies of BEYOND THE BULL   @ $28.95 per copy _____

Shipping and handling   @ $ 6.05 per copy _____

(CALL FOR COSTS ON MULTIPLE ORDERS)   GRAND TOTAL $ _____

_____Check Enclosed (make checks payable to *Pendleton Round-Up Cookbook*)

_____ VISA _____
              Card Number   Expiration Date

_____ MasterCard _____
              Card Number   Expiration Date

Signature _____

_____ Check here if gift wrapping is desired at $2.00 each (includes a gift card).